To the Accrington Sodomite!

Love & Solidarity

Janno

Minnie Lansbury:
Suffragette, Socialist,
Rebel Councillor

GW00481853

Minnie Lansbury:
Suffragette, Socialist,
Rebel Councillor

Janine Booth

Five Leaves Publications

Minnie Lansbury: Suffragette, Socialist, Rebel Councillor
by Janine Booth

Published in 2018 by Five Leaves Publications
14a Long Row, Nottingham NG1 2DH
www.fiveleaves.co.uk
www.fiveleavesbookshop. co.uk

ISBN: 978-1-910170-55-7

Printed in Great Britain

Contents

Foreword

The story of Minnie Lansbury may be a century old, but it is the story of modern, British political struggle. Like many of those on the frontline of today's fight for fair pay, terms and treatment at work, Minnie was from a migrant background. Her Jewish family had not long before fled from Poland to the melting pot of London's East End. Then, like now, foreign workers were being identified — by both elements of the popular press and mainstream political discourse — as outsiders who not only take jobs but undercut wages and conditions. Of course there are subtle nuances with this analysis. Many on the left today are quick to explain that although this is true, it is employers themselves, emboldened by decades of anti-trade union legislation, who use migrant workers to undercut 'British workers'.

But inherent in this analysis is the underlying notion of 'them and us' — as if the struggles of British workers and migrant workers were somehow separate, somehow different. Although considered as champions of equality, the historical relationship between trades unions and migrant workers has varied, from the solidarity shown to the 'strikers in saris' at Grunswick to darker chapters where the forerunner of Unite, the TGWU colluded with employers to bar West Indian bus drivers.

The reality is, as Labour history has shown, foreign workers are the working class. Their struggles are our struggles. Their treatment today is what is planned for us all tomorrow.

And therein lies the beauty of this work on Minnie Lansbury. It is a history that focuses on a woman whose struggle so often encapsulated the multi-dimensional reality of intersectional class struggle — one that is more relevant today than ever. Working class and Jewish; against war but supported its victims; socialist and feminist; Labour Party member and Communist; a unifier and a rebel; a suffragette who didn't stop when some women got the vote.

The struggle against oppression in all its forms has a long and rich history in our movement. But it is not a foregone conclusion this will always be so. Division and sectarianism on the left is never far away. This wonderful history of Minnie Lansbury reminds us what can be achieved when it is rejected and solidarity with all who struggle, embraced.

Clive Lewis MP
Labour, Norwich South

The Search for Minnie Lansbury: introduction and acknowledgements

I first 'met' Minnie Lansbury when reading about the Poplar Council rates rebellion which shook London in the aftermath of the First World War. Of the thirty councillors who went to prison to win a significant redistribution of the capital's local government funding, she was the youngest and the first to die. A memorial clock on Bow Road bore her name, but few people seemed to be aware of who she was and what she did. I thought that East Enders, historians and left-wing activists could benefit from knowing more about her, and that recording the contribution of a woman, a second-generation immigrant and a Jew would help a labour movement which still struggles to involve and fight effectively for these groups.

The more I learned about Minnie, the more I uncovered the fascinating backstory of this daughter of impoverished Polish Jews who grew up among rebels and became part of the radical East End labour movement. She worked behind the scenes but still found herself thrust into the limelight, most notoriously in the manufactured scandal with which this book opens. This was one alongside many other tensions in Minnie's life: between tradition and modernity; religion and secularism; being married and remaining independent; her immigrant community and her host country; her quiet personality and her need to speak out.

Tensions presented choices, and Minnie shaped her life by the choices she made. She chose to campaign for votes for all not just for 'ladies', to leave her teaching job and work full-time for the East London suffragettes, and to break the law and not back down when faced with prison. On other issues, she rejected the apparent dichotomy and refused to choose one option over another: she opposed war but still supported its victims; joined both the Labour and the Communist Parties; and was both a socialist and a feminist.

Some biographers face the onerous task of sifting through a large quantity of material about their subject and selecting the most interesting and relevant. Writing the life of Minnie Lansbury, however, presented the opposite challenge. Minnie left little record of her life. She was not a writer or a public speaker, and only in the last two years of her life held public office for which records survive. Moreover, the recorded history of the labour movement tends to focus on male leaders, and that of the suffragette movement on well-heeled women. Minnie was neither.

Uncovering her story therefore involved seeking out every snippet available from every possible source. I owe great appreciation in this to the various archives listed in the bibliography and their always-helpful staff. I offer a special mention to Malcolm Barr-Hamilton, recently retired from Tower Hamlets Local History Library and Archive, who has supported my research into Minnie's life for several years.

Collecting every snippet still left gaps in her record. Filling these required a little informed speculation. For example, the page of Chicksand Street School's Admission and Discharge Register for the year that Minnie started school is missing, but those for all six of Minnie's surviving siblings are preserved, so although there is no record for Minnie herself, we can confidently conclude that she took the same short walk to the same school as her sisters and brothers. Other speculation is based on records of similar lives and knowledge of the places and cultures in which she lived and worked, but I have tried to avoid wild guessing!

Most of the written personal descriptions we have of Minnie are written by Sylvia Pankhurst, who penned vivid descriptions of her black, sparkling eyes and gay demeanour. This was very much Sylvia's writing style, and Minnie featured strongly in her life for several years. The other indispensable source of more personal information about Minnie's life came from her great-niece Dr Selina Gellert, who has become a good friend as well as a great help. Thanks are also due to other relatives of Minnie's fellow Poplar Councillors, specifically Nigel Whiskin, Terry Lansbury, Steven Warren and Chris Sumner.

Telling Minnie Lansbury's story has become something of a mission for me. I have been sustained in this by the various people and organisations who have provided a platform for me to talk and write about her, including the Jewish Socialists' Group, Workers' Liberty, Islington Libraries, Central Foundation Girls' School, Tower Hamlets Ideas Stores, the East London History Society, the East London Women's Museum, *The Clarion* magazine and the Jewish East End Celebration Society.

I could not have pursued this research to its conclusion in this book without the tolerance and support of my partner John, sons Alex, Joe and Harrison, and parents Jean and David. And the book itself would have been of poorer quality without guidance from Dr Catherine Fletcher.

A biography is rarely the story just of the individual, but also tells of the communities, movements and places in which she or he lived.

Through telling the story of Minnie Lansbury, we can both memorialise a remarkable woman and learn again the stories and the lessons of the struggles of which she was part, and of the events and times in which she lived, fought and died.

Janine Booth
October 2018

Prologue: Chocolate Diamonds in London's East End

It was August 1920, and in the living room of a small house in Wellington Road, just off Bow Road in London's East End, a small, dark-haired, thirty-one-year-old woman sat opposite a jewel dealer. On the table between them were unset Russian diamonds, and they were discussing what price the dealer would be willing to pay for them. Although the home was modest, the gems were impressive, worth thousands of pounds. The dealer examined the stones and made an offer, but it was not enough. The woman wanted a good price for the diamonds, and if she could not get it from him, she would get it elsewhere, with the help of her family. The dealer left empty-handed.[1]

The woman was Minnie Lansbury, and she was trying to convert to cash a substantial donation to her father-in-law's socialist newspaper. The donation was from the young and beleaguered Bolshevik government in Russia, the country from whose empire her Jewish parents had fled over three decades previously.

Minnie's father-in-law was George Lansbury, editor of the *Daily Herald*, read each day by over three hundred thousand working-class people eager for a newspaper that took their side.[2] The *Herald* reported positively on workers' struggles and had supported the suffragette movement in which Minnie had been heavily involved. Like her, it had opposed the Great War which had raged until less than two years previously whilst demanding rights and care for the men who fought in it and the families who depended on them. And like her, it championed the 'Hands Off Russia' campaign against the British government's participation in war against the new Soviet Union.

The *Daily Herald* waged a different sort of war: a constant battle against insolvency. The working-class people who read it had little money and the capitalists who could afford to fund it despised its socialist politics and its rousing of rebellion against their privileges. The *Herald* begged and borrowed, scrimped but never saved, and even appeared on unusually-shaped paper on occasion.[3] Meanwhile, the

---

[1]   *Edinburgh Evening News*, 23rd September 1920.

[2]   The *Daily Herald*'s audited circulation in 1919 was 329,869.

[3]   For a detailed history of the *Daily Herald*, see George Lansbury, *The Miracle of Fleet Street*, 1925, Victoria House; and Huw Richards, *The Bloody Circus*, 1997, Pluto Press.

hard-pressed Bolshevik government valued those in foreign lands who gave it supportive coverage and who campaigned to stop their own governments' military aggression towards Russia. Add these two situations together and it is no surprise that the Bolsheviks wanted to give financial help to the paper.

But although, like Minnie, the *Herald* was a 'staunch supporter of Soviet causes',[4] unlike her, its editor was not a revolutionary. George Lansbury had visited Russia earlier that year and reported favourably on what he saw, but he believed that in Britain, revolution was not necessary to bring about socialism: a radical Labour government backed by an active and militant labour movement could do that. But while George was not a communist, his son Edgar and Edgar's wife Minnie were. And so was Francis Meynell, the *Herald*'s youngest director and a firm friend with Minnie and Edgar.

Earlier that summer, Meynell had met with Maxim Litvinov, the Soviet government's roving envoy, in Copenhagen. Litvinov had offered the *Herald* £75,000, 'no strings attached'. Moving a sum of that size from Moscow, or even Copenhagen, to London in those days was a difficult business, so Meynell accepted the gift in the form of pearls and diamonds. He then bought a box of expensive chocolate creams, inserted a gem into each chocolate in the two lower tiers and posted the box to his only suitable contact in London whose address he could remember in full, the philosopher Cyril Joad. Fearful that Joad – a 'greedy eater' – would consume them, Meynell left for England immediately so that he would arrive before the jewel-filled confectionery. His plan was to convert the jewels into cash in London, and only then tell George Lansbury of the newspaper's windfall. But that would also be a tricky business. Meynell enlisted the help of his friends, as he later described in his autobiography:

> My close friends Edgar Lansbury and his wife Minnie lived in the East End and could make easy contact with unorthodox but honest jewel brokers with Hatton Garden connexions. Through them, I sold all the jewels.[5]

Minnie was the crucial 'connexion', the link between the well-known socialist Lansbury family and the East End's Jewish community and its jewel traders. Her parents, Isaac and Annie Glassman, had recently

---

4   Morgan, 2006, pp.34-5.

5   Meynell, 1971, pp.120-2.

moved to Golders Green, among the first of many Jews who relocated to that part of north London once they had the resources to escape the impoverished East End. But they still ran Isaac's business from the east London house in which Minnie had grown up, in Chicksand Street, two miles west of Minnie's marital home in Wellington Road. Minnie might have taken that two-mile journey by the District Railway from Bow Road Station, just round the corner from her house, to Whitechapel Station. Or she might have ridden on an electric tram or walked along Bow Road, a busy thoroughfare that changed its name to Mile End Road and Whitechapel Road as her journey progressed.

Minnie's parents' business dealt in coal, not jewels, so when Minnie asked them to help convert the diamonds to cash, they sought further help. Annie approached a Mr. Zuidenseld, who owned a small drapery shop in Stamford Hill, an area with a significant Jewish population some four miles north of Whitechapel. Zuidenseld recalled that:

> Mrs. Glassman mentioned to me that she had some loose diamonds she wished to sell. I do not know anything about jewels, but Mrs. Glassman asked me if I knew any diamond merchants, and I remembered that I knew a Mr. Blitz, of Hatton-garden. I suggested I should introduce Mr. Blitz to her. She agreed. I went to Mr. Blitz's office and arranged a meeting. We met one evening at a private house. Mrs. Glassman brought the jewels, and they were spread out on a table. ... I heard it mentioned once that the stones came from Russia: but, of course, there is no harm in that.[6]

Annie Glassman sold a 'conspicuously large portion' of the jewels, including one transaction in the small parlour at the back of the Chicksand Street premises, 'Mrs. Glassman making the sale while Mr. Glassman was in the public part of the shop engaged in the more prosaic task of weighing black diamonds [ie.coal] for his customers.'[7] Zuidenseld took another batch of jewels to the office of Blitz and his partner Kartun, at Ely Place in the City of London.

Francis Meynell had hoped that Minnie and her family's dealing on his behalf would remain unnoticed, but he had not reckoned on the fact that Russian jewellers cut their diamonds in a unique style, and so the appearance on the London market of such a large quantity came to the attention of Special Branch and thence, according to historian Kevin

6   *Nottingham Evening Post*, 22nd September 1920.

7   *Aberdeen Daily Journal*, 22nd September 1920.

Morgan, the British state deliberately put the story into the public sphere. In September 1920, *The Times* – the house newspaper of the British ruling class – exposed the events as a scandal, as though trading diamonds were somehow outrageous rather than a lawful activity forced upon people who would rather have acted openly by the very anti-Bolshevik sentiment and administrative obstruction that *The Times* supported.

Provincial newspapers snapped up the story, the *Western Gazette* denouncing the *Daily Herald* as a 'Bolshevic rag' and the *Edinburgh Evening News* sneeringly referring to Zuidenseld as 'the kerbstone broker'.[8] From the other side of the world, the *Sydney Sun* was keen to point out, with dubious accuracy and heavy innuendo, that Minnie's mother Annie Glassman was 'an orthodox Jewess'.[9] The conservative *Morning Post* wrote of 'odious and disgraceful intrigue' and 'nauseous hypocrisy',[10] but its attack on the *Herald* and the Glassman family perhaps had a particular pernicious motivation. The *Morning Post*'s editor, H.A. Gwynne, believed that Bolshevism was the latest project of a centuries-old Jewish conspiracy to dominate the world. By Gwynne's own admission, by 1920 the paper had been known for three years as being 'anti-Jew', and just two months before denouncing the *Herald* over the Russian jewels, it had published a series of articles based on the antisemitic forgery *The Protocols of the Elders of Zion*.[11] The *Daily Herald*'s rivals and enemies used the suggestion of Jewish dirty dealing to attack the paper and its socialist politics. Their antisemitic undertone focused on the role of the English George Lansbury's Jewish daughter-in-law Minnie and her family.

George claimed to have known nothing of the Russian donation until it was exposed and used against him, although not everyone believed this. British state intelligence services noted that the diamonds 'were actually displayed in Edgar Lansbury's house. As George Lansbury breakfasts with his son every morning it is inconceivable that he was ignorant of the transaction.'[12]

The police interviewed Edgar Lansbury and others, but they had done nothing illegal and no charges were brought. Despite the subterfuge and

---

[8]   22nd September 1920.

[9]   21st September 1920.

[10]   24th September 1920.

[11]   Wilson, 1985.

[12]   Home Office memorandum, CAB 24/111/88

scenes that could have come from a 'penny dreadful' (the cheap, sensationalist story books that had been popular until quite recently), it is hard to see that Edgar, Minnie or her family had done anything morally wrong either. The *Daily Herald* competed in a capitalist media market which had plenty of slippery financial practices of its own, and Lansbury's paper had received financial help from rich philanthropists (such as US steel tycoon Andrew Carnegie) without any taint or denunciation for hypocrisy. Moreover, the sums involved may have been large to a permanently-broke labour movement newspaper, but they were a metaphorical drop in the ocean to the capitalist system that Minnie, Edgar, George and the rest of the labour movement were battling against. As historian Kevin Morgan observes, 'There were certainly stranger and deeper wells to have drawn from than Lenin and Trotsky's.' The labour movement rank and file seem to have seen through the manufactured outrage. When the 'scandal' broke, George Lansbury received a 'fine reception' in Trafalgar Square, with journalist H.W. Nevinson reporting that 'Cries of Bolshevik Gold & Chinese Bonds have only done him good.'[13] Francis Meynell wrote that 'as an internationalist I, and surely he [GL], would see no objection to the *Daily Herald* having help from Russia.'[14]

But George Lansbury took a different view. The *Daily Herald* asked its readers whether the paper should accept the money, but even when they answered a clear 'yes', George successfully urged the directors to reject it anyway. He explained later that he did not object to Russian money but he did object to secrecy, so acted to ensure that 'the *Daily Herald* is clear of the taint which has fallen upon those who dared to carry jewels embedded in chocolates, and those who turned the funds into money.'[15]

Unlike the non-religious Minnie, Christian socialist George Lansbury had a large dollop of religiosity in his socialism, which perhaps made him prone to a certain degree of hand-wringing. It seems that on this occasion he was prepared to allow his son, his daughter-in-law and her family to carry a 'taint' so long as his newspaper did not. Why not simply face down the right-wing newspapers and their hypocritical denunciations rather than appear

---

[13] Morgan, 2006, pp.196, 106.

[14] 1971, p.121.

[15] 1928, p.194.

to accept that there was some substance to their opprobrium? We can only imagine the arguments that may have taken place within the Lansbury family, whether over breakfast at Minnie and Edgar's house, or a little further along Bow Road at George and his wife Bessie's.

Chapter 1 – Born to Struggle

A Girl Named Rebel

> 'It was a cold hard winter in 1888-9. Men roamed the shabby thoroughfares of Stepney looking for work – native and immigrant alike sharing the realities of hunger and want.'[16]

The men, and the women, of London's East End also challenged the system that left them jobless and starved. Conceived in 1888 by a strike of women and girls who made matches at Bryant and May's factory in Bow, New Unionism was born in the East End in 1889 as thousands of workers joined trade unions, marched and struck for their rights. Gas workers won a cut in working hours from twelve to eight per day; ten thousand tailors took strike action in the summer; jam makers, brewery workers, coal porters, rope makers, printers' labourers and others joined the uprising. Most remembered by history, the East End's dockers held a determined and effective strike to improve their pay and conditions. Between them, these actions showed that 'unskilled' workers could and would rebel.

Also conceived in 1888, Minnie Glassman was born into this cauldron of class conflict on 9th February 1889 at 32 Grey Eagle Street, which ran to the rear of Truman's Black Eagle Brewery in Brick Lane. A visiting journalist wrote that the brewery 'exhibit[s] a magnificence unspeakable … a most elegant and church-like structure, one of the largest of its kind in London … we were struck by the beauty and utility'. [17] Those who lived next to it were more likely to be struck by its smell, noise and traffic, as the massive steam engines powered the brewing process and work started at four o'clock each morning, with foremen watching over draymen loading the barrels onto their horse-drawn wagons to take their ale and porter around London and beyond.

The Glassmans were one of several Jewish families living in Grey Eagle Street, a road which featured in Charles Booth's notebooks as the place where 'the Jews began to predominate beyond a largely Irish area'. It was located in Spitalfields, an area which hosted successive waves of immigrants. Before the Irish and then the Jews came, French Protestants, the Huguenots, had fled Roman Catholic persecution and found sanctuary there, and since the 1970s, Bangladeshis have settled

---

16   Fishman 2004/1975, p.162.

17   Alfred Barnard, 1889, www.zythophile.co.uk

in the area. The Old Truman Brewery is now an arts and media quarter, after beer-making stopped in 1989, exactly one hundred years after Minnie's birth.

Social researcher and reformer Charles Booth (no relation to this author!) mapped the East End of the late nineteenth century, colour-coding each section of each street to indicate the conditions in which people lived. Booth was a wealthy shipowner who began investigating the East End in order to disprove socialist claims that a quarter of its residents lived in poverty. He found that the claim was an understatement, as more than one third were abjectly poor. His notebooks, drawn up from over three hundred walks by social investigators accompanying police officers around their beats, described Grey Eagle Street as 'poor but fairly respectable', containing some 'model buildings' (dwellings commissioned by philanthropists to improve the living standards of the poor). The houses were two and three storeys high. Describing the street as 'overcrowded', Booth showed one family of six – parents aged thirty and twenty-nine, plus children aged six months, three, eight and twelve years – living together in a single room and paying three shillings a week for the privilege. That sum could be a full week's wages for an unskilled shirt-finisher in the local clothing trade, and up to a quarter or more of the wage of a skilled worker.[18]

Around the time of Minnie's birth, Spitalfields was considered to be one of London's worst criminal 'rookeries' – the popular name for a slum area of impoverished people crammed into poorly-constructed multiple-storey buildings on narrow and insanitary streets and alleyways, whose residents had little choice but to work on the streets, in sweatshops or as prostitutes, or to steal what they needed to live.

Isaac and Annie Glassman, already parents of toddler Selina, who had been born in June 1887, named their second child Minnie, a name with several origins and contested meanings. The one best-suited to its newborn bearer was the pet form of the Hebrew name Miryam, meaning 'rebellion'.

Fleeing the Tsar

Minnie's father Isaac had been born on 14th June 1866 to Hyman and Selina Glassman, in a place in the Warsaw district of Poland, then part of the Russian empire, named in Isaac's naturalisation papers in 1913 as

---

[18] www.victorianlondon.org, citing *Toilers in London*, 1889.

'Tuchrachine'. No town with this spelling exists, and the papers were probably written by an official approximating what Isaac said, so my best guess is that his home town was Zakroczym.

At the time of Isaac Glassman's birth, Jews constituted over half of Zakroczym's population, two of its newest additions being Isaac and his future wife Hannah Goodkindt. Standing on the right bank of the river Vistula, the town – named from the ancient Polish word Zakrot, meaning river crossing – dated back to 1065, but by the early nineteenth century had declined due to a barrage of wars, invasions, fires and epidemics. From 1815 though, the town grew, including an increasing population of Jews.

Zakroczym's Jewish population increased as the Russian Tsar's repressive regime expelled Jews from the countryside into towns where they could be contained in ghettos. This was just one of the many antisemitic policies of Nicholas I, Tsar of Russia in the mid nineteenth century, in pursuit of his plan to systematically repress Jews and rid Russia of Judaism lest it threaten the supremacy of the Russian Orthodox (Christian) Church. The Jews also provided a useful scapegoat for a backward and corrupt government. So the Tsar's regime forced Jews into unpopular jobs as estate administrators and economic 'middlemen', entrenching a stereotype of Jews as money-dealers that persists to this day. Compulsory military service took Jews, including children, into Russia's armed forces for up to three decades, with many never returning. The state barred Jews from election as Mayors, censored Hebrew literature, burned Hebrew books, shut Jewish printing presses and compelled Jews to renounce their religion and convert to Christianity. The huge majority of Jews suffered worsening living conditions as they were ostracised socially and oppressed politically.

Tsarist antisemitism had started long before Nicholas' reign began in 1825, had stepped up with the inclusion of Jews in Russia's empire following Poland's partition in 1772, and continued after his death in 1855. Following the assassination of Nicholas' successor Alexander II by a group including one Jewish woman in 1881, antisemitic agitation and violence reached fever pitch. In the fourteen months from April of that year, nearly a quarter of a million Jewish families left Russia in the first – but by no means the last – mass exodus from the land of oppression. Most travelled to the USA, many others to London. In the mid-1880s, young newly-weds Isaac and Hannah (known as Annie) Glassman left Zakroczym and joined this exodus. Despite wanting rid of the Jews, the Russian authorities made it a torturous process for them to leave, and their voyages were often fearfully dangerous. But at least the Glassmans had escaped Tsarist tyranny, made it to the East End of London, and found a home in Grey Eagle Street.

Thus, Minnie Glassman was born in London's East End to Jewish parents who had arrived from Polish Russia. Introducing a collection of Jewish women's personal memories, the Jewish Women in London group wrote in the 1980s that:

> central to Jewish experience, is a history of migration, as immigrants and refugees or as the daughters of immigrants and refugees … it is a common Jewish experience that mothers and daughters are not born and brought up in the same place … For these Jewish women there is not only the difference of generation that separates them from the experiences of their mothers but also the dislocation of migration, their mothers' or their own.[19]

With the exception of the dramatic episode of the Russian jewels in 1920, Annie Glassman does not feature much in this story of her daughter's life, as there is so little record of what she did or what she was like. Perhaps this is because history remembers women less than it does men, perhaps because her life was lived out of the public sphere, keeping a home and husband and raising seven children within a self-contained, Yiddish-speaking community. Minnie Glassman's life would take a very different, more public and political, path from her mother's.

Making Boots in the Jewish East End

In 1876, Jewish socialist Aron Lieberman asked rhetorically,

> In the narrow, crooked streets of Whitechapel, in the smelly and dirty holes and corners of the workshops working twelve to fourteen hours a day for a paltry starvation wage … here have the Jewish workers of Poland, Russia, Germany, Austria … found their better life?[20]

The Glassmans did not stay in Grey Eagle Street for long, and before she was a year old, Minnie, her older sister Selina, her mother Annie and her father Isaac moved to 20 Newman's Buildings in nearby Pelham

[19]   Jewish Women in London group, 1989, p.10.

[20]   Quoted in Fishman, 2004/1975, p.103.

Street (since renamed Woodseer Street). Booth coded the street purple, indicating that it was 'mixed: some comfortable, others poor', and described Newman's Buildings thus: 'Nearly all Jews in these buildings – a poor class – women usually work.' The Glassman family took in a lodger to help pay the rent: Solomon Cohen, like Isaac and Annie a Jewish immigrant from Poland.

Pelham Street ran south of the brewery from Spitalfields into Whitechapel, also a Jewish area, whose name came from the church of St. Mary Matfelon. An 1899 photograph[21] taken from Commercial Street shows the white chapel of St. Mary's dominating the eastern end of Whitechapel High Street, standing where Altab Ali Park now lies. It also shows horse-drawn omnibuses on the cobbled road bearing adverts for Nestlé's Milk and Cadbury's Cocoa; carts pulled by horses or pushed by hand; businessmen in suits and bowler hats and working men in rolled-up shirt sleeves and flat caps.

Away from the main roads, the back streets were less photogenic. This was the district in which the 'Jack the Ripper' murders took place during the autumn before Minnie was born. The killings put pressure on the Board of Works to install gas lights in the unlit streets. In his *The Nether World*, George Gissing described Whitechapel in 1889 in melodramatic language:

> Over the pest-stricken regions of East London, sweltering in sunshine which served only to reveal the intimacies of abomination; across miles of a city of the damned, such as though never conceived before this age of ours, above streets swarming with a nameless populace, cruelly exposed by the unwonted light of heaven …[22]

Isaac Glassman was a 'greener' – or *griner* in the Yiddish language that the Jewish immigrants spoke – a newly-arrived Jew in need of work. He became a boot finisher, as did his lodger Solomon Cohen. Finishing was the last of the four stages of the process of making boots. After the clickers had patterned and cut the leather, the closers had stitched and shaped it into uppers, and the lasters had attached the uppers to the lower parts, Isaac and his fellow finishers took the completed but rough-edged shoes and turned them into marketable footwear. They trimmed the soles; attached heels; blacked, rubbed, and polished the finished article; and applied the finishing touches.

[21] Ramsey 1997, p.118.

[22] Quoted in Ramsey 1997, p.197.

The availability of work in the bootmaking trade varied from season to season, with slack times in the late summer and winter. When they could get work, boot finishers carried it out in conditions described by Charles Booth as 'cellar accommodation and huddled misery' and by American-Israeli scholar of Jewish history Lloyd Gartner (1927-2011) as causing widespread tuberculosis and being second only to the mines in their unwholesomeness.[23] Tuberculosis (TB) is a bacterial infection of the lungs, which once active in an infected person causes fever, coughing up blood, night sweats and the dramatic weight loss that gave TB its common name of 'consumption'. After this painful deterioration, many TB victims died. Known then as the 'white plague', it was preventable and curable, but poor living conditions nurtured it, and the treatments available to working-class city-dwellers were sparse, not very effective, and reliant on charity. The fight against tuberculosis would be one of the causes to which the adult Minnie Lansbury would lend her campaigning zeal.

East London housing was cramped, poor and temporary, and three years after their move to Pelham Street, the Glassmans again moved a short distance, this time to 23 Chicksand Street, where, on 10th January 1892, their third child, Katie, was born. The family would remain living on the same street, although not in the same house, for nearly thirty years.

Chicksand Street ran off Brick Lane in what was then called Mile End New Town. The street had formed at the start of the nineteenth century, since when it had 'humbly and irregularly built up with small two-storey dwellings'.[24] Young Minnie's home was located in the area, comprising St. George-in-the-East, Whitechapel and southern parts of Bethnal Green, which was populated by immigrant Jewish bootmakers and their families, while English bootmakers were to be found in Shoreditch, Bow and outlying parts of Bethnal Green. Booth described Chicksand Street in his notebooks as characterised by 'Jews, tailors, clean windows' and 'Respectable hard working people on the whole – mixed with Jews'; his map coded it purple.

In the census year of 1891, Isaac Glassman was one of 1,560 male and 31 female Russian or Polish (ie. immigrant Jewish) boot and shoe workers in London's East End. Nationally, the trade employed over two hundred thousand men and nearly fifty thousand women, of whom

[23] Booth, 1889, pp.221-5, quoted in Fishman, 2004/1975; Gartner, 1960, p.160.

[24] Survey of London, 30th March 2017.

fewer than ten thousand were Jewish,[25] suggesting that the claim made by both right-wing nationalists and some trade unionists that Jewish immigrants were pushing out native British workers did not stand up to the facts.

From the mid-1880s, the oppressed, over-worked, underpaid, sweated boot finishers began to organise to improve their lot. But into the 1890s, the bootmaking in which Isaac Glassman worked was becoming a less reliable source of subsistence, as a greater use of machinery gave employers a pretext to hold down wages and dispense with workers. Some bootmakers would eke out an extra income during slack periods by selling their products or taking on odd jobs, and for some of them, this might develop into a business. They would find it easier to leave sweated work by this route than by getting work with other employers, most of whom were English and beyond their reach due to barriers of language or prejudice.

By the middle of the decade, while Minnie was still a young child, Isaac had left the bootmaking trade and taken up work as a coal and coke dealer, based at his family home in Chicksand Street, from where he drove his horse and cart around the East End selling fuel. He was no longer a sweated worker, but he and his family still shared the working-class living standard of his fellow East Enders, Jewish and English.

Going to School

The Glassman family continued to grow, with fourth daughter Rachel (known as Ray) arriving in 1894. By this time, Minnie and her family had moved to another house on the same road, 37 Chicksand Street. Their new house stood on the north-east corner with Casson Street, opposite the Lord Collingwood, a pub which had quenched the locals' thirst since 1819 but which would close in 1900. Daughter Leah followed two years after Ray, then sons Louis in 1898 and finally Hyman in 1903.

At some time during these years, Isaac and Annie also had a baby who died – a tragic experience, although common at that time. The baby's birth and death were mentioned but not dated in the 1911 census, the first census which included a record of families having had a baby who died. Given that the gap between the births of Louis and Hyman is longer than that between any other consecutive pair of Glassman babies, it is likely that the unfortunate child was born between 1899 and 1902.

[25] Gartner, 1960, p.75.

Around these years, more than half of the babies born in the East End died before they were a year old (compared with around one in six West End babies). American author Jack London, who wrote a first-hand account of East End poverty in 1902 called *The People of the Abyss*, added to this dreadful statistic that, 'there are streets in London where out of every one hundred children born in a year, fifty die during the next year, and of the fifty that remain, twenty-five die before they are five years old. Slaughter! Herod did not do quite so badly.'[26] It seems that with seven of their eight children growing to adulthood, the Glassmans did quite well.

All the Glassman children who lived attended Chicksand Street primary school at the eastern end of their road. This was an elementary school, the equivalent of a primary school today, and the only schooling provided by the state and compulsory for children to attend. Minnie and other children started infants' classes at the age of four, with boys and girls learning in the same classes but not always learning the same subjects. While Minnie and the other girls were practising needlework, the boys in her infants' class would be learning to draw. Two years later, the children were divided into separate boys' and girls' sections. You can see the evidence on school buildings dating back to that era: the words 'girls' and 'boys' inscribed in stone lintels above separate entrances. The syllabus studied by Minnie and the other girls became even more different from that followed by the boys, with a heavy emphasis on domestic duties and household skills such as cleanliness and knitting. Chicksand Street School had over one thousand pupils, with a head teacher and seven assistant (ie. classroom) teachers in each of its boys', girls' and infants' departments, assisted by eight teenage pupil teachers. It had opened in 1878, replacing a 'ragged school' on the site, and one of many schools established in the wake of the 1870 Education Act, which heralded the beginning of compulsory state education for all children. The new building had three storeys, but was 'comparatively low, undemonstrative and without a hall'. A new building was added for the Infants' Department in 1886-7, in good time for the arrival of the younger Glassmans.[27]

At first, Jewish children made up fewer than half of the school's pupils, but as the area became more Jewish, so did the school. A family named

---

[26] 1903/2016, p.103.

[27] Survey of London, 30th March 2017.

Karbatznick, who had also fled antisemitic persecution in Polish Russia, also lived in Chicksand Street, and their oldest child was the same age as the Glassmans' youngest. Their family history website[28] records the children's memories:

> The children later recalled those childhood years with affection, growing up in a *frum* [particularly devout religious Jewish] family. The Karbatznick household was poor but the children knew no different. …

> Miriam recalled with great affection her days at Chicksand Street School, … and Dora had a twinkle in her eye when she recalled how 'everything happened on the doorstep'.

> In a 1993 interview, preserved on DVD, Dora said [that] 'many children would have to run around the streets barefoot.'

Modern historian Louise Raw points out that 'oral history accounts make clear that despite material conditions, the East End was not solely a place of bleak despair. For all the horrors of overcrowding, and its inevitably destructive effect on family bonds, many people, even while recalling the privations of their childhoods, also remembered the comfort of close family and friends.'[29] Booth described Whitechapel as 'poor' but having 'a remarkable air of cheerfulness & bustle.' While crediting the 'large foreign element' – the immigrant Jews – with bringing 'life & colour to the busy streets,' he also blamed them for the poor conditions in which they lived in terms that we would now consider bigoted:

> The excessive crowding is largely attributed to the presence of the foreign Jews who pay little or no attention to sanitary matters & appear able to live under conditions which would be impossible to any other nationality.[30]

For young Minnie Glassman, Whitechapel and its surrounding area provided an education both in its schools and in its political struggles.

---

[28] www.karbatznick.com

[29] Raw, 2009, p.80.

[30] BOOTH/B/343, pp.3,7.

Minnie Glassman grew up in an East End racked with poverty but bubbling with rebellion. She also grew up in an East End Jewish community which was both finding freedom and facing hostility. That community, with its background of oppression and its share of radicals, would find a mixture of solidarity and rejection from the English left and labour movement.

For working-class people – whether newly-arrived Jews, longer-settled Irish, or native English – living in the East End often meant families sharing a single room in a decrepit building infested with vermin and sharing a water pump and an outdoor toilet with several other families. Overcrowding worsened as thousands of homes were torn down in the name of slum clearance, to make room for roads, railways, businesses and schools. Landlords were quick to take advantage of new arrivals, Jewish historian Lloyd Gartner recording that 'rents probably rose fifty per cent. or sixty per cent. when a street turned Jewish, with the entire difference pocketed by speculating or rack-renting landlords and partially made back by tenants who took in lodgers.'[31]

Respectable London shuddered at the district on its doorstep that caused it both revulsion and alarm, as East London suffragette historians Sarah Jackson and Rosemary Taylor wrote: 'it was too close for comfort, and many feared that the political activism, industrial action and religious dissent which were also a hallmark of the area would seep westward.'[32] The dissent from religion – which would attract Minnie as she grew older – was perhaps to be expected when, as William Fishman argued, 'God appeared either indifferent or incapable of meeting the demand for daily bread. Unrequited want decreed that socialists got a hearing too.'[33] Fishman (1921-2014) was an author of several studies of the Jewish East End, and was himself the son of a Russian tailor father and a Ukrainian mother, both immigrants to East London.

The first Jewish socialist organisation in the East End had been the *Agudain Hasozialistim Chaverim*, the Hebrew Socialist Union, founded in Whitechapel in 1876 by Aron Lieberman, who had arrived from Russia the previous year. As working-class struggle heightened and New Unionism spawned, Jewish workers set up trade unions, many short-

---

[31] 1960, pp.156-7.

[32] 2014, p.7.

[33] 2004/1975, p.93.

lived and most desiring unity with English unions but compelled to exist separately for the time being due to social and cultural differences and the informal segregation of industry. In trades such as Isaac Glassman's bootmaking, Jews worked alongside Jews, English alongside English.

But even while they organised separately, Jewish and English workers marched together. Half-a-million people attended London's first May Day demonstration in 1890, which thereafter became an annual event hugely significant in the labour movement calendar. Minnie Glassman's future husband Edgar Lansbury recalled the May Day gatherings he attended as a boy, including their Jewish sections:

> From every part of London branches of trade unions, co-operative societies, socialist parties and all kinds of reformers would congregate on Victoria Embankment and with banners flying and bands playing march to Hyde Park to demonstrate the solidarity of the workers throughout the world. ...

> And how we all-too-English boys from Bow would stare in wonder at the curious cosmopolitan crowd that formed the Stepney and Whitechapel contingent, with their strange clothes, lean and dark faces, their ugly scowls, untidy gait – shuffling along arm in arm, women like men and men like women, chanting their revolutionary songs to strange music in strange tongues. I wonder if we ever saw Lenin or Trotsky, Stalin, or Litvinoff in those processions![34]

Perhaps Edgar also saw his future wife.

The Jewish establishment already in England expressed its disdain for the new immigrants and their rebellious ways. When, a month after Minnie's birth in 1889, over two thousand working-class Jews marched through the East End against poverty and unemployment, the *Jewish Chronicle* declared that due to their actions, they were 'not Jews'.[35] The mass arrival of distressed Jews from Tsarist Russia had initially met with sympathy, but this soon turned to hostility, including from those Jews whose place in English society had been established over several generations. In 1893, Chief Rabbi Dr. Adler offered his assurance that Anglo-Jewish leaders were using 'every possible influence to prevent immigrants coming over here from Russia and Poland.'[36]

---

[34] E. Lansbury, 1934, pp.95-6.

[35] Gartner, 1960, p.116.

[36] Fishman 2005/1975, p.215.

By the time of the mass immigration and the Glassmans' arrival in London, Britain had repealed its laws explicitly discriminating against Jews, including those excluding them from the legal and other professions and from being elected to public positions. However, prejudice continued and as Jewish immigration increased so did antipathy to the new arrivals. 1887 saw the first recorded public meeting at which the ratepayers of Mile End – a district named for being one mile to the east of the White Chapel – were invited to petition the government to exclude destitute foreigners (then commonly known as 'aliens') from Britain. The newcomers faced opposition both as Jews and as immigrants, the two prejudices often stirred together.

On a Friday evening in May 1896, Isaac Glassman was driving his horse and cart along Stratford High Street, when 42-year-old John Dooley violently assaulted him. Over a century on, we cannot be certain that the attack on Isaac by Dooley and his accomplice James Sergeant was antisemitic in motivation, but the news report headlined it 'Unprovoked Assault on a Jew'.[37] Minnie was by then seven years old and her father Isaac had given up finishing boots and was now a coal and coke dealer. Dooley grabbed Isaac's horse's head, then:

> He was remonstrated with, and Dooley gave him [Isaac] a savage smack in the face. He screamed for the police, when both the men attacked him, Constable Hutchinson, 617 K, seeing the assaults as he came up. On the road to the station Dooley got away from the police, and again hit Glassman, who was a perfect stranger to both of them. There was no apparent cause for the assaults, and prisoners said it was not feasible they would hit the man for nothing.

John Dooley, aged forty-two, a carman (like Isaac, a driver of horse-drawn vehicles for transporting goods) of 8 Hadley Road, Old Ford, and nineteen-year-old James Sergeant, a cooper (barrel-maker) who lived at 1 Napier Road, Stratford, were found guilty of assaulting Isaac Glassman. The court fined Dooley twenty shillings and Sergeant ten shillings, both with costs. This may not have been Dooley's first time in court: a John Dooley is listed in the 1881 census as resident at HM Prison Springfield; then a dock labourer from Stratford, born in 1854, his details fit those of Isaac's assailant.

According to one study,[38] East End Jews had little contact with the

---

[37] *Lloyd's Weekly Newspaper*, 24th May 1896.

[38] Englander, 2010.

police, who saw them as 'peaceable, sober and relatively free of criminality', and moreover, the Jews and the police viewed each other with considerable suspicion. But on this occasion, Isaac and his cart had ventured out of his Jewish home patch, and the constable had witnessed the event so had little choice but to intervene.

Many British socialists welcomed and showed solidarity with the Jewish immigrants. William Morris, now more famous for the wallpaper designs that remained popular long after his death, was then leading the Socialist League, which worked closely with East End Jewish socialists. Eleanor Marx (daughter of Karl) campaigned against antisemitism and learned Yiddish so that she could help Jewish working-class women in Whitechapel to organise against oppression. Others, though, were hostile. The Social Democratic Federation was Britain's first socialist organisation, set up in 1890, and was avowedly Marxist, but its leader, H.M. (Henry Mayers) Hyndman, was hostile to Jews. Dockers' union leader Ben Tillett deployed stereotypes of Jews in advocating restrictions on immigration in Minnie's birth year of 1889, seeming to blame Jews for their own exploitation:

> The influx of continental pauperism aggravates and multiplies the number of ills which press so heavily on us ... Foreigners come to London in large numbers, herd together in habitations unfit for beasts, the sweating system allowing the more grasping and shrewd a life of comparative ease in superintending the work.[39]

In fact, the 'sweating' system – compelling workers to toil for long hours in terrible conditions for very low pay – had existed before mass Jewish immigration and still plagued industries where there were no Jewish employers or workers. As social reformer and labour historian (and Charles Booth's cousin) Beatrice Webb pointed out, 'if every foreign Jew resident in England had been sent back to his birthplace, the bulk of sweated workers would not have been affected, whether for better or for worse.'[40]

Minnie Glassman was growing up in a Jewish part of a working-class district and alongside socialists and trade unionists some of whom were hostile to her family and her community even being there. If those were the only socialists and trade unionists she had encountered, it seems unlikely that she would have joined their ranks. Fortunately, she also

---

[39] Quoted in Fishman 2004/1975, p.80.

[40] Beatrice Webb, My Apprenticeship, quoted in Fishman 2004/1975, p.80.

came across those who rejected prejudice and showed solidarity towards the Jewish immigrants, including the dominant figure among East End socialists, her future father-in-law George Lansbury. Looking back in 1935, George would write that:

> The foreign Jews and others have done and still do a great deal to keep the true spirit of internationalism and brotherhood alive ... always they come forward cheerfully to help any cause needing assistance ... As I consider the change in East London's population I am convinced that it is nonsense to pretend we have been injured by the huge Jewish immigration. I think we have become better.[41]

The Jews' Free School

Just before her eighth birthday in February 1897, Minnie Glassman left Chicksand Street School and was admitted to the Jews' Free School. Instead of walking to the end of her street, she would now walk for ten minutes to 23 Bell Lane, on the other side of the busy Commercial Street and close to Spitalfields wholesale fruit and vegetable market. Perhaps she walked to school with her older sister Selina, who had enrolled at the school two years previously after finishing her infant schooling at Chicksand Street.

The Jews' Free School had been established in 1732 as the Talmud Torah (boys' religious school) of the Great Synagogue of London. It moved to Bell Lane in 1822 and took on the task of educating the children of Jewish immigrants. By the time that Selina and then Minnie enrolled there, they were among some 3,400 children who attended every day – around one third of all Jewish children in London. When Jewish socialist Israel Zangwill wrote his classic work *Children of the Ghetto* in the early 1890s, his 'great Ghetto school' surely represented the Jews' Free School, at which he had previously worked at a teacher. He wrote of the mass of children – soon to include Minnie and her sister – responding to its bell 'summoning its pupils from the reeking courts and alleys, from the garrets and the cellars, calling them to come and be Anglicized.'

> And they came in a great straggling procession recruited from every lane and by-way, big children and little children, boys in blackened corduroy, and girls in washed-out cotton; tidy

[41] 1935, p.219.

children and ragged children; children in great shapeless boots
gaping at the toes; sickly children, and sturdy children, and
diseased children; bright-eyed children and hollow-eyed
children; quaint sallow foreign-looking children, and fresh-
colored English-looking children; with great pumpkin heads,
with oval heads, with pear-shaped heads; with old men's faces,
with cherubs' faces, with monkeys' faces; cold and famished
children, and warm and well-fed children; children conning
their lessons and children romping carelessly; the demure and
the anaemic; the boisterous and the blackguardly, the insolent,
the idiotic, the vicious, the intelligent, the exemplary, the full –
spawn of all countries – all hastening at the inexorable clang of
the big school-bell to be ground in the same great, blind,
inexorable Governmental machine.[42]

Perhaps when Minnie and Selina arrived each morning, they ate the
'hearty breakfast' of hot milk and bread provided by the school some
years before state schools provided meals for their pupils. Perhaps they
also accepted the clothes, boots and even pocket money that the school
offered. The Jews' Free School was a charitable endeavour, in particular
funded by Lord Rothschild, who received thanks and deference in
return. A typical newspaper article[43] described his generosity with
awestruck admiration rather than questioning a system under which
one person could be so rich while others were so poor.

The school stood in what the *East End News* had in 1888 called 'the
worst area in all London'. With eight hundred people crammed into each
acre, Bell Lane's residential housing had been considered for over a
decade as unfit for human habitation.[44] Bursting at its seams, the school
had cause to complain about insanitary neighbours, and repeatedly
sought to acquire adjacent land, but still suffered from inadequate
accommodation. The girls' section of the school developed cracks in its
ceiling while Minnie was still studying there in 1901, and two years later
the school was looking for estimates for pulling down and rebuilding
the part of the girls' section that had become unstable.[45]

---

[42] 1893, p.30.

[43] *Sheffield Independent*, 13th January 1897.

[44] Quoted in Ramsey, 1997, p.108.

[45] Minutes, Jews' Free School Executive, 4th May and 1st November 1899,
LMA/4046/A/05; letter, Jews' Free School to unnamed building contractor,
4th May 1903, LMA/4046/A/10/002.

When Selina and Minnie started at the school, the head teacher was Moses Angel, who was passionate about integrating Jewish children into English society. At the end of 1897, Louis Barnett Abrahams became their new head teacher, and continued Angel's anglicisation crusade. For him, this including weaning the children off Yiddish, the language that was spoken in most of their homes, including the Glassmans'. At a 1905 school prize-giving event, Abrahams would describe Yiddish as 'that miserable jargon which was not a language at all.'[46]

This unconcealed contempt for the immigrants' language suggests that assimilation, while it may have helped the new arrivals in some ways, had a darker side too. Yiddish was the language of millions of working-class Jews across Europe, but not of those Jews who had become part of the property-owning, capitalist class, who spoke the language of their 'host' country. Jewish socialist Julia Bard wrote nearly a century later that 'The influx of such poor, working-class Jews, many of them bringing revolutionary ideas from Russia and Poland, was a clear threat to the Jewish establishment's carefully constructed image and relationship with the British state. ... In Britain the upper- and middle-class establishment did not encourage Yiddish-speaking Jews to come. Indeed, they co-operated in turning some back to face persecution under the Tsar, then concentrated on keeping those who did come under control.'[47]

Living in a Jewish enclave in the English capital, learning English habits in a Jewish school, speaking English with her teachers and schoolmates but Yiddish with her parents, Minnie was in the same position as Esther Ansell, the fictional twelve-year-old child of Israel Zangwill's ghetto, who 'led a double life, just as she spoke two tongues. The knowledge that she was a Jewish child, whose people had a special history, was always at the back of her consciousness ... But far more vividly did she realize that she was an English girl.'[48]

While Minnie Glassman studied at the Jews' Free School, Jewish people continued to flee antisemitism in Eastern Europe only to find it in their new home as well. As unemployment rose from 1901, it was somehow easier to blame poor immigrants rather than employers or the government, and both East London and Britain generally saw a new rise

---

[46] Oxford Dictionary of National Biography, OUP.

[47] Bard, 1991, pp.87, 88.

[48] Zangwill, 1893, pp.80-1.

in hostility to the recent arrivals. Tory MP for Stepney, Major William Evans-Gordon, led the charge, setting up the anti-immigration British Brothers League in 1900 and the following year moving an amendment to the King's Speech opposing immigration.

In 1895, several of the Jewish trade unions jointly published an appeal to the British trade union movement in response to the anti-immigration resolution passed at that year's Trades Union Congress. The pamphlet, *A Voice from the Aliens*, pointed out that many more people were leaving England than arriving here, and that the Board of Trade (the government department concerned with commerce and industry) had found that Jewish immigrants' work in the boot and shoe trades did not drive English workers out of their jobs: if the likes of Isaac Glassman were not doing this work in London, it would not be done. The Jewish unions argued that, 'To punish the alien worker for the sin of the native capitalist is like the man who struck the boy because he was not strong enough to strike his father.'

Hostility to migration from within the native labour movement helped to smooth the way for the Conservative government to pass the Aliens Act in 1905, Britain's first law restricting immigration. However, putting up border controls did not address the cause of mass Jewish migration. In the same year, revolution in Russia forced Tsar Nicholas II to concede limited democratic reforms but also prompted him to unleash a new wave of political repression, which in turn led to a new wave of Jewish emigrants, among them many socialists and anarchists.

By then, Minnie Glassman's compulsory education had ended and she needed to decide what to do next.

Coborn School for Girls[49]

In 1902, Minnie turned thirteen, and was no longer required to attend school. She was now at the age at which working-class children like her either looked for funding to continue their studies or, far more commonly, left school and looked for work. Secondary schooling was not even part of the state system until the Education Act passed in that year, and only a single-figure percentage of children 'stayed on' at school to pursue a secondary education. One of that small fraction was Minnie Glassman.

---

[49] Unless otherwise specified, references in this section are to the Coborn School for Girls archive.

Why did Minnie choose to set her sights 'higher' than those of other girls of her age and background, most of whom finished their compulsory elementary education and started work for wages, helped look after their families, or did both? Perhaps she was inspired by her father's upward mobility, having seen him give up sweated boot finishing and set himself up as a coal merchant. Perhaps she was aware of her abilities and enjoyed learning. Maybe she already rejected the traditional subservience expected of her sex, the religious conservatism of some in her community, and the low expectations that society held of immigrant East Enders. Most probably, it was a combination of all of these.

Secondary schools charged fees, so with parents who were not wealthy enough to pay, Minnie needed to win both a scholarship and a place in a secondary school. Her chosen place of learning was Coborn School for Girls in Bow. It offered scholarships to girls who had been attending a public elementary school in Bow, Bromley or Stepney for the previous three years, but Minnie had been attending a Jewish charitable school, so she did not qualify. But she was eligible to apply for a scholarship from Samuel Butler's Educational Charity, which had been set up in 1854 by the philanthropist whose name it bears. The charity – which still exists – paid fees and maintenance allowances for the schooling of boys and girls aged twelve to fourteen who were residents of thirteen East End parishes named in its founding documents. Minnie's home in Chicksand Street was in one of those parishes: Christ Church with All Saints, Spitalfields.

To get her Butler scholarship, Minnie would have to pass the Preliminary Examination for the LCC's Junior County Scholarships and then score not less than two hundred marks in the Preliminary and Final Examinations taken together, with Scripture as one of her recognised subjects. The Junior County Scholarship system was a forerunner of the later 'eleven-plus' examination, but even more exclusive. It had been devised to allow some working-class youngsters to continue into education, but only in exceptional cases: the 'Hadow Report' on the Education of the Adolescent[50] referred to scholarship children as 'supernormal'. This was the top level of entry to post-elementary education: students who did quite well in the exam but not well enough to achieve a scholarship could get a place at a 'central school' and receive a technical education; those who failed, or who were not even entered, might have stayed a little longer at elementary school but mostly left education.

---

[50] Board of Education, 1927.

The Butler charity also required confirmation from the Jews' Free School on her attendance, conduct and progress in learning while she had been there, and when it received this and her exam scores, the charity awarded Minnie her scholarship. She was the only Butler scholar at Coborn School for Girls in 1902, and went on to have her award extended for a further year in 1903.

Another local Jewish schoolgirl, Jenny Judelson, explained that, 'if you got a scholarship you were regarded a somebody, you know, quite special.'[51] She added that some parents might not allow their children to take up a scholarship place even if they got one, as they would not be able to afford to fund them to continue beyond the two years of the scholarship. But Minnie had parents who supported her continuing her education, and after the two years of her Butler scholarship, she would have a new plan to continue her studies and a new source of funding.

Coborn School dated from around 1703, set up with a bequest from Prisca Coborn, a Bow brewery owner who had died the previous year with no dependants, plenty of wealth and a passion for education. The school moved between various locations until 1892, when it established itself at 86 Bow Road. By now, it was named Coborn School for Girls, with a separate boys' school also established, Cooper's Company's Grammar School. The separation of boys and girls into two distinct schools went against the original stipulation of Prisca Coborn that the school be mixed-sex.[52] In 1898, Coborn School for Girls moved along Bow Road to the building which today houses Central Foundation Girls' School.[53] Then newly-built and now listed for its historical interest, the school building is in a striking red brick, with white stone dressings, a slate roof, and features including architraves and turrets.

In a cool and rather wet September 1902, Minnie walked up the balustraded stair to the main entrance and joined class LIVa (lower fourth form). She progressed to the upper fourth form in January 1903 and gained distinctions in drawing and needlework (general and patching). Government regulations still required schools to teach girls household skills. Coborn School was required to send half-yearly reports

[51] Audio interview with Jenny Judelson, Tower Hamlets Local History Library and Archive.

[52] Francella, 1973, p.2-4.

[53] In 1973, Coborn School relocated to Upminster, now renamed Coopers' Company and Coborn School, and once again educating boys and girls together.

to the Butler charity on Minnie's conduct and educational progress, on pain of losing her funding if these were repeatedly unsatisfactory. They were not.

Minnie's journey to school took her the short distance from Chicksand Street to Whitechapel Road, then two miles east along the busy thoroughfare, which became Mile End Road and then Bow Road. For the first time, Minnie's daily life took her out of the immigrant Jewish area of Spitalfields and Whitechapel. It also took her across the border from the Borough of Stepney into the Borough of Poplar, municipal units only recently formed, each bringing together several of the parishes which had been the base units of nineteenth-century local administration. Also for the first time, Minnie was attending a school where Jewish children were very much a minority: there were only a handful of girls named Jacobs, Solomon or Baruch among many more English Fishers, Allens and Bells and some Irish Murphys. If Minnie's family were religious, they were not separatist.

In 1904, the London County Council (LCC) took over responsibility for schools in London, and embarked on ten years of 'unification and consolidation', at the end of which it declared that:

> It is now possible for a child of the humblest of parents to gain
> a scholarship from one of the elementary schools at the age of
> 11, to spend 5 years at a secondary school as a junior scholar
> and then at the age of 18 to proceed to a university.[54]

One of those children of the humblest of parents, Minnie Glassman, now aged fifteen, had completed her first two years at the school and now needed a new source of funding to continue her studies. She sat exams at the Stepney Centre and succeeded in the 'competition' to become a London County Council probationary scholar, and so receive free tuition and a maintenance grant of fifteen pounds per year, enough to pay for her school materials and probably to make a small contribution to her family's household.[55]

With other girls also receiving LCC scholarships, Coborn School's pupil population rose to two hundred and sixty. And with their school now recognised by the Board of Education, Minnie and her classmates had to wear school uniform:

[54] The London County Council and Education. A Ten Years' Retrospect 1904-1914 (draft), LCC/EO/GEN/1/146.

[55] LCC Education Committee minutes, 20th July 1904.

navy-blue gym tunics, red blouses in winter and white ones in summer. A plain straw or navy velour hat was worn according to the season, with the school hat-band on which was a badge of Prisca Coborn's coat-of-arms. The uniform could be made at home or bought from the school tailor.[56]

The school year ran from January to December, and Minnie was now one of sixteen pupils in the lower fifth form. They were taught for four-and-a-half hours per day, Monday to Friday: from 9.30am until 12.45pm (with a fifteen-minute break at 11am) and from 2 until 3.30pm, after which Minnie and her fellow lower fifth form pupils were expected to do an hour and a half of homework each day. They studied in buildings described by a 1904 University of London report as 'modern and well designed', with 'bright and pleasant' classrooms and 'well chosen pictures'. The school used its 'fine hall' for drawing, singing and drill (physical exercise). There was 'a good playground' and Minnie and her fellow pupils played games, including tennis and basketball, for an hour after school each week. Coborn School was, however, hampered by a lack of easels, blackboards, physics equipment and wall cupboards, and cookery and science classes had to share the same room.

The University's report recorded a 'very favourable' impression of the education that Minnie and her schoolmates received, particularly praising teaching in English literature, language and composition; modern languages; chemistry; art; and mathematics. It lauded Minnie's headmistress, Miss Emma Cawthorne, as 'enlightened and progressive'; the teachers for working 'loyally and conscientiously'; and the pupils for taking 'genuine interest in their work'. However, it seems that the school's appreciation of its teachers was not reflected in their rates of pay, as the report recorded that: 'The salaries are hardly high enough to be considered satisfactory. There is no pension scheme.'

By the time the report was published, Miss Cawthorne had left her post in order to get married.[57] The expectation that women would not keep working as teachers once they married would confront Minnie Glassman as she became Minnie Lansbury a decade later. Coborn School's new headmistress was a Miss J.W. Holland, who was paid an annual salary of one hundred pounds, less than half of what a headmaster of a boys' school might expect.

---

[56] Francella, 1973.

[57] *East London Observer*, 25th April 1903.

Meanwhile, Minnie continued her progress, passing her Junior Cambridge University Local Examination and winning a school prize. Her achievement was recognised at a prize-giving event in the very wet and dull month of June 1905, chaired by local MP and Chair of Governors Sir Harry Samuel, at which presentations were made by (the first) Mrs. Bertrand Russell – American-born Quaker relief organiser Alys Pearsall Smith. Minnie was again awarded a London County Council scholarship.

The annual prize-giving was an important event in the school's calendar, and included musical performances by the pupils. Local dignitaries attended, including the Rector of Bow, the Reverend Henry Kitcat. This may have been the first event at which he and Minnie were both present, but it would not be the last. Over the next fifteen years, they would, despite their political differences, work together supporting war victims and serving on the local borough council. Prize-giving was a grand affair, on which local newspapers reported and at which Coborn School showed its patrons 'all the enthusiasm and freshness which characterises this sound scholastic institution.' Minnie and the other pupils wore 'white dresses, relieved with a rosette of geranium bloom, [and] looked particularly neat and intelligent – a credit to the school.'[58]

Harry Samuel was a Conservative, one of a succession of Tories and Liberals who represented East London seats in Parliament. They represented those who were entitled to vote – men of property – while the working class, mostly voteless, organised and fought against the capitalists' domination of politics. Anarchists were active among the Jewish community in which Minnie lived, led by Rudolf Rocker. Not himself a Jew, German-born Rocker nonetheless dedicated his political life to organising and supporting Jewish working-class struggle and culture. Rocker and others opened the Workers' Friend Club, first in Berner Street and then in Jubilee Street, less than a mile from Minnie's home and near the Royal London Hospital, the great medical centre which had stood in and served Whitechapel for over one hundred and fifty years and which still does today. The club ran social functions, educational classes and chess competitions; provided a bar and cheap refreshments; and hosted debates. Jewish socialist historian William Fishman argued that the Workers' Friend Club's influence may even have exceeded that of the more famous Toynbee Hall, the charitable settlement of social reformers on nearby Commercial Street, adding that

---

[58] *East London Observer*, 2nd June 1906.

the club 'was rarely empty, attracting the young (the majority) and old, the political and apolitical, the informed and the ignorant.'[59] Vladimir Lenin visited the Club in 1907 and 1908, and other revolutionary visitors to the area included Leon Trotsky, Louise Michel and Peter Kropotkin; the Russian Bolsheviks held a congress in Whitechapel in May 1907. Perhaps Minnie read about or even saw some of these people and events.

The East End in which Minnie Glassman was growing up was fizzing with rebel politics. The British labour and socialist movement was surging, and it would be this, rather than a specifically Jewish movement, in which Minnie would involve herself. Moreover, it was a labour movement in which working-class women were playing an increasing role, exposing and opposing their low wages, long hours, insanitary conditions and burdensome responsibilities at home.

The options for working-class girls leaving school were not great. If Minnie had left education after elementary school, she might have found work in a shop, or as a feather dresser, bookbinder or artificial flower maker. Or she might have worked in a factory or at home, making ties, matchboxes or other goods, usually for meagre wages and in unsafe conditions. Domestic service would have been an unlikely choice, as relatively few Jewish girls and women worked for pay in another person's home.[60] And although Minnie had already shown herself willing to break some Jewish conventions and would go on to break more, domestic service would probably not have figured as a principle worth breaking. Society at that time considered itself to have a 'servant problem': for families wanting to employ servants, it was a problem of finding willing workers; for the servants themselves, the problem was low wages, low status and unpleasant conditions.[61] Girls, it seems, preferred the freedom and enjoyment offered by shop, mill or factory work. In London, over one hundred thousand girls and women worked as milliners and dressmakers. Minnie Glassman's elder sister Selina had become a milliner, and went on to work for several theatrical companies.

Minnie, however, had continued her education to secondary level, which opened up more opportunities and choices. Most secondary school girls took up jobs such as clerical work or teaching, which were paid at a modest but not poverty level, and in which a young woman

---

[59]   2004/1975, p.267.

[60]   Walter, 2010.

[61]   Schwartz, 2015.

could have a career and a degree of independence without competing with men.[62] As a young woman who had herself enjoyed and benefited from education, and at a time when schooling was expanding and educators were in demand, Minnie Glassman decided to become a school teacher.

---

[62] Gillard, 2018.

Chapter 2 – Student, Suffragette and School Teacher

Teaching the Teachers

Zangwill's Esther Ansell wanted to become a teacher, but feared that she was too poor and not clever enough.[63] If Minnie Glassman had these anxieties, she would have to tackle them through repeatedly passing examinations and winning scholarships.

The route into teaching began at secondary school as a 'pupil teacher'. This system dated back to 1839, but at the start of the twentieth century became more structured. Minnie Glassman was one of the first generation to prepare for teaching under the new system. She was also one of the aspiring teachers to benefit from a new move to make provision for non-Anglicans to join the profession. Following lobbying from the National Union of Teachers, this had been added to the 1902 Education Act,[64] which had given control of education to county and municipal authorities. The following year, new Pupil-Teacher Regulations stipulated that pupil-teachership began at sixteen years of age and involved both teaching and being taught how to teach. The former took place only in schools approved for the purpose and the latter in Pupil-Teacher Centres where possible.

Implementing the new rules, the London County Council (LCC) devised a system for teacher training. Between fourteen and sixteen years of age, the aspiring teacher would attend secondary school funded by a probationer scholarship, then from sixteen until eighteen years of age, s/he would become a pupil teacher, receive a pupil-teacher grant and gain some teaching experience.

Coborn School's application for approval of its Pupil-Teacher Centre set out its proposal to recruit pupil-teachers from among the girls in its own upper forms and to send them to practise teaching in a local elementary school for one term. It would take around thirty girls (fifteen each year), and at that point, half of the school's fifty probationer scholars were competing for places starting the following September.[65] The Centre opened in 1906, and among its first intake was Minnie

---

[63] 1893, p.89.

[64] Cloake, 2018, p.13.

[65] LCC Clerk's Department: Coborn School, 1906-08 Recognition, EO/PS/3/139.

Glassman, who had completed her two years as a probationary scholar and succeeded in the competition for pupil teachership. She would have received a grant of £20.16.0 in her first year and £26 in her second year, significantly less than the boys' pupil-teacher rate of £32 and £39.[66]

By now, Coborn School's student population had grown to over three hundred and the school was turning away some applicants. That year, the school inspector reported that it 'continues to do increasing good work' while still struggling with a 'want of proper accommodation and furnishing' and in need of new buildings and outside areas. The inspector's report praised the school's drill and remedial work for 'satisfactory results' in 'back-straightening among London County Council scholars ... most encouraging.' The LCC scholars, among them Minnie Glassman, were the working-class children who studied alongside fee-paying pupils from wealthier backgrounds, and it seems that the impoverished conditions of London's East End had bent their backs by their early teens. Coborn School was also concerned about the lack of open spaces in the local area, so it increased the time its pupils spent playing games to two hours after school per week. It also reduced homework and dispensed with summer term exams, as girls 'take examinations much more seriously than boys' and girls were frequently dropping out of school 'through being overdone' [ie. exhausted].[67]

Minnie passed her Senior Cambridge exam in 1907 with distinction in religious knowledge, and left school aged eighteen in December to spend the spring and summer terms teaching in a local elementary school. I have not been able to confirm which school this was, but it may have been Oban Street School, as this was mentioned in one of her obituaries as a school in which she taught.

In 1908, Minnie was among twenty-one students from the upper fifth and sixth forms named on the school's honours list. She had successfully completed her pupil teachership and could now move on to the higher-level training to qualify as a teacher. As Minnie left, her youngest sister Leah began at Coborn School, the only one of her siblings to do so. Leah was a month short of her fourteenth birthday when she joined the upper third form in September 1908, leaving four years later 'owing to ill-health' to work at home as a shorthand typist.[68]

---

[66] LCC press release, 1906, LCC/EO/TRA/1/30.

[67] Correspondence, Coborn School for Girls to Board of Education, 16th November 1906.

[68] Coborn School archive – admissions record.

As Minnie left and Leah arrived, the school's increased pupil numbers and workload – still without a much-needed extension of its premises – had caused the headmistress Miss Holland a 'temporary breakdown in health', and she was absent for most of the first two terms of the 1908/09 school year. The LCC's inspector recommended double-glazed windows be installed at the front of the building, as 'The noise of the traffic ... is very nerve exhausting.'[69]

In the decade since the turn of the century, the Bow Road on which Minnie attended school had changed from a genteel thoroughfare to a cacophony of motor-traffic. A photograph from the beginning of the decade shows the stretch of Bow Road on which Coborn School stood, known then as 'The Promenade'. True to its name, it had wide pavements, along which gentlemen in suits and top hats and ladies in bonnets and full dresses walked, either side of a cobbled road along which horses pulled carts. But the horse-drawn vehicles were not fast enough, and the development of electric traction and of motor vehicles were about to drive dramatic change. The new Whitechapel and Bow Railway extended the District Railway (now London Underground's District line) through new stations at Stepney Green, Mile End and Bow Road, where it emerged above ground. The line opened in 1902, the year in which Minnie began her daily journey along the road to Coborn School, and was electrified in 1905, two years after the London County Council inaugurated its new electric tramway. In his book, *The East End: Then and Now*, Winston G. Ramsey writes that, 'horses were fighting a losing battle with the internal combustion engine which was under threat from electric power. The decade saw a tremendous revolution in transport methods as each vied with the other for popular favour.'[70] Minnie made her first journeys to secondary school alongside horse-drawn vehicles but her last ones alongside motor-cars and electric trams.

As well as being a loud and busy thoroughfare, Bow Road was also a regular stage for the rebel political activism in which the young Minnie Glassman would go on to involve herself. Alongside the emerging Labour Party and the ongoing battles waged by trade unionists, working-class women were organising for better conditions and the right to vote.

---

[69] LCC Education Committee Higher Education Sub-Committee report, 1908/09.

[70] Ramsey, 1997, pp.277, 53.

Votes for Women

Through the nineteenth century, a series of Reform Acts had extended the Parliamentary voting franchise to wider categories of men. The last, in 1884, extended it to men who owned a house, but still left vast numbers of men – and all women – voteless, ruled by people whom they had had no say in electing. By the end of the century, single (and some married) women ratepayers were eligible to vote in elections to local councils, a political sphere concerned with education and social care, considered more suitable to the female nature than the masculine sphere of Parliament and its deliberations on economics and war.

Those who supported votes for women did not so much demand the franchise as politely request it from those who had no intention of giving it, but in 1889, the Pankhurst family set up the Women's Franchise League to provide a more assertive approach. But still the only two government parties of the era, the Conservatives and the Liberals, stubbornly refused the women's claims. In 1897, the more polite suffrage campaigners established the National Union of Women's Suffrage Societies (NUWSS). In 1903, again frustrated by slow progress, the Pankhursts and others set up the Women's Social and Political Union (WSPU).

From 1905, the WSPU stepped up its militancy, with members breaking windows and taking other direct actions. Over a thousand campaigners served prison sentences over the following nine years. *Daily Mail* writer Charles Hands distinguished the militant women from their less confrontational suffragist sisters by labelling them 'suffragettes', a badge the women wore with pride.

In 1906, while seventeen-year-old Minnie Glassman pursued her pupil teachership, twenty-four-year-old Sylvia Pankhurst made her first journey to London's East End. Along with fellow suffragette Annie Kenney, she paid a visit to George Lansbury at his home in St. Stephen's Road in Bow, just half a mile from Minnie's school, to the north. George was one of the highest-profile male supporters of votes for women, and the leading socialist in the East End. Sylvia recalled that Lansbury lived in 'a little house adjoining the family woodyard', and added that, 'He introduced us to his son, Edgar, of whom he was obviously proud, whilst we endeavoured, not very successfully, to break the ice with his daughters, who, perhaps because they were so many, were not introduced.'[71]

---

[71] Pankhurst, 1931/77, p.198.

This was also around the time that Minnie Glassman met George's son Edgar, her future husband, who was two years older than her.[72] Moreover, it was around the time that their fathers Isaac and George first met.[73] So, did Minnie and Edgar meet through their father, or did George and Isaac meet through their son and daughter? Sadly, we do not know.

Sylvia would return to the area in 1912 to establish a WSPU branch that Minnie would join and that would organise 'Not by the secret militancy of a few enthusiasts, but by the rousing of the masses.'[74] She would be doing so in an area where the masses were already considerably roused.

Teacher Training

In 1908, with her pupil teachership successfully completed, nineteen-year-old Minnie Glassman could apply for the two-year course to obtain the Certificate of Education that would qualify her to teach in a state elementary school. Aspiring teachers had the choice of several training colleges across London dedicated solely to teacher education, but there was a further option too. Goldsmiths' College in New Cross was the only teacher training centre maintained by a University, had begun accepting student teachers in 1905, and had become the largest teacher training college in Britain. It was also the first at which men and women studied together and, crucially for Minnie Glassman, it was the first non-denominational teacher training college. A Jewish woman like Minnie could learn alongside women and men of all faiths and none.[75] Goldsmiths' was the obvious choice for Minnie to train as a teacher, so long as she could win a place.

Minnie applied alongside two hundred and fifty others from across London for an LCC-funded place at Goldsmiths' starting in autumn 1908 and was one of ninety-five who were successful. She began travelling daily across the River Thames to study, quite possibly on a

---

[72] A letter from Edgar to Minnie's sister Katie, undated but written between 1922 and 1923, referred to having met Minnie seventeen years previously.

[73] Stated by George when he testified to Isaac's suitability for naturalisation as a British citizen, 1912.

[74] Pankhurst, 1931/77, p.416.

[75] www.sites.gold.ac.uk/goldsmithshistory

steam train along the East London Railway (now London Overground) from Whitechapel to New Cross, to the grand, red-brick, Victorian college building.

In their first year, Minnie and her classmates pursued a 'general education', to bring them all to the level of academic knowledge needed to teach children. They studied English language and literature, arithmetic, science, history, geography, physical training, music and drawing. Women took domestic training (including needlework); men took manual training (including woodwork). Women and men even studied a different mathematics syllabus.

These subjects continued into the second year, alongside education in how to teach: the theory and history of teaching, and practical issues of physiology and hygiene at school. Minnie planned to teach the youngest elementary school children, and as an 'Intending Infant Teacher', studied how to teach needlework through sewing on coarse canvas, the aim being 'to familiarize little children with the use of needle and scissors, and the manipulation of material, convincing them at the beginning of the practical utility of needlework.' Minnie and her fellow Intending Infant Teachers also learned about taking children on excursions to study nature in Greenwich Park or elsewhere, and were given suggestions 'for lessons on animals and interests which surround them'.[76]

Among the friends that Minnie made at College was Edith Hellowy, known as 'Deano', who later wrote of their 'happy time there together'. Their friendship continued for several years beyond their graduation, but eventually they drifted apart, largely due to their differences of opinion, particularly on religion. Edith was a devout Christian, but as Minnie said to her, 'It's no good Deano, I'm not religious.'[77] Minnie had grown up in a Jewish community, but in a family which was less religiously strict than others, which supported her in attending a Christian secondary school, and which itself interacted with non-Jews, for example in her father Isaac's business dealings. She had studied science and other subjects, including excelling in Christian-based religious knowledge, a subject which she had chosen to learn when she could have refused to do so by exercising her the right to withdraw. She had thought and learned about religion, and had rejected it not through ignorance or moral apathy but through understanding.

76 Goldsmith's information book, 1908/09 and 1909/10.

77 Letter, Edith Hellowy to George Lansbury, 22th January 1922, LSE Lansbury collection.

Minnie's London County Council scholarship brought with it a grant of twenty pounds per year (men received twenty-five pounds)[78] and a signed undertaking from the student that she would teach in an LCC public elementary school for two years after qualifying. The value of the student grant was not the only way in which men and women were treated differently. They had separate entrances to the college buildings, separate corridors, separate lunch sittings and separate times in the gym and swimming pool. The men who lodged at the college had a curfew of 10pm while the women had to be in by 8pm; the college was closed to women after 7pm and all day Saturdays, but closed to men only on Saturday mornings; the Pavilion was out of bounds for women; and smoking was allowed in the men's common room but not in the women's.[79]

Perhaps this contributed to Minnie's growing awareness of women's disadvantage and her decision to fight against it. If so, she had opportunities to discuss these issues while at Goldsmiths'. The College's Women's Society formed in November 1909, 'for the object of discussing social problems especially relating to women,' open to all college members on the 'Women's Side' who paid a two pence subscription and regularly attended the meetings, which took place every third Thursday during the dinner hour. Invited speakers introduced discussions on subjects including the Poor Law Guardians and women, married women's work, and women in local government,[80] three areas which would be very relevant to Minnie's future work and activism.

Debate also raged at the College about votes for women. The college's quarterly magazine, *The Goldsmithian*, published 'a point of view' from a Miss C.E.M. Todd in favour of women's suffrage in its November 1908 issue, prompting another, opposing point of view in the following issue three months later:

> [M]an has to deal with … questions such as declarations of war, where cool, hard thinking is necessary, and when sentimentality has to be thrown on one side. I venture to say that, with very few exceptions, women can not throw sentiment aside and give a calm decision, the outcome of careful thought.

---

[78] LCC press release, 1906, LCC/EO/TRA/1/30.

[79] Goldsmith's College Training Department Students' Handbook 1910-11.

[80] *The Goldsmithian*, December 1910, July 1910.

The writer concluded by recommending that 'all women have their confidence in man, their natural protectors, restored; and … follow their proper lives and vocations allotted to them by Nature.' By the time that *The Goldsmithian* published a further, pro-suffrage reply in its June issue, Goldsmiths' College had a Women's Suffrage Society. At the end of that year, around four hundred people attended the Literary and Debating Society's debate on the issue, the majority of whom endorsed the resolution, 'that women ought not to possess the Parliamentary Suffrage'. But for Minnie Glassman, the struggle for the vote would take place in the streets of the East End more than in University debating rooms.

At the end of her course, Minnie obtained her Board of Education Teachers' Certificate with distinction in music.[81] She had excelled in learning to teach music to infants at a time when this consisted almost entirely of singing. As a teacher, she would be expected to lead her class in singing hymns and patriotic songs, seen as part of their moral and physical, as well as their cultural, development. Minnie's distinction in music coincided with the final years of the 'Romantic' period in classical music, and increased popular interest in jazz and English folk songs. Her own background would have included Yiddish folk music.

Having qualified as a teacher, Minnie began looking for work in the East End: a more difficult task than you might expect.

Finding Work at Fairclough Street

It would take Minnie Glassman a year to get a job as a teacher, facing the same struggle as hundreds of others did in a year when teacher unemployment was the 'political "hot potato"'.[82] The London County Council had required trainee teachers to commit to teaching in its schools, but did not commit itself to provide the jobs for them to do so.

London's unemployed teachers took a deputation to the LCC in August 1910 protesting at its failure to employ the teachers whom it had itself trained. A spokesperson for the jobless teachers explained that they 'had been lured into the profession, bribed by bursaries, scholarships and Press advertisements,' and said that 'if they were not actually promised they were insidiously led to expect employment at the end of their training.' The unemployed teachers made clear that they were 'not sitting still. They have elected a fighting Executive who are enthusiastic with the enthusiasm of

[81] Coborn School archive, press clipping, December 1910.

[82] www.leicesternut.org.uk/docs/history.php

desperation, and who will not rest content until they have secured justice for their most unfortunate comrades.[83] The Organisation Committee of the Unemployed listed those who had obtained their Certificate of Education but not yet got a job, including Minnie Glassman.

The situation became so bad that it began to deter young women from even applying for teacher training. By 1911-12, Goldsmiths' had its lowest proportion of women teacher trainees yet, attributing this to women being 'more affected than the men by the temporary (and for the most part local) unemployment of newly-trained teachers which has prevailed during the last two or three years.'[84]

For a year after qualifying as a teacher, Minnie looked for a job, while still living with her parents, probably helping with their business and with her siblings, the youngest of whom, Hyman, was now eight years old. Finally, she got a job. Minnie began working in the infants' department of Fairclough Street LCC School in an unusually rainy June 1911, replacing a Miss Stilliard, who had moved to Findlay Street School.[85] With the crisis of teacher unemployment, she may not have had much choice over which school she worked at, but to the extent to which she did, choosing a Jewish school near her home made sense.

Fairclough Street elementary school had opened at the start of that academic year, in a brand new building on the former site of Dutfield's Yard, where 'Jack the Ripper' had murdered Elizabeth Stride in 1888, the year before Minnie was born. Her ten-minute, southward walk from home to school took her across the two main highways, Whitechapel Road and Commercial Road (the western part of East India Dock Road). Like most new schools in London and other big cities, Fairclough Street was housed in a triple-decker building, with infants on the ground floor, boys on the next and girls at the top. Arthur Conan Doyle had his famous fictional detective Sherlock Holmes describe them (in *The Naval Treaty*) as 'big isolated clumps of buildings, rising above the slates like brick islands in a lead coloured sea – lighthouses, beacons of the future, capsules with hundreds of bright little seeds in each, out of which will spring the wiser, better England of the future.' Pevsner's architecture guide described Fairclough Street School's cookery and laundry block as 'charmingly detailed'.[86]

[83]   *School Government Chronicle*, 28th August 1910.

[84]   Goldsmith's College Old Students' Association Year Book, 1911-12.

[85]   Register of teachers, Council schools, 1911-15, LMA, LCC/EO/STA.

Fairclough Street School has since been renamed Harry Gosling Primary School, after the docker and trade unionist whom Minnie would get to know as she became more involved in East End labour politics. It still stands, educating new generations of mainly Bengali local children after having taught mainly Jewish children through the first part of the twentieth century. A later Jewish pupil of the school explained that she had to walk past a school nearer to her home to attend Fairclough Street School, as 'I guess the "powers that be" decided to organise it so that all the Jewish children went to Fairclough Street. In fact, most of the teachers there ... were Jewish and we had our own 'prayers' every morning, in Hebrew.'[87] The LCC recognised that certain of its schools were de facto Jewish schools, and arranged for these to have different holiday periods from other schools, to allow the observation of Jewish festivals.

The school that Minnie joined had modern buildings and a spacious playground, but it struggled through its first few years. The LCC's inspector reported in 1913 that it had been beset with 'marked' difficulties:

> The type of pupil with which the school was originally filled was not very good; the regular normal flow of children through the departments from the Infant grades to the Senior classes is not by any means established yet; and there have been considerable difficulties in the staffing. In addition it has been found necessary to use the Infants' Hall for feeding purposes.

What was this 'not very good' 'type of pupil' whom Minnie taught? Did the inspector mean poor, or immigrant, or Jewish, or working-class, or, most likely, all of these? If so, then Minnie was teaching children who were like she had been at that age.

The inspector was pleased to see that the infants' department, in which Minnie taught, benefited from a headmistress, Miss G.E. Jenkins, who had been a 'brilliant teacher of infants' at her previous school in Hackney, and was 'well read in modern methods of teaching'. Since Minnie's own elementary education, much had changed. Either side of the 1902 Education Act, the government had set out for the first time a list of subjects that each teacher would deliver to the children in her class, including English, arithmetic, geography and history. Schools now

---

[86] www.stgiteshistory.org.uk

[87] Ruth Migdale, www.jewisheastend.com/christianstreet.html, accessed 22nd June 2014.

also paid more attention to children's well-being: they began to provide meals and medical inspections. The government's Board of Education explained that:

> The purpose of the school is education in the fullest sense of the word: the high function of the teacher is to prepare the child for the life of a good citizen, to create or foster the aptitude for work and for the intelligent use of leisure, and to develop those features of character which are most readily influenced by school life, such as loyalty to comrades, loyalty to institutions, unselfishness and an orderly and disciplined habit of mind.[88]

Fairclough Street School accommodated around one thousand pupils and employed one head and eight assistant teachers in each of its boys', girls' and infants' departments. Minnie – 'Miss Glassman' at school – would have sat at the front of a class of around fifty young children. She wrote on a blackboard with chalk and taught her young charges to write first with their fingers in sand trays, later progressing to a slate and pencil. It was no doubt difficult to keep such as large class in order, even with the assistance of her handbell. But at least Minnie would not be administering any punishment that inflicted bodily pain, as this was barred in infants' departments. Perhaps she detained children at the end of the school day, perhaps she made some wear the widely-used 'dunce's hat', but none would be caned until they progressed out of her care and into the junior departments.

Fairclough Street School's struggle to establish itself was taking its toll on headmistress Miss Jenkins, and the inspector, fulsome in his praise but anxious for her well-being, recommended that she be transferred to a 'less exacting school'. Minnie had studied in a secondary school whose headmistress had become ill through workload and pressure; now she was teaching in an infants' school where the same was happening.

Teacher Trade Unionist

Miss Jenkins was paid one hundred and fifty pounds per year, rather less than the two hundred pounds paid to Mr. Pinhorn, the headmaster of the junior departments. The difference in pay between men and women applied also to the classroom teachers. Minnie Glassman's wage was ninety pounds per year when she started (giving her the spending

---

[88] Handbook of Suggestions for the Consideration of Teachers and others concerned with the Work of the Public Elementary Schools, 1905, HMSO.

power of around eleven-and-half thousand pounds today), rising by four pounds annually. Had she been a man, it would have been ninety-five pounds, and would have risen by a higher figure.[89] Women's pay was less than men's throughout the teaching profession, despite men and women having passed the same qualifying examinations, having spent two or three years often at a mixed training college, and frequently teaching in mixed schools in adjacent classrooms.

Minnie could accept this inequality or challenge it. She chose to challenge it. The obvious place for a woman teacher to look to for support in doing this would be her trade union, and for certificated elementary school teachers, this was the National Union of Teachers (NUT). Minnie joined the NUT and its local branch, the East London Teachers' Association (ELTA). By 1914, she was a 'collector' for the union at Fairclough Street School, collecting union subscription fees from the four other members at the school, all of whom were women. The union had few members there and had not had a collector at the school until Minnie took up the post. By the following year, NUT membership at Fairclough Street had risen to six, one quarter of the number of assistant teachers at the school. Minnie attended ELTA meetings at Bromley Public Hall, a large, impressive building in a classical Italianate style, with round arched windows and an arched porch leading to its front door. ELTA elected Minnie to represent it at the conference of the newly-formed London Teachers' Association for 1914-15.[90]

Women made up the majority of members of the NUT nationally, and the union was making efforts to attract and involve more women. From 1909, its 'Ladies Committee' began holding a women's meeting at the annual NUT Conference and in 1910, the union elected its first female President, Miss Conway. In her study of women teachers,[91] Alison Oram asserts that they 'were more densely unionised … and took a greater part in union affairs than probably any other body of women workers in this period', elementary teachers even more so than secondary teachers. By 1914, seventy-five per cent of women certificated elementary teachers were NUT members, alongside over ninety per cent of men.

---

[89] Register of Teachers in Council schools, LCC/EO/STA/4/63.

[90] ELTA Year Books, 1914 and 1915; minutes, LTA Local Committee 1914/15.

[91] Oram, 1996.

But while it was making organisational efforts, was the union fighting for the demands that mattered to women teachers like Minnie, in the first place pay rates equal to those of their male colleagues? Sadly not. In 1904, a group of NUT members had formed an Equal Pay League, which two years later became the National Federation of Women Teachers (NFWT), but it would take many more years to win the union to a policy supporting equal pay and even longer to seriously fighting for it. NUT Conference repeatedly voted against resolutions calling for equal pay, a stance that the NFWT pointed out was against the interests of men teachers as well as women, comparing male teachers' attitudes unfavourably with those of male doctors:

> When women began to practise medicine and surgery, medical men saw the danger to their professional incomes and status that might possibly arise, and they wisely insisted that women doctors be paid on the same scale as themselves. How different is the attitude of men teachers to their women colleagues! They not only begrudge equal pay for equal qualifications and skill, but promote scales of salaries, showing glaring inconsistencies, and press these upon Local Education Authorities![92]

At the East London Teachers' Association (ELTA) quarterly general meeting on 6th December 1913, Minnie Glassman successfully proposed that the meeting debate a resolution to NUT conference supporting the principle of equal pay for men and women teachers of the same professional status. The minutes record what happened next:

> After discussion a vote was taken and as the voting was close the Chairman [Mr. Keddell] called for another vote appealing to all members to vote. The Chairman declared the Resolution Lost by 25 for and 26 against. A division was claimed for but not agreed to by the Chairman who declared the meeting adjourned to Friday December 12th …

A division is a method of accurately determining the result of a close vote by requiring each member in turn to declare 'for' or 'against' (or 'abstain'). At the reconvened meeting on 12th December, Mr. Keddell explained his reason for refusing a division when members had requested it, but while the meeting accepted the explanation, the minutes did not record what it was!

ELTA's leaders apparently wanted to avoid any repeat of such embarrassment, so at the Annual General Meeting (AGM) in February

[92] Presidential address, NFWT handbook, 1914, p.15.

1914, they proposed to alter the rules so that a division would be held only if twenty – rather than the existing three – members requested it. Minnie saw a problem with this proposal: it would make it easier for branch leaders to declare that votes had gone a different way than they actually had, and harder for members to challenge this. So she proposed an amendment to the rule change proposal, seconded by Miss Gritton, to replace 'twenty' members required for a division with 'ten'. Perhaps she thought that tactically, she would be more likely to succeed with this than with outright opposition to the rule change; perhaps she thought ten to be the most reasonable and democratic figure. Either way, the meeting defeated Minnie's amendment and agreed the leaders' proposed rule change.

We can see from this episode how astute and developed Minnie Glassman had already become as a political activist. As well as fighting for her beliefs – in this case, equal pay – against stiff opposition, she could see the machinations of trade union bureaucracy at a branch level and fought for democracy against attempts to stifle it. Maybe this was something she could see for herself, or maybe she had learned something about democratic ways of organising from the local suffragettes.

Would the union be better on the issue of women's suffrage? Even if women did not deserve to be paid as much as men, surely they did deserve a vote? The same ELTA meeting in December 1913 that (officially) voted down the equal pay resolution also carried by 38 votes (including Minnie's) to 22 a resolution to NUT Conference that it 'express its sympathy with those members of the N.U.T. who desire to possess and exercise the Parliamentary Franchise, but, because they are women, and for that reason alone, are debarred from doing so.' This overturned the previous position of the branch, carried in December 1911, that 'the discussion of such a political subject should have no place at Conference.' Perhaps the irony of men and women voting on this on equal terms at their trade union branch meeting was not lost on them.

Minnie was not a delegate to the 1914 NUT Conference which debated the pro-suffrage resolution. When it did so, the resolution appeared to be carried on a show of hands, but a 'card vote' (in which each constituent association casts a number of votes equal to the number of its members) was called and it was defeated. An amendment stating that women's suffrage was outside the scope of the objects of the union was carried by 46,000 (card) votes to 27,000, to the great disappointment and anger of feminist delegates and amid 'much disorder'.[93] Reflecting on this and similar incidents the following year, ELTA's outgoing and incoming Presidents told the Association that:

> On more than one occasion recently, when a certain motion ... was brought before meetings of teachers, a parrot cry would go up 'No politics,' although every teacher is forced to recognise that citizenship and education are indissolubly connected ... let us drop the traditional cant about 'no politics' in school.[94]

Unlike most mixed trade unions, the NUT made no formal differentiation in the rights or status of its male and female members, but involvement in the union was a frustrating experience for Minnie and other women who wanted to advance equality. The union's prolonged obstruction of women teachers' claims for equality eventually led to a split, with the National Union of Women Teachers separating from the NUT in 1920, but the women teachers' battles also brought them a greater part in the larger struggle for women's enfranchisement.

Minnie Glassman would become part of that broader struggle. But in the meantime, her family was becoming officially British, with her father citing Minnie's job as one of his reasons.

Becoming British[95]

The police report attached to Isaac Glassman's application for naturalisation, dated 13th January 1913, describes his residence and settled place of business, 37 Chicksand Street, as consisting of:

> a shop and five rooms, for which he pays a rental of 16/- per week ... the rooms are clean, well furnished and appear to be in good sanitary condition. ... There are five children under age residing with Memorialist [ie. applicant: Isaac], all of whom appear to be healthy and well cared for.

Minnie, now aged twenty-three, was the sole over-age child living at the address, her older sister Selina having married Abraham Lazarus in 1910 and given birth to a daughter, Ruth, two years later (a son, Harold, would follow in 1916). Minnie came home from work each day to a house busy with business activity and with her five younger sisters and brothers, Kate, Ray, Leah, Louis and Hyman.

---

[93] *Daily Herald*, 17th April 1914.

[94] ELTA Year Book 1915.

[95] Unless referenced otherwise, information in this section is from Isaac Glassman's naturalisation papers, HO 144/1243/231498 C615098.

As well as 37 Chicksand Street, Isaac also rented a stable in the next parallel road to the north, Heneage Street, described by Charles Booth as a 'Decent class street – long established Jews'. The stable's rent was nineteen shillings and sixpence per week. If it seems odd that Isaac was charged more to house his horse than the sixteen shillings per week that he paid to house his whole family, we can perhaps infer that the stable's rent included the upkeep of the horse.

'Glassman Isaac, coal dealer' had first appeared in the Post Office's London Directory in 1898, when Minnie was nine, and by the time of his application for citizenship, his headed notepaper boasted that he was a 'CARMAN AND CONTRACTOR Coal & Coke Merchant – Removals done at the shortest notice'. So, he was a man with a (horse-drawn) van and a deliverer of fuel and other goods. Households would buy their fuel from the coalman who delivered around their area and would store it in a cupboard until it was needed for the fire or the stove.

Isaac was by no means the only businessperson on Chicksand Street. On the road where Minnie lived, there were confectioners, furniture makers, timber merchants, beer retailers, a trimming seller, dairy, bottle merchant, cigar manufacturer, whipmaker, butcher and more, all trading from the premises in which they also lived. Most were Jewish, judging from names including Jacob Lipshitz at number 12, Lazarus Goldman at number 47 and Zalic Rubinstein at number 49a.[96] Mrs. Hannah Lazarus at number 9 ran one of the street's several chandler's shops, selling candles to a population still not served by electricity. Even the streets were lit by gas lamps, as described by an East End resident:

> In the early days of the [twentieth] century, when the air was laden with factory and locomotive smoke, which caused frequent fogs, the main street lighting was by gas light. A regular sight was to see the attendant walking through thoroughfares, carrying a pole on his shoulder, long enough to reach the gas lamp, at the top of the lamp post. He made his rounds at dusk, putting on the light with the pole, and at dawn putting it out by the same method.[97]

Isaac's business appeared to be doing well, and as it expanded, he needed help both in its premises – which doubled as his family home – and in making deliveries, so by the census year of 1911, he was employing one person for each. He had gone from greener to guv'nor. His domestic

---

[96] Post Office London Directory, 1898.

[97] Blake, 1977/95, pp.18-19.

servant, fifty-four-year-old Elizabeth Read, lived with the Glassmans, and was one of many Irish women then doing such work in London.[98] In that year, domestic service was the largest occupation for workers across England and Wales, employing over a million men and (mainly) women.

As an employer, had Isaac been British, he would now qualify to vote. So, more than twenty years after arriving in London, Isaac Glassman applied for naturalisation as a British citizen, citing as his reason: 'a desire to vote and for the benefit of [his] children, one of whom [Minnie] is a School Teacher at Fairclough Street, L.C.C. School London East.'

Naturalisation was the process by which a foreign-born person – known as an alien – changed his nationality to that of the country in which he now lived, thereby gaining the same legal rights and status as a natural-born citizen. In Britain at this time, the process was governed by the 1890 Naturalisation Act and was a tough road to take, perhaps another contributory factor to Isaac's long delay in applying. As William Fishman explained, 'The immigrant was scarcely allowed to forget that he was an unwanted foreigner, and naturalisation was a long and costly affair.'[99] There were various routes by which a person could qualify to apply, the primary one being residence in Britain for five years. Pursuing this route, Isaac submitted a 'memorial' to the Home Office, giving his name, address, date and place of birth, parents' names, occupation and names and ages of his dependent children. He engaged the support of Powell & Smith, Naturalisation Agents (and mortgage and insurance brokers) of 6 St. Swithin's Lane opposite Bank Tube station in the heart of the City of London, a short distance but a world apart from Whitechapel.

The police tested Isaac's mastery of the language, and reported that he 'speaks English fairly well, but reads it with difficulty, and cannot write it from dictation. He however understood the meaning of a newspaper paragraph copied correctly by him.' The paragraph – both the newspaper clipping and Isaac's sloping, loopy, carefully-crafted handwritten copy of it, written on his business headed paper – was attached to the report. It reads: 'Naylor's fine fighting speech against the Bill as amended, was of no avail, and the discussion was practically guillotined.'

[98]   Walter, 2010.

[99]   2004/1975, p.302.

Four 'respectable and responsible persons, householders and natural-born British Subjects' signed a statement that 'from our respective acquaintance with the manners, habits and mode of life of said Isaac Glassman we do confidently vouch for his loyalty and respectability' and support his application for naturalisation. Among his four signed supporters was George Lansbury, then (in 1912) the Member of Parliament for Bow and Bromley. Lansbury had known Isaac since 1906. Perhaps they met through business, Isaac delivering coal to the Lansburys' timber yard, perhaps through politics, perhaps through their children. They would gain a family connection in 1914 when Isaac's daughter Minnie married George's son Edgar.

Having completed the process, signed the Oath of Allegiance and paid a fee of five pounds (equivalent to around £560 today), Isaac Glassman was issued his certificate of naturalised British citizenship on 6th May 1913. This conferred British citizenship on his wife Annie as well, with all the (lack of) rights of a British-born woman. Minnie and her younger siblings were already British, having been born in Britain.

A Family Fighting for Women's and Workers' Rights

Minnie was one of many school teachers who pursued the cause of women's right to vote, making up substantial contingents on suffrage processions and taking up posts in local branches of both the WSPU and the Women's Freedom League (WFL), which had split from the WSPU to form a democratic, militant suffrage organisation. Minnie joined the WFL,[100] which focused its campaigning on the relationship between women and the state; feminist Alison Oram argues that this gave it 'particular meaning for women teachers who ... were employed by the state, but were barred, on the basis of their sex, from the political processes which determined the discriminatory conditions of that employment.'[101]

Her future husband was also active in the fight for women's suffrage. Edgar Lansbury followed his father George into left-wing activism, later recalling that:

> On Saturday afternoons five or six of us children would go with father to Victoria Park, where he would mount the socialist

---

[100] *The Vote*, 14th November 1919.

[101] 1996, p.121.

platform and sway the masses while we mooched about on the outskirts of the meeting selling pamphlets and a weekly journal entitled *Justice, the Organ of Social Democracy*.

… [George] never tried to exercise compulsion upon any of us, or to persuade us to plan our lives according to his views … [but] Of course, he liked to think that we would all grow up into good socialists.[102]

Edgar took dramatic action when necessary, including at a huge rally in 1913 in support of locked-out Dublin workers, held at the Albert Hall, which has four tiers of seating above the ground level of its great circular interior. His friend and fellow socialist Francis Meynell recollected that:

Edgar Lansbury … and I were in charge of the stewards. No easy task, for there were thousands of supporters unable to get into the overcrowded hall and there were also some scores of university students who had managed to force their way in, hoping to break up the meeting. (Yes, the students then were on the side of the Establishment.) Edgar and I swung down from one tier to another of the Albert Hall (a thing I couldn't do in

Edgar, Minnie and George Lansbury

[102] 1934, pp.91,137.

cold blood) as the quickest way of dealing with troublemakers below.[103]

In 1910, George Lansbury had become the Labour MP for Bow and Bromley, two adjoining districts lying east of Bethnal Green, west of Stratford and north of Poplar. George had taken the battle for women's suffrage onto the floor of the House of Commons, while also campaigning 'on the stump', marching and speaking in support of the suffragettes.

Political campaigning was a family affair for the Lansburys. Edgar's brother William – known as Willie – served two months in Pentonville prison and sister Annie a month in Holloway, both for smashing windows in pursuit of women's suffrage. In February 1913, the Thames Police Court sentenced Edgar, his sister Daisy, and four others to two months in prison with hard labour, the heaviest sentences thus far imposed in London for comparable property damage in the cause of women's votes. Magistrate Mr. Leycester, in passing the sentences, said that 'if the defendants chose to behave like common riff-raff they must be treated like common riff-raff.'[104] Daisy used to act as a decoy so that Sylvia Pankhurst could escape arrest after speaking at public meetings, and decades later would regale friends with the stories. In the 1960s, a journalist profiling Daisy and her husband Raymond Postgate wrote that:

> I know few other women who can make their guests laugh so uncontrollably at the relation of happenings that couldn't have been other than grim at the time … Daisy telling of her arrest, when she refused to give her name, until the sergeant who, like everyone in the district revered her father, said irritably, 'Well, Miss Lansbury, if you won't tell me who you are, I shall have to get your father down to the station to identify you', is a delight to dinner parties.[105]

With George Lansbury articulating their case in Parliament and campaigners voicing it in the streets, parks and public halls, it was an active East End that Sylvia Pankhurst made her base and her home. She persuaded the WSPU to invest some resources there, as she saw its class composition and location as a fertile combination: 'The East End was

---

[103] Meynell, 1971, p.81.

[104] *East London Advertiser.*

[105] Pamela Vandyke Price in *Wine & Food*, June/July 1969, POSTGATE 2/9.

Minnie (left), her older sister Selina (right) and Selina's daughter Ruth (centre)

the greatest homogenous working-class area accessible to the House of Commons by popular demonstrations. The creation of a woman's movement in that great abyss of poverty would be a call and a rallying cry to the rise of similar movements in all parts of the country.' 'Filled with such aspirations,' wrote her son Richard, some sixty-seven years later, 'she walked down the Bow Road in 1912 in search of offices. Finding an empty building she rented it, mounted a ladder and wrote in gilt letters the words 'VOTES FOR WOMEN',[106] where Minnie and any other passers-by could see and be inspired by them.

The building was number 198, a disused baker's shop opposite St. Mary's Church, the striking place of worship that occupies a traffic island passed on either side by Bow Road. It was 'an architecturally charming little old place ... with a bay window painted and grained in quiet and pleasant brown.'[107] Timber merchants Edgar and Willie Lansbury helped to renovate the new WSPU base, from which flowed a continuous stream of activity, as speakers attended trade union meetings and addressed open-air gatherings.

But in late 1912, a bold political move by George Lansbury in support of women's suffrage would misfire and would bring to the surface the

---

[106] Pankhurst, 1931/77, p.426; introduction, p.xviii.

[107] Pankhurst, 1931/77, p.417.

tension between class-focused labour activists and wealthy feminists. By then, George was at odds with his fellow Labour MPs, who seemed more committed to propping up the Liberal government than to advancing socialism, and despite Party policy in support of votes for women, did little to fight for it. Lansbury suggested that Labour oppose every government measure until the Liberals conceded on women's suffrage. His colleagues refused.

George travelled to Paris to confer with exiled WSPU leader Christabel Pankhurst, who persuaded him to resign his seat in Parliament and fight the consequent by-election on a women's suffrage platform. The national Labour Party, cross at what it saw as Lansbury's disloyalty, disowned his candidature, but the local labour movement and the wider suffrage movement mobilised strongly through the dull, drizzly, misty month of November, with Joe Banks as campaign organiser and Edgar Lansbury as treasurer. Banks was hostile to the WSPU, and on election day, Tuesday 26th November, a dispute between them led to vehicles not being made available to take voters through the rain to the polling stations until late in the day. The only other candidate, Conservative Reginald Blair, won by 751 votes, and used his first speech in Parliament to oppose women's suffrage.

Once he had decided to resign, George's by-election effort was spearheaded by those whom we might now call socialist-feminists, people who saw women's and workers' emancipation as parts of the same

Minnie with George and other Lansburys

struggle. But on one flank, they had wealthy suffragettes who held working-class people in disdain or disinterest, and on the other flank Labour men who did their class a disservice by their intolerance of assertive women. George's resignation may have been principled but it was misguided, suggested as it was not by socialist suffragists in Bow but by a rightward-moving WSPU leadership in Paris. Edgar wrote that his father had 'burned his boats by resigning his seat', George with hindsight said that 'It was not a wise political decision.'[108]

After the by-election defeat, the WSPU withdrew from the East End and within a year, Christabel and Emmeline's alliance with George Lansbury was over, Sylvia's explanation being that 'his temperament was too volatile, theirs too ruthless for its continuance.'[109] Emmeline and Christabel's 'ruthless' leadership of the WSPU had already prompted several splits and would go on to provoke more. In 1913, they stepped up the WSPU's militancy, adding arson to window-breaking. While the East London suffragettes were partial to some window-smashing, they were not keen on this latest escalation, and kept their focus on mass popular agitation and mobilisation.

The East London suffragettes continued their campaigning without the support of the national WSPU, setting up branches in Bow, Bromley, Stepney, Limehouse, Bethnal Green and Poplar, which together formed the East London Federation of the WSPU. They opened a new shop and office at 321 Roman Road, a bustling street of colourful market stalls and shops with a high metal arch at one end, known locally as 'the Roman' and located just under two miles to the east of the Glassmans' home in Chicksand Street. Sylvia described the new premises as 'a little place with a parlour behind the shop, a tiny scullery-kitchen, and three small rooms upstairs.' It had a broken window and holes in the floor, which the landlord refused to repair.[110]

With the suffrage movement dominated by wealthy women, and the WSPU's move from support for Labour to hostility, many in working-class communities rejected, or at least distrusted, the suffragettes as wanting only 'Votes for ladies'. The WSPU's demand for women to be enfranchised only on the same terms as men was in practice a demand for men and women of property to have the vote, leaving millions of

[108] E.Lansbury, 1934, pp.40-1; G.Lansbury, 1935, p.98.

[109] 1931/1977, p.489-90.

[110] Pankhurst, 1931/1977, p.438; *East London Advertiser*, 20th November 1915.

working-class women and men without it. It may seem odd today that those so militant in their pursuit of votes for women did not support votes for all, but some women's suffrage campaigners argued that universal adult suffrage (votes for all) was a utopian proposal that would delay votes for women, and some no doubt believed that only the 'better class' deserved the franchise. Minnie Glassman was not one of them.

A Working-Class Women's Movement

Into 1913, the East London suffragettes were busy: disrupting the Bow and Bromley Conservatives' annual meeting; breaking windows of anti-suffrage political groups and banks; marching from the grand East India Dock Gates to the two-hundred-acre Victoria Park for 'Women's May Day'. Their opponents rallied too, one hundred people attending a public meeting in Bow hosted by the National League for Opposing Woman Suffrage. Local newspaper the *East London Advertiser* took the side of the antis, pronouncing in March that 'Women's suffrage is for the present dead, killed by the insane outrages of those who avow themselves its supporters,' and adding that '"hunger strikers" must be taught that they need expect no mercy.'[111]

The *Advertiser*'s temper had been stirred by an escalation of suffragette militancy across the country. The government had promised that its Suffrage Bill would allow amendments to legislate votes for women, but then blocked any such amendments being debated. Frustrated to breaking point, WSPU suffragettes burned down Kew Gardens tea house, destroyed golf greens and cut telegraph wires. When suffragettes were imprisoned, they often refused food – and sometimes water as well. The government, keen to avoid the embarrassment of suffragettes starving themselves to death, authorised the prisons to force-feed them.

But the public did not like the brutal force-feeding of suffragette prisoners, so in May 1913 the government introduced the Prisoners (Temporary Discharge for Ill-Health) Bill, allowing hunger strikers to be released when they became ill, only to be re-arrested and returned to prison once they showed signs of recovery. Suffragettes dubbed it the 'Cat and Mouse Act'. In the East End, Sylvia Pankhurst was in and out of prison, tailed by police every time she was released as a 'mouse' and protected from re-arrest by crowds of supporters.

---

[111] *East London Advertiser*, 15th February, 22nd February, 4th January, 8th March 1913.

Minnie Glassman managed not to be arrested for her suffrage campaigning, perhaps by good luck, more likely by choosing to avoid law-breaking. Although many women teachers like Minnie were active suffragettes, they tended to avoid the more militant actions, some concerned for the respectability of their profession, others concerned not to lose their jobs. Their fears seem to have been justified: in 1910, a woman teacher at a Deptford school was reprimanded for absenteeism when she missed work in order to attend a suffrage demonstration and was later made to resign because she had been sent to prison.[112]

Interestingly, legend took hold that Minnie was not only arrested but imprisoned as a suffragette. Her great-niece Selina Gellert heard this from her other great-aunts, Minnie's sisters Ray and Kate Glassman, in the 1960s.[113] As it passed down orally through the generations, the story probably became confused with the time that Minnie would spend in prison later in her life for her actions in defence of impoverished East Enders. History tends to remember as heroes those who were imprisoned in fighting for causes that were subsequently won, such as votes for women, but to equivocate about those whose cause is still outstanding, such as the abolition of poverty. As Selina says, 'There was a kind of romantic idea that she went to prison as a suffragette, whereas the reality is that she was fighting for the poor people.'

The East London suffragettes differed from the national WSPU leadership not just about the nature of their militancy, but about democracy, politics and the role of working-class women. Finally, at the start of 1914, Christabel could tolerate the differences no longer, and told her sister Sylvia that the East End movement could no longer be part of the WSPU. Christabel's pretext was that Sylvia had spoken at a rally at the Albert Hall in solidarity with locked-out Dublin workers, which a large number of East London suffragettes had attended. At this rally, Irish socialist James Connolly had spoken of the common struggle 'against the domination of nation over nation, class over class, and sex over sex,'[114] but Christabel insisted that the WSPU would make no such alliances.

Thus, the East London Federation of the WSPU became the East London Federation of the Suffragettes (ELFS), and stepped up

---

[112] Oram 1996, p.122.

[113] Interview with author.

[114] Connelly, 2013, p.57.

campaigning, including many activities in which those like Minnie who wanted to avoid arrest could involve themselves: door-to-door canvassing to recruit members; outdoor meetings; and several large marches. ELFS began publishing its own newspaper, the *Woman's Dreadnought*, in March 1914, selling it for half a penny then after four days giving away any copies remaining from the twenty thousand printed. ELFS members talked with local women about their concerns and aired their grievances in the *Dreadnought*.

By this time, Poplar Borough Council had banned pro-suffrage events in its venues. In late 1913, the police had violently attacked two suffrage meetings held at Bow Baths Hall, an impressive building towards the eastern end of the busy Roman Road, where local people went to wash their bodies and their clothes, to swim, and to take part in great meetings for which the pool was covered with wooden slats. Poplar Council responded to the violence not by calling the police to account but by banning the suffragettes. The Council suggested that it might revoke the ban if the women promised not to make militant speeches, but the women refused to do so. As suffragette Nellie Best pointed out, 'Every speech of every reformer is militant from the viewpoint of those opposed to the particular reform.'[115]

Poplar Council was dominated by the Poplar Borough Municipal Alliance (PBMA), which had formed in 1905, claiming to be 'a non-party organisation'[116] but enjoying the support of the Tories and Liberals. At each election, it offered candidates to the property-owning electorate: business owners and others whom it could trust to defend their interests, hold tight to the purse-strings and oppose any rebellion. It vehemently opposed socialism and would repeatedly attack the efforts of Minnie and her comrades when they entered local government a few years later.

When the Labour minority on the council challenged the ban on the suffragettes using the public halls in March 1913, the majority refused to even discuss it. Enraged, members of the public threw bags of yellow and blue powder at the Municipal Alliance councillors, invaded the Council Chamber and tipped over inkstands and water bottles. The Mayor adjourned the meeting, and the suffragette protesters made speeches and sang songs. Over the following months, Labour kept up its efforts to overturn the Council's ban, with Edgar and George Lansbury leading the charge, Edgar earning himself a rebuke from

[115] Letter, *Daily Herald*, 29th January 1914.

[116] PBMA, 1925.

Alderman Bussey, who called him 'a child ... [who] could be treated with contempt.'[117]

This 'child' was in fact a grown man, who in May 1914 became Minnie Glassman's husband.

---

[117] *East London Advertiser*, 14th February 1914; *Daily Herald*, 27th March 1914; *East London Advertiser*, 28th March 1914; *Daily Herald*, 7th April 1914.

Minnie's husband, Edgar Lansbury

Chapter 3 – Wedding and War

A Loving and Low-Key Wedding

We know roughly when Minnie Glassman and Edgar Lansbury first met – around 1906. We may not know exactly where or how they met, but we do know where they first kissed: sitting together on a seat in the East End's iconic open space, Victoria Park. In the letter in which he recalled this precious memory, Edgar also wrote of his and Minnie's 'passion and love of those days' and assures the reader that 'we never lost the mystery & the excitement of first love.' It is a beautiful letter, sent to Minnie's sister Katie after their brother Louis' early death in the 1920s and kept by the Glassman family ever since.

Although teaching was a profession which gave women a pretext to remain single, marriage was still the expected route for a young woman – and if like Minnie she were Jewish, she would be expected to marry a Jewish man. Although there would often be family pressure to marry, this seemed not to be the case in the Glassman family, as two of Minnie's sisters and both of her brothers never married. However, her other two sisters married Jews, as did those of their children who married. We can safely conclude that Minnie married not because or to whom she was expected to, but for love and from her own choice.

The wedding took place in the early morning of Thursday 9th April 1914 at the Poplar registrar's office in the council premises on Poplar High Street. It was one of fewer than a quarter of marriages made that year at a civil rather than a religious ceremony, a ratio that is almost reversed today, with just under a quarter of marriage ceremonies being religious.[118] Like his bride but unlike his father, Edgar Lansbury was not religious. When his children were young, George had rejected religion and become a rationalist for a number of years – one or two years according to George; ten according to Edgar. When he later rejoined the church in 1900, his sons and daughters did not necessarily follow, his son-in-law Raymond Postgate writing that 'there was what might almost be called a mass-baptism of young Lansburys, [and] one of the children at least was so established in her freethinking views as to spend the rest of the day under the bed nursing her resentment.'[119]

---

[118] 24.1%; Office for National Statistics.

[119] 1951, p.55.

Although the council building that hosted it was elaborate – built in a High Victorian free Gothic style with a copper-domed octagonal tower – the wedding was a small and simple affair. George Lansbury and Isaac Glassman were present, as were Edgar's sister Daisy and sister-in-law Jessie. Edgar's best man was his friend Will Yoxley, and there were no bridesmaids.[120]

Although there is no record of why the wedding was so low-key, it is likely to have been because Minnie, a Jewish woman, was marrying a gentile (non-Jewish) man. The Glassman family thought very highly of Edgar, and Minnie's sisters 'always talked warmly about Edgar and what a lovely man he was,' according to her older sister Selina's granddaughter. Minnie's parents gave the wedding their approval through Isaac's attendance, and Edgar later acknowledged that they 'never were bound by silly conventionalism,'[121] but they may have felt that a big public display of their daughter 'marrying out' would have alienated them from the Jewish community in which they lived. Minnie's great-niece Selina explained to me that:

> Nowadays, intermarriages are two a penny and nobody bats an eyelid. But in those days, it would have been almost a scandal, and a lot of families would have been so horrified by it that they would refuse to talk to you again. In the real extreme, they would say that if you marry out, you are dead to me, and they would quite literally sit *shiva* [the seven-day mourning period observed in Judaism] as if the person had died. It's dreadful, but that's the length that people took it to. They felt that you had to stick with tradition. So the sheer fact that my great-grandfather went to their wedding, I see as quite positive for those times.

Edgar later wrote privately that 'for many months – even for two or three years – Minnie and I got no approval or help from anybody, except [Minnie's family] and Father. But we just went on because we knew how sure and safe we ourselves were.' For Edgar, 'No two people were ever so exactly suited' as he and Minnie, and he was determined not to allow any social hostility to undermine them, writing that, 'when I met Minnie and found that I loved her, I dashed everything else to the wall and made the world see that compared with our love it was less than nothing.'[122]

---

[120] *The Post*, April 1914.

[121] Letter, Edgar Lansbury to Annie and Katie Glassman, 17th November 1923.

[122] Letter, Edgar Lansbury to Annie and Katie Glassman, 17th November 1923.

Edgar had been born and brought up in Poplar, had attended the local board school,[123] then studied at King's College to qualify for the civil service, which he joined as a boy clerk. In 1910, he left this post to take over the running of his family's timber business – Stratford Veneer Mills, inherited from his maternal grandfather Isaac Brine – with his older brother Willie. Edgar was elected to Poplar Borough Council as a Labour representative of Bow North ward in 1912.

Edgar Lansbury was 'a considerable fellow' in both stature and character. Considered very handsome, he stood five feet eleven tall and was broad across the shoulders. Several sources record that he was notably gentle, and fellow Poplar Councillor George Cressall described him as 'a most lovable young man and a splendid specimen of a man.'[124]

Edgar was the fifth of Bessie and George Lansbury's twelve children – the others, in birth order, being Bessie, Annie, George (who died in childhood), William, Dorothy, Daisy, Nellie, twins Constance and Doreen (the latter dying in childhood), Violet and Eric. After Bessie junior died in 1909, the family also cared for her three children. Just as Edgar did, several of his siblings married politically compatible partners: Willie's wife Jessie was an active suffragette; Daisy married socialist journalist Raymond Postgate; Dorothy's husband Ernest Thurtle became Labour MP for Shoreditch; Nellie married Albert Hawkins, industrial organiser and business manager of the *Workers' Weekly* and *Sunday Worker*; and Violet married first Russian socialist Abraham Rigozhim and later communist Clemens Palme Dutt. Postgate, the first of George Lansbury's biographers, described the household in 1910 thus: 'the Lansbury family was no longer a poverty-stricken family, it is true, but it was never well-to-do. Its standard of living remained throughout his life working-class.'[125]

It was a huge and demanding family, the care of which fell squarely on the shoulders of Minnie's new mother-in-law, Bessie. On top of the working-class woman's usual burden of housework and child-rearing, Bessie often had to manage alone due to George's busy political schedule. Edgar wrote that:

> Father writes of the long week-ends spent away from his home. There were also the long evenings after work during which

[123] A state school run by a board elected by local ratepayers.

[124] Gottfried, 1999, pp.10,19; *East End News*, 31st May 1935.

[125] Postgate, 1951, p.104.

mother wrestled with a difficult and sometimes turbulent family, with father miles away lecturing and debating on Socialism and public affairs generally, or sitting for hours on committees and councils fighting the battles of the poor.[126]

Edgar considered how the Pankhursts must have viewed the Lansbury family arrangements, thinking that they 'looked askance at our household' and wondered what sort of suffragist man would keep his wife 'in subjection' and what sort of suffragist woman would let him. It seems, though, that Bessie raised her daughters to aspire to more than this, as one of their nieces described them as 'an extraordinary group of women … extremely intelligent, independent, forceful women who … made something of their lives.'[127] Bessie herself 'believed ardently enough in votes for women,' although this 'did not extend to enthusiastic support for the well-heeled feminists of the WSPU.' Her son Edgar described her as 'far and away more courageous politically than most men,' having joined the Marxist Social Democratic Federation and sticking to its 'uncompromising Socialism' until the end of her life.[128]

Many sources confirm that Edgar was the closest of George's children to their father, variously calling him 'in a very real sense, the son of his father', 'the one with whom [George] discussed politics regularly, and who was his obvious successor'; who 'certainly worshipped but was never intimidated by GL.'[129] The Lansburys' house on Bow Road was a hive of not only family life but also of political and community activity, 'Almost daily … called at by men and women who were in legal, personal or financial difficulties and wanted "G.L." (the initials were by now commonly used) to advise and help.'[130] Perhaps this provided a model for Minnie's future work with war orphans, widows and others.

Moving to Poplar

The newly-married Edgar and Minnie Lansbury received the congratulations of, among others, Poplar Borough Council. They were

---

[126] E.Lansbury, 1934, p.88.

[127] Angela Lansbury, daughter of Edgar's second marriage, quoted in Gottfried, 1999, p.4.

[128] E.Lansbury, 1934, p.142; Shepherd, 2002, p.130.

[129] *Star*, 29th May 1935; Morgan, 2006, p.299; Gottfried, 1999, p.19.

[130] Postgate, 1951, p.104; parentheses original

'a devoted couple, never happy out of each other's company,' and George and Bessie Lansbury held their new daughter-in-law 'in great affection.'[131]

Returning from their honeymoon in the country and in mild and sunny weather, Minnie and Edgar moved into 25 Mornington Road, where they would live for the next three years. Mornington Road ran off Bow Road, with the grand Presbyterian Chapel standing on the south-east corner of the two streets and next to the Bow County Court. A short distance to the west was Bow Road Station – such a short distance, in fact, that some of Mornington Road's grand and quite new houses had been demolished to make way for the new station's opening in 1902. Of an 'elegant' street of forty-eight homes, nineteen were flattened and 'the road turned into a fractured remnant of the original.'[132] Number 25 had survived the demolition, although part of its garden had been lost to the new railway. As this was the place where the District Railway came up from underground, it would not have been a quiet place to live!

Minnie had left her childhood home in Whitechapel and had moved two-and-a-bit miles eastwards into Bow, an area she already knew well having attended school there: in fact, her new home was just five minutes' walk from Coborn School. However, their marital home was much nearer to where Edgar had grown up than to where Minnie had: they had chosen to live in his community rather than hers.

Bow was named after the bow-shaped bridge over the River Lea at its eastern boundary, and formed the northern part of the London Borough of Poplar. The borough extended south from Bow, through Bromley and into the dockland area of Poplar itself. Named after the poplar trees which grew in large numbers before the docks were built, Poplar was bordered on three sides by the Thames, nestling in the big bend in the river which is so noticeable on any map of London. The borough which took its name would now be the centre of Minnie's personal and political life.

Poplar Borough covered more than two thousand acres, bordered by Hackney to the north, Bethnal Green and Stepney to the west as well as by the rivers Lea and Thames. Minnie Lansbury would serve it in various capacities, always championing the working class which constituted virtually its entire population. The *Daily News*[133] described

---

[131] *Daily Herald*, 7th January 1922.

[132] www.morningtongrove.com

75

it thus: 'Poplar, by common consent of its inhabitants and its exploiters, of those who make a living in it and those who make a living out of it, is a place that ought not to exist. In the jargon of sociologists, it is a homogeneous area of poverty, which simply means that nobody except a stray philanthropist would live there if he could possibly live anywhere else.'

Minnie took 20th April to 1st May off work to enjoy her honeymoon and was deducted £3.9s.3d in wages. She chose to return to her teaching post even though it would have been more usual for a woman to leave her job once married. Teachers were the only employees whom the London County Council did not require to resign following their marriage, although many women teachers did so anyway, following convention. Alison Oram argues that women teachers had a professional identity which was constructed as being incompatible with marriage, and that as teaching involved caring for children, it was thought an acceptable alternative to being married.[134] Even after the coming war saw a huge influx of women into employment, and even among the women readers of the left-wing *Daily Herald*, the majority still favoured a married woman staying away from waged work. They argued that 'No decent man would allow his wife to work, and no decent woman would do it if she knew the harm she was doing the widows and single girls who are *looking* for work ... Put the married women out [of work], send them home to clean their houses and look after the men they married.' Supporters of married women working argued that it gave a '[g]reater feeling of independence towards the employer for both husband and wife,' that it was 'most useful in times of financial difficulty' such as strikes, and that '[m]any women feel cramped and lonely in the home.'[135]

The London Married Women Teachers' Association campaigned for better treatment and security for those who stayed in their jobs, holding a meeting of one hundred people in June 1914. By then, Mrs. Minnie Lansbury – once again defying custom to be an independent, modern woman – was back at work and back to campaigning for women workers' rights.

---

[133] 11th February 1924.

[134] 1996, pp.53-4.

[135] *Daily Herald*, 31st October 1919.

Great Unrest

Still barred from using Poplar Council's public halls, the East London Federation of Suffragettes (ELFS) opened a hall of its own. Located at 400 Old Ford Road, next to Victoria Park, it was a place where Minnie Lansbury would spend a lot of her political time over the following years. The building had previously been used as a school and was in poor condition. Sylvia Pankhurst later wrote that it included a 'ramshackle little meeting hall' at the back and that:

> At the rear of the house a queer flat-roofed building, which served as our general office, communicated with a small hall, a poor mean edifice, its interior walls of unplastered brick merely brightened with a rough colour-wash. At one end of the hall was a low platform; at the other, a wooden archway, with niches holding plaster casts of Homer, the Venus of Milo and the Delphic Apollo.[136]

The new premises were refurbished by volunteers organised by Minnie's brother-in-law Willie Lansbury, and the newly-named Women's Hall became ELFS headquarters, a four-hundred-capacity venue for meetings and events, an assembly point for demonstrations, a calling place for people who needed help, and home to leading suffragettes Sylvia Pankhurst, Mr. and Mrs. Payne and Norah Smyth.

As well as providing a platform for working women to voice their grievances, the East London suffragettes supported them when they fought for improvements. In 1914, a flurry of strikes in the East End saw workers walk out of the Johnnie Walker's bottling factory, Bach's asbestos works and Morton's preserves and tea-packing factory. The wave of strikes across the country at this time became known as The Great Unrest. It saw trade union membership increase to four million workers, a sixty percent rise on four years previously. One of its most significant struggles in London was the builders' lockout, to which Minnie lent her active support.

Construction industry employers, emboldened by their fellow bosses' victory in the previous year's Dublin lockout, tried to compel London's building workers to renounce their trade unions. When this failed, the workers refused to work alongside non-union builders and the employers appealed to union officials to call a halt to such antics. But the building workers were not going to be told by their own unions to stop protecting union strength in the workplace, so the bosses insisted

---

[136] Pankhurst, 1932/87, pp.12,21.

that every worker sign an individual contract promising to work peaceably with non-unionists. They had to sign by 24th January 1914, on pain of being deemed to have resigned. They did not sign. The bosses locked them out of work.

So began a long and bitter struggle which plunged already poor building workers and their families into even more desperate distress. Minnie Lansbury joined the effort to raise funds and support for the locked-out workers, making her marital home in Mornington Road the base for the Bow Women and Children's Distress Committee.

Every few months, the employers would offer a concession or two, some union leaders would recommend accepting it, but the workers were not willing to concede their ground. The employers were bemused by the resolution of men and their families whom they thought they could defeat but who were made of sterner stuff:

> In rags themselves they also had to bear the anguish of seeing their children bewildered and suffering privation for principles they were too young to understand. But these conditions, which might logically have been expected to degrade them and weaken their resolve, strengthened their determination to defy employers who were trying to starve them into submission.[137]

Minnie organised not only fundraising but also entertainment for the locked-out builders' children. On Saturday 20th June, Minnie, her sister-in-law Daisy Lansbury, socialist postman Albert Farr and one or two other adults took forty of the children to the Surrey green belt village of Ashtead, to a birthday party for Ivan Seruya, the one-year-old son of suffragette Sime Seruya, where they 'roamed over the common and woods … [and] thoroughly enjoyed the swings and roundabouts, and, not least, the excellent food that was provided.'[138]

Sime Seruya was a socialist, a pacifist and, unusually for the time, a vegetarian. She had been imprisoned three times for suffrage actions, and had opened the International Suffrage Shop in Covent Garden in 1910. The *Daily Herald* hoped that with such a mother, and with the early introduction to solidarity provided by the party that Minnie and others had organised, young Ivan would grow up to be a leading rebel. There is evidence that he did. In 1932, at the time of anti-poverty marches and at eighteen years of age, he was charged with being in the garden of the Prime Minister's house for an unlawful purpose, carrying

---

[137] Hilton, 1963, p.208.

[138] *Daily Herald*, 23rd June 1914.

a brick in his hand and two under his arm. And in 1960, he was one of the original signatories of the Committee of 100 sworn to civil disobedience against war. We can be confident that Minnie Lansbury would have approved.

Minnie's support for the locked-out building workers took the form of fundraising and entertainment, relatively respectable political activities, albeit in solidarity with a rebellious cause. Over the next few years, she would venture into more confrontational forms of activism. In the meantime, one of the fundraising events Minnie organised was a whist drive at the Ethical Hall on Libra Road on Saturday 27th June,[139] the day before the assassination of Archduke Franz Ferdinand, the event that led to the vast, bloody conflict known as The Great War.

To War

As the rumble of approaching war grew louder, the labour movement mobilised against it. On Sunday 2nd August, ten thousand people gathered in a rain-lashed Trafalgar Square to show their opposition to war. The next day, Britain gave Germany an ultimatum to withdraw its invading army from Belgium, and when the midnight deadline passed without response, on Tuesday 4th August Britain declared war on Germany, which was already at war with Russia and France. Immediately, most of the labour movement gave its support to the government's war, including even some who had attended the anti-war rally, such as dockers' leader Ben Tillett and SDF leader H.M. Hyndman. Labour MPs involved themselves in Parliament's Recruiting Committee and some would join the wartime coalition governments. In Ralph Miliband's words, 'the labour movement remained committed until the very last stages of the war to the doctrine of peace through slaughter.'[140] However, some socialists did oppose the war, including Sylvia Pankhurst, Keir Hardie, Ramsay MacDonald and Minnie Lansbury.

The outbreak of war split the women's suffrage movement. The United Suffragists (a recent split from the WSPU) kept campaigning for the vote, although with a low profile, and kept publishing *Votes For Women*. The Women's Freedom League, of which Minnie was a member, also continued its suffrage work. The National Union of Women's Suffrage

---

[139] *Daily Herald*, 26th June 1914.

[140] Miliband, 1961/2009, p.53.

Societies suspended its campaigning for the vote and set up a Women's Active Service Corps. Emmeline Pankhurst led the WSPU to become, in the words of her grandson Richard, 'one of the most vociferous of the pro-war factions.' Its members placed white feathers in the buttonholes of men who did not enlist and it accepted funds to run pro-war rallies from the same government that had been its bitter enemy before the war. Its newspaper, renamed *Britannia*, 'attacked the idea of any compromise with a vehemence equal to that earlier reserved for Suffragette militancy.'[141]

The East End socialist suffragettes had no intention of stopping their campaigning for votes for women, but had more difficulty in deciding their attitude to the war itself. ELFS held a special meeting two days after Britain declared war. Although leading figures such as Sylvia Pankhurst, Melvina Walker, Elsie Lagsding and the Lansbury women opposed the war, many members supported it, perhaps especially those with husbands, boyfriends, sons or brothers enlisted in the armed forces. An unstoppable wave of war enthusiasm had engulfed even the East End:

> When War was declared, everybody who was 'anybody' in Poplar threw himself or herself into the job of recruiting …

> Down came three or four 'buses filled with soldiers, and bands playing … 'Rule Britannia' and other such songs to stir up the people. Each 'bus displayed a white banner inscribed: 'Roll Up Boys, A Free Ride to Berlin'.

> Hundreds of men and women gathered round. Every man who walked up the steps to 'sign on' was treated as a hero; cheers were continually rising.[142]

In this atmosphere, to take a position either for or against the war would have split ELFS in two, undoing the powerful unity for women's and workers' rights that it had built. It decided instead on a three-pronged policy of continuing its suffrage campaigning, helping those suffering distress, and making political points.

The start of war threw many workers out of their jobs. Virtually all the East End's factories, except those connected with the prosecution of war, either closed or significantly curtailed their production and consequently the hours and pay of their employees. The textile and clothing industries slumped, pushing many women out of work. In the

---

[141] R. Pankhurst, Introduction to E.S. Pankhurst, 1932/87, pp.xx,xxi.

[142] *Workers' Dreadnought*, 17th April 1920.

first month of the war, the *Woman's Dreadnought* reported the dramatic change from getting by to being cast adrift:

> Up and down the Old Ford Road, under our windows, women were wont to hurry past, pushing babies' perambulators or rough packing cases on wheels, laden with trousers, coats and waistcoats that they were making for the factories. But now, with their little conveyances all empty, they linger hopeless. 'Any work?' a woman always asks her neighbour, as she meets her. The answer is always 'No'.[143]

For Minnie Lansbury, there was more work rather than less, as the London County Council reopened its schools a fortnight earlier than scheduled after a summer break of just two weeks. Despite the absence of about a thousand teachers either called up as reservists or away on holdiay, London schools reopened on an unseasonably cool Saturday 8th August, keeping children in the state's care while their fathers enlisted to fight in the war and their mothers dealt with the impact of war on family life.

The outbreak of war also prompted some retailers to hike their charges. Just four days after Britain declared war, local newspaper the *East London Advertiser* complained of 'greedy traders' making 'a wicked attempt to take advantage of the war scare to increase the price of food unduly.' ELFS wanted to take direct action against this appalling profiteering, and agreed a proposal 'that someone should go into a shop and ask for food at normal price and if it were refused go and get a member to back her up and go & take it.'[144] Members did this on a few occasions, but with morale at a low ebb, it did not become a mass action.

Sharply rising prices were accompanied by food shortages; shortages meant queueing; and queueing impacted gravely on local working-class women and their children. Suffragette Melvina Walker recalled that during a shortage of potatoes:

> [O]ne could hear the tramp and clatter of women hurrying past at five o'clock in the morning. They had heard that a certain shop had got potatoes and was going to open at nine, and they found it necessary to line up outside before six because they had learnt by experience that if they came even a little later the potatoes were sold out before their turn was reached. So the women hurried out with their market bags before day-break, leaving the

---

[143] *The Woman's Dreadnought*, 22nd August 1914.

[144] ELFS Minute book, 6th August 1914.

> children and young babies behind, and we constantly heard of
> children being absent from school, and children being scalded
> or burnt whilst their mother was waiting in the queue.[145]

Later in the war, Minnie Lansbury would witness, and report to her fellow socialist suffragettes with delight, that East End women had found a more collective and confrontational way of forcing traders to part with their potatoes.

Working-class women urgently needed relief from the distress into which war had plunged them and their families. ELFS set up a Distress Bureau at the Women's Hall and then at its other offices around the East End, at 319 East India Dock Road; Crowder Hall on Bow Road; Poplar Women's Hall at 20 Railway Street; 53 St. Leonard's Street in Bromley; and later in Canning Town. Immediately the war began, ELFS organised a Baby Clinic at the Women's Hall on Old Ford Road, giving out sixteen quarts (four gallons) of milk each day. Within a short time, the Federation extended this to a further three centres.

At the end of August, ELFS opened a Cost-Price Restaurant, also at its Women's Hall, which was soon followed by a second, then more. The restaurant provided up to two hundred dinners per day, each obtained with a ticket for which most women paid two pence but the most destitute were given for free. The 'tuppence dinner' comprised 'Suet dumplings, well-fried onions, thick brown gravy and bread, followed by large baked apples.' In the evenings, soup was served at a penny a pint.[146]

ELFS set up an employment bureau to help women find work, and by October turned to creating work itself. In ELFS workrooms, women made clothes and other items for a wage of five pence per hour or one pound per week (the minimum wage of unskilled labouring men in the area and half of what Minnie earned as a teacher), while their children were cared for in a crèche. One such workplace was the ELFS toy factory at 45 Norman Road, Bow, an address which today carries a plaque to remember the good use to which the suffragettes put it. By early 1915, it employed over twenty women and girls, making 'quaint representations of humans, animals, and fowls, … designed by a Belgian refugee.' The Federation repeatedly stressed the point that 'What these women want is work not charity.'[147]

---

[145] *Workers' Dreadnought* supplement, 'East London in War Time', 17th April 1920.

[146] *East London Advertiser*, 3rd and 31st October 1914.

[147] *East London Advertiser*, 13th March and 10th October 1914.

In pursuit of this principle, ELFS campaigned for the government and its contractors to pay at least the same wage that ELFS paid to women workers. It held public meetings both indoors and outdoors, and staged protests to press its demands. Sylvia Pankhurst spoke at practically all these meetings and protests. Other suffragettes spoke as well, but Minnie Lansbury did not. She was already a committed campaigner and trade unionist, and would become an effective and popular organiser and advocate, but she would not become a public speaker until near the end of her life. Many years later, a friend of Minnie's named Rosie told her great-nephew that Minnie had 'a certain air of reserve' about her; she was not exactly quiet or shy, but she had to push herself to speak to any audience.[148] Although her own sisters remembered her as 'feisty',[149] her friend Rosie gave the impression that Minnie's feistiness was 'in a concrete, operational sort of way' rather than in an oratorical way. Many women did speak in public in the fight for the vote and their rights, but many more were committed to the cause but less confident to speak out for it. Sylvia Pankhurst's description of a meeting in Bethnal Green in the early days of suffragette organising shows local working-class supporters reluctant to put themselves forward:

> In the front seats to the left there sat a number of Jewish girls, whose ages ranged from about seventeen to twenty-five. They were well nourished and full of vitality, with fine dark eyes, clear olive skin, and an abundance of dark glossy hair. Their spirits were so high that they found it difficult to sit still.
>
> To the right there sat some tired faded looking women, poorly dressed, with babies in their arms. In the back rows were several men and boys, as well as numbers of women of all ages.
>
> I had spoken many times to this same audience and many of the women had joined our organisation. I thought it was time that some of them should learn to speak for themselves. And so, after few words, I asked which of them would make a speech.
>
> There was a pause, many headshakes, murmurs of "I can't," shouts of "You, Mrs. So-and-So," and replies of "Oh no, not me," giggling from the Jewish girls, laughter and shouts from the men and boys – a general uproar.[150]

---

[148] Interview: author with Steven Warren.

[149] Interview: author with Selina Gellert.

[150] Sylvia Pankhurst Papers, IISH, 124.

Fighting for Maintenance

A week into the war, Parliament empowered the Board of Trade to commandeer foodstuffs which it believed were being unreasonably withheld from the market. But this was limited in its scope and bureaucratic in its procedures. Chancellor of the Exchequer David Lloyd George adopted a recommended price list for food but took advice on the price levels from the companies which stood to gain from keeping them high. Sugar and margarine now sold for double their pre-war price. An ELFS deputation to Board of Trade President Walter Runciman suggested that he instead convene a committee of 'they who know what the people of the nation can afford.'[151]

A government-appointed Coal Committee found that coal prices were also too high, but also did precious little to lower them. London's wholesale coal merchants switched their supply away from small dealers such as Isaac Glassman and prioritised instead their bulk customers in wealthy households and institutions. Isaac and others made up for their loss of trade by delivering flour and other goods as well as coal. Landlords were no less ruthless than price-setters, evicting tenants who fell into rent arrears at such speed that Parliament felt obliged to pass a law at the end of August requiring landlords to obtain a magistrate's order before doing so. ELFS representatives accompanied women to court to help plead their case against eviction. Across a street near Old Ford Road hung 'a rudely lettered calico banner' adorned with the words:

> Please, landlord, don't be offended
> Don't come for the rent till the War is ended[152]

The government acted much more decisively in clamping down on dissent and delinquency. Two Defence of the Realm Acts in the first month of the war made it a criminal offence to spread 'reports likely to cause disaffection or alarm.' Women were banned from pubs at certain hours, and there was police surveillance of soldiers' and sailors' wives. The *East London Advertiser* reflected the prejudices that motivated these latter moves, conjuring a picture of feral women let loose by war:

> There never was a time when the working woman needed to be
> saved from herself so much as at the present moment. The

---

[151] *Daily Herald*, 7th September 1914.

[152] Pankhurst, 1932/1987, p.19.

restraining influence of husbands, sons and fathers has been removed by the absence at the front of male members of the family and many women find themselves, thanks to the liberal separation allowances, with more money and greater freedom than they have ever had before in their lives.[153]

Raymond Postgate's description was very different and much more accurate:

Their allowances were inadequate, they were deprived of reliefs to which they were entitled, the forms they were given and the questions they were asked seemed to them … inquisitory, they were not infrequently insultingly treated.[154]

It was in this context that the socialist suffragettes of the East End of London organised their fellow working-class women to fight for their rights. This would be the focus of Minnie Lansbury's activism and public service during the war.

The government set up a National Relief Fund to give money to those in distress via local committees. Allowances were to be paid to the wives of soldiers, but at more than twice the rate for officers' wives (2s3d per day) than for sergeants', corporals' or privates' (1s1d per day). There would be an additional two pence for each child, four pence for those without a mother. Soldiers were expected to supplement this by sending money home from their wages. Sailors' wives were to receive no separation allowance, only what their husbands sent.

However, getting even these meagre payments was difficult. The authorities would not make payments to those who could not prove that their distress was caused directly by the war, and they stopped payments to families as punishment for soldiers' misdemeanours. They required women to provide marriage and birth certificates, which they had to pay for, and refused allowances for children born less than nine months after their parents' marriage. Servicemen's dependents ought to have received extra help from the Soldiers' and Sailors' Families Association charity, but it too was keeping women waiting for payments or refusing to make them at all.

Help seemed to be on offer with the establishment of the Queen Mary's Fund to create work for women. But it set a pay rate of just ten shillings per week (half the rate that ELFS paid), and just five shillings

---

[153] 30th October 1915.

[154] Postgate, 1951, p.153.

for young women under seventeen years of age. The Fund's workrooms continued only until February 1915, by which time women made unemployed by the war were working in war industries or replacing men who had gone to the front, but the low wages it had set ensured that women would be underpaid throughout the war.

The East London suffragettes knew that it was not enough for them to fill the yawning gaps left by the official funds with their self-organised services. They would also have to demand representation on the bodies that ran those official funds. Socialists, although disagreeing with each other about the war itself, could at least unite to insist on labour representation on war distress committees. The government, buoyed by mainstream Labour's assistance with its war effort, was keen to co-opt them into its mean 'relief' schemes and readily agreed, while keeping them outnumbered by conservative councillors and charity-mongers.

As the war dragged on much longer than the quick victory predicted, more such bodies would be set up including, in 1916, War Pensions Committees. Minnie Lansbury would become a member of her local committee and would win enormous community support and appreciation for her efforts to obtain decent maintenance for the victims of war. Minnie was one of the labour representatives who defied the government's expectation of compliance, typifying historian Julia Bush's argument that 'Labour was rarely prepared to be a mere token presence. It persisted in stridently voicing its own point of view, which showed a regrettable [for 'the local hierarchy'] tendency to be a socialist one.'[155]

Joining the Committee

The East London Federation of the Suffragettes saw in the new year of 1915 with a huge children's party at Bow Baths Hall on Saturday 2nd January. Over fifteen hundred local youngsters, their daily lives dragged down by poverty and war, received presents donated by supporters, while 'Actresses, singers [and] musicians provided entertainment for children and grown-ups with all the old brilliance of the Suffragette movement.'[156] Ten days later ELFS hosted a further children's party in one of the ample-sized halls in the substantial and ornate Poplar Town Hall, which stood on Newby Place, about four hundred yards from the East India Import Dock.

---

[155] Bush, 1984, p.53.

[156] Pankhurst, 1932/1987, p.126.

In the first week of the new year, ELFS held its annual conference and made an important change to its constitution. It replaced its stated object 'to secure the Parliamentary vote for women on the same terms as men,' which it had inherited from the WSPU, with 'to secure the vote for every woman over twenty-one.' In doing so, ELFS was making a firmer commitment to universal suffrage – votes for all – and explicitly rejecting 'Votes for Ladies'.

The conference also elected a new committee, including Minnie Lansbury. Minnie had chosen – and had been chosen by members – to join the leading body of a very large, well supported, intensely busy, belligerently assertive organisation rooted in a lively, dense, impoverished and struggling populace. East London was a community in which she had been born if not bred, had lived her whole life, had campaigned for, and for which she would now work and advocate.

One of her first responsibilities in her new committee role was as Assistant Secretary of the Mothers' Arms. A weapons factory on Old Ford Road had expanded to meet its boom in demand, but its neighbouring pub, the Gunmakers' Arms, had lost its licence and closed. The suffragettes took it over and transformed it, its brochure declaring that:

> The Gunmakers' Arms is now the Mothers' Arms, a Children's Day Nursery and Mother and Infant Clinic and Milk House. If there is sunshine anywhere you will find it there. The walls of the rooms are white with gay pictures. Friends from the country send flowers to the Mothers' Arms.

Minnie brought to the role her experience not just of living locally but of several years of activity in her trade union and in suffrage campaigning. She knew how to organise and how to argue. Her husband Edgar was the Treasurer of the project, Sylvia Pankhurst its Secretary, and with them, Minnie – who was still working as a school teacher – oversaw its development while a dedicated staff ran it day to day.

The Mothers' Arms cared for children from eight o'clock in the morning until seven o'clock in the evening for a charge of three pence. The staff bathed the babies and dressed them in fine clothes donated by wealthy supporters, then provided them with good food, play, and a daily outing to Victoria Park. Photographs survive of the Mothers' Arms and other ELFS services for children, one showing a thin and malnourished infant on a nurse's lap. The photo, says East London feminist historian Sarah Jackson, 'punctures the picture of the "jolly poverty" of the East End'.[157] The transformation of pub into playcentre was symbolic as well as practical, Israel Zangwill declaring that, 'The hope of the world lies in changing the "Gunmakers' Arms" into the "Mothers' Arms".'[158] Its site is now a housing estate, but a plaque records that the Mothers' Arms once stood there.

The Mothers' Arms was not simply an act of charity. It provided employment at a decent wage for those who worked there and enabled its young charges' mothers to work. Even so, Minnie and the other East End suffragettes knew that such projects were, though necessary, a sticking plaster on a broken social system. Edgar wrote about Minnie that, 'Although she strove hard to alleviate suffering, she always looked forward to the day when preventible misery and economic injustice would be no more.' Local head teacher and Poplar councillor Charles Key said that Minnie 'never lost sight of the fact that justice could not be done until capitalism had been swept away'.[159]

A Union for the Victims of War

Nevertheless, there was a gulf between the relief that Minnie and the East London suffragettes provided and the socialism they wished for, and they realised that only working-class self-organisation for political demands could bridge that gap. Servicemen's dependents needed their own organisation. This could connect the services run by the socialist suffrage campaigners to their goal of changing society, and cast women as fighters not just as victims: as collective self-liberators. Moreover, the existing non-governmental organisation that sought to support armed forces dependants – the Soldiers' and Sailors' Families Association (SSFA) – seemed 'inadequate' to Minnie and Sylvia.[160]

ELFS took the initiative and decided to form the League of Rights for Soldiers' and Sailors' Wives and Relatives. It was launched by the unanimous vote of a 'large and enthusiastic' meeting of soldiers' and sailors' dependants at the Women's Hall on Monday 1st February 1915.

---

[157] Talk at Tower Hamlets Local History Archive, August 2015.

[158] Pankhurst, 1932/1987, p.429.

[159] Report of Minnie Lansbury memorial meeting, *East London Advertiser*, 14th January 1922.

[160] Winslow, 1996, p.94.

George Lansbury later recorded that, 'long before anyone else either cared or thought of soldiers' wives, children, and dependents, Sylvia Pankhurst, Mrs. Despard [founder of the Women's Freedom League], my wife, Minnie Lansbury, and others formed the League of Rights.'[161] With Sylvia Pankhurst and Charlotte Despard having many other responsibilities, and Bessie Lansbury tied to her home, the work of building and running the League fell to Minnie and others.

Servicemen's family members paid a penny per month to be members of the League, which stipulated that two-thirds of its committee and of its branches' committees must consist of servicemen's dependents. These would mostly be women, but men – such as soldiers' fathers – were also welcome to join. The League set up branches, and many wives became Honorary Secretaries of their branch. Minnie Lansbury, although not a serviceman's dependant, became Honorary Secretary of the Bow branch, which met at the Women's Hall at 400 Old Ford Road at eight o'clock every Tuesday evening, helping individuals and organising to pressure the authorities.

The League's strategy was that Minnie and its other branch secretaries would 'by constant practice become experts, and their expert knowledge will be at the disposal of others.' One of Minnie's duties as secretary was to convene a 'visiting committee' of League members to whom she would supply the names and addresses of 'comrades who may be in trouble' and who may benefit from being called on. The League aimed to 'act as the family lawyer does in the case of well-to-do people, and as the trade union does in the case of miners, railwaymen and others.'[162] The branches dealt with many cases of people treated dreadfully by the authorities, arranging for others like them to fight their corner, often successfully. The League pressured government to adopt more compassionate policies, and when government conceded, it fought to ensure that it kept its promises. By May, the League had more than a dozen branches and was regularly receiving requests to form more. However, Sylvia's biographer Barbara Winslow contends that 'this organization was not accompanied by the flashy success of the suffrage days. The meetings were attended by "quiet, earnest little women, who joined the organization with diffidence and in modest numbers. The dark streets [due to the wartime blackout] were a growing deterrent."'[163]

[161] G.Lansbury, 1928, p.208.

[162] *The Woman's Dreadnought*, 17th April and 11th September 1915.

For Minnie Lansbury, this was more than just 'casework': it was solidarity in action. Her approach was reflected in her growing popularity in the community. Edgar later recalled that, 'The unemployed and the destitute were to her not cases but real friends whom she loved … That they addressed her as "Minnie" was a joy to her always.'[164]

At a time when administration was carried on with more formality even than now, it would have been rare indeed for a woman in this sort of role to be on first-name terms with those whom she was helping. Even militant suffragettes tended to refer to each other by title – Mrs. Savoy, Miss Pankhurst, and so on – and with Minnie being a school teacher married to a local councillor, people would certainly have expected to call her 'Mrs. Lansbury'. The fact that they called her 'Minnie' suggests that she was informal, friendly and approachable, and perhaps more importantly that she saw them as equals, as comrades rather than clients. It had the added bonus of distinguishing her from the other Mrs. Lansburys, Bessie and (Willie's wife) Jessie.

Leaving the Classroom

As 1915 began, Minnie Lansbury was still working as an infants' teacher at Fairclough Street School. War was making a tough job even tougher. With hundreds of London's male teachers departed to war, and hundreds more ready to follow them, conditions in schools deteriorated. The National Union of Teachers (NUT) complained that 'Depleted staffs, shortage of the usual provision in apparatus and material, and above all, children excited and worried by the absence of fathers and brothers doing duty in the firing line all tend to make the work harder and more exhausting.' Moreover, the London County Council had an 'overruling passion … to save money on education', making economies by measures such as not heating classrooms and merging classes so that in many cases, teachers were teaching over a hundred children at a time.[165]

The NUT did not, however, allow the worsening conditions of teachers to dull its enthusiasm for the war. Every issue of its journal, *The Schoolmaster*, carried tales of the exploits of teacher-soldiers and

---

[163] 1996, p.94, quoting Sylvia Pankhurst.

[164] Letter to memorial meeting, *East London Advertiser,* 14th January 1922.

[165] *The Schoolmaster*, 20th November and 4th December 1915.

reported with pride on the union's contribution to the war effort. Minnie Lansbury seconded a motion proposed by a Miss Dawson at a local NUT meeting, 'That we view with much concern the great loss to Education that is being felt through the loss of Teachers from the schools on account of Military Service,' only to see the motion defeated in a vote.[166] The motion had not even opposed the war: it had merely expressed worry about schooling suffering by the absence of teachers in khaki. Even that was too much for the NUT patriots.

Minnie's fellow East London Teachers' Association members also remained resistant to the idea that women teachers be paid as much as men, voting down a conference resolution from Miss Tysack and Minnie in December 1915 to support 'the principle of Equal Pay for men and women of the same professional status.' The union nationally adopted recommended pay scales for male teachers of £100-£250 and for female teachers of £90-£200,[167] showing itself not just unwilling to fight for equal pay but positively in favour of unequal pay. Still, its lady members could enjoy the regular 'Hints for women' in *The Schoolmaster*, including 'a word about hats', 'rainproof silks', 'winter blouses' and 'fashions up to date'.

Perhaps it was because of her growing responsibilities at ELFS and the League of Rights; perhaps it was the increasingly strenuous conditions at Fairclough Street School; perhaps community activism and advocacy seemed a more productive arena for Minnie to pursue her political views than repeatedly losing battles in teachers' trade union meetings. Whatever the reason, at Easter 1915, one term short of four years' service as a teacher, Minnie Lansbury left her post at Fairclough Street School and became a full-time campaigner and organiser. Sylvia Pankhurst explained the characteristics that made Minnie so valuable:

> I induced [George Lansbury's] son Edgar's wife, née Minnie Glassman, to leave her work as an elementary school teacher and help me as assistant honorary secretary of our Federation. She devoted herself mainly to our distress work, and to the League of Rights. She knew the district and people, and in accordance with the first principle of work in our Federation, she was prepared to make herself unreservedly the advocate of the people, and to get the best she could for them. So many

---

[166] Minutes, London Teachers' Association local meeting, Stepney Division, 24th February 1915.

[167] *The Schoolmaster*, 4th December 1915.

would-be uplifters of the poor allow their critical faculties to run amuck, and begin to fancy that after all, "poor people like that" can manage on very short commons. I always felt I could trust Minnie to realise that under the veneer we humans are all very much alike; and that the most we could get for our poor, was very much less than we all of us need – and a wretched makeshift, indeed, for the social equality and assurance we desire. I was more than glad of her aid. A dear girl I thought her, and think so still though I lost touch with her towards the close of her brief life.[168]

Minnie joined the staff of ELFS, which paid its full-time organisers thirty shillings per week each, about a quarter less than Minnie's wage as a teacher. She was convinced that the sacrifice was worthwhile.

Getting Registered

There was plenty for Minnie to do in her new role. In July 1915, ELFS staged a procession to Parliament demanding price controls, better wages and equal pay. The following month, it led a 'great protest' against low wages and the taxation of necessities. But as the conflict bled into its second year, it had another fight on its hands: the battle against conscription. The numbers of men volunteering to fight had slowed, and the government worried that not enough were coming forward to replace those being killed or wounded. It needed to find more fodder for the cannons.

Its first step was to create a National Register. All men and women aged between fifteen and sixty-five years of age had to fill in a form with their personal details, on pain of a heavy fine for delaying or failing to do so. The government wanted to know how many, and which, men were available to go to the trenches, and how many women were available to replace them in industry. It also hoped that the National Register would shame some men into enlisting voluntarily.

The Register came into force on 15th August 1915, and was met by a protest called by ELFS, trade union branches and others. Despite the TUC's support for the war, it opposed conscription, and the National Register was, as ELFS labelled it, 'the thin end of the conscription wedge'.[169] The TUC's approach typified a much larger and more vocal opposition to forcing men to join the war than to the war itself.

---

[168] Pankhurst, 1932/1987, pp.132-3.

[169] ELFS Annual Report, 1914/15.

On the first day of 1916, the government announced that it would introduce a conscription bill, and a week later, the *Dreadnought* published a detailed case against conscription, which it also issued as a leaflet. A week after that, the anti-conscription campaigners began holding daily open-air meetings, and were no doubt relieved to find the weather unusually dry and mild. By the end of the month, they had held demonstrations in both Hyde Park and Victoria Park.[170]

The Military Conscription Act came into force on 2nd March 1916. From then on, all men aged eighteen to forty-one were liable to be called up to the Army unless they were married, widowed with children, serving in the Navy, a minister of religion, or working in a reserved occupation. Two months later, married men were included, bringing Minnie's husband Edgar into its scope; two years later, the upper age limit was raised to fifty-one. The government did not include Ireland (which was then part of the UK) in the scope of conscription, for fear of the strength of opposition. It already faced significant rebellion from those who wanted Ireland to become an independent country, rebellion which would erupt that same spring in the Easter Rising in Dublin.

Despite strong labour movement opposition, half of the Labour Party's MPs had voted for the Military Conscription Bill. Thirteen voted against it, along with some Liberals and the Irish Nationalists.

New Year, New Name, New Horizons

A second New Year under the cloud of war saw the East London Federation of Suffragettes once again bring a glimpse of sunshine. Six hundred supporters attended a celebration at Bow Baths Hall as the old year drew to a close, with toasts given by suffragettes Barbara Tchaykovsky, Mrs. Savoy and Sylvia Pankhurst, and by teetotaller George Lansbury, who raised a (non-alcoholic) glass to ELFS, 'the very best working women's organisation in the country.' A fortnight later, nearly a thousand children enjoyed an ELFS party at the same venue, featuring a marionette show, a Spring Pageant, milk, buns and a toy for every child. The *East London Advertiser* admitted that 'the gathering served to prove the popularity of the Suffragists' Federation in East London.'[171]

But ELFS was ready to expand its horizons beyond East London. With the main women's suffrage organisations either dropping campaigning

---

[170] WSF report, 1st January 1916 – 31st March 1917.

[171] *East London Advertiser*, 1st and 15th January 1916.

because of the war or tainted with their support for 'Votes for Ladies', the Federation began discussing the need for a national body dedicated to universal adult suffrage and drawing up plans to become that body.

The WSPU, in contrast, was now demanding that the government give the vote to soldiers and take it away from those who refused to fight: Conscientious Objectors. Having previously opposed the call for votes for everyone because it detracted from the fight for women's suffrage, the WSPU now opposed it because it would detract from the demand for votes for the fighting men! Minnie, Sylvia and ELFS insisted that there was no need for this hierarchy of suffrage: the straightforward answer was for all adults to have the vote.

Sylvia took these thoughts to the January meeting of the ELFS Committee, proposing that the organisation change its name to 'one that was not so local' and which emphasised universal suffrage. The Committee, including Minnie, agreed. On Saturday 26th February, the annual conference of ELFS agreed as well, and changed its name to the Workers' Suffrage Federation (WSF). It elected Minnie Lansbury as Honorary Assistant Secretary, Sylvia Pankhurst as Honorary Secretary, Barbara Tchaykovsky as Honorary Treasurer and Norah Smyth as Honorary Financial Secretary. The four office-holders issued a notice setting out the political basis of their refounded organisation, drawing together the threads of women's political emancipation, the impact of the war, and the centrality of the working class. The four wrote that 'as a result of this war and the economic pressure that will follow it, the forces of oppression will be more powerfully lined up against the forces of democracy and that women are bound to play a larger part in the industrial and social struggle than ever before.' Minnie and the others contended that the 'older Suffrage Societies' were not up to the job of fighting for franchise reform, '[h]eld back' as they were by limiting their demands to votes for women on equal terms with men, a demand which failed to enfranchise 'Women of the working class [who] are the chief sufferers by any property barriers to the franchise.' For the WSF, 'It is imperative that a strong working-class suffrage organisation should be built up to press for the sweeping away of property qualifications, for women as well as men.'

The notice concluded by urging those reading and agreeing with it to join the WSF, subscribe to the propaganda fund, and either join an existing branch or help set up a new one. This was an organisation determined to grow and to organise effectively, and its Assistant

Secretary, Minnie Lansbury, would take a central role in making that happen. In its first year, the WSF spread beyond the East End to other parts of London, establishing branches in St. Pancras, Leyton, Willesden and elsewhere. It also built a presence around the country, with branches in Durham, Birmingham, Southampton, Leeds, Newcastle, Nottingham, Sheffield, Glasgow and several more towns and cities. During that year, the Federation held over a thousand meetings in London, around two-thirds of them in the open air.

Minnie Lansbury was working full-time for the cause and regularly attending WSF Committee meetings. When the WSF's 1916 conference discussed organising a special conference about women in industry and politics, Minnie proposed tackling Parliament's Select Committee on the issue as soon as it formed. She gave practical help to branches when needed, for example filling in when the organisers were indisposed. When Miss Lynch began working on building the WSF outside London, Minnie helped Miss Price in taking over the organising work in Bow.[172] When Poplar organiser Miss Stephens was away in August 1916 and was then due to attend September's Trade Union Congress, the committee delegated Minnie to 'go to Poplar on Tuesdays to see any cases who want advice.' Keeping the branches under its watchful eye, the committee sought to help them through difficulties, and Minnie was often the one who proposed practical measures to assist. In October 1916, it thought the London branches to be 'very unsatisfactory', with both Bow and Poplar having 'good numbers, but no-one to take responsibility', West Ham being 'too large a district to be run as one branch', and even Canning Town, previously 'the most self-supporting branch', now having problems. It was Minnie who stepped up with a proposal that could facilitate a new branch being set up in part of West Ham and could overcome the interpersonal difficulties between some local organisers.

Minnie and the WSF also took an interest in wider social issues. Since the end of the nineteenth century, the 'garden cities' movement had won support for its plans to build communities including substantial open spaces as an alternative to the congestion of the usual urban environment. Minnie organised a visit by East London WSF members to the new garden city in Golder's Green, which would become known as Hampstead Garden Suburb, on Sunday 27th August. The Hampstead branch of the Independent Labour Party – the socialist organisation formed in 1893 to promote working-class political representation –

---

[172] *Woman's Dreadnought*, 20th May 1916.

arranged tea for the visiting WSF delegation, who were doubtless impressed by this spacious and pleasant new initiative in urban planning.[173] Garden cities were supposed to become home to people of all classes, and when Minnie later joined Poplar Council, it would follow some of the movement's ideas.

The Workers' Suffrage Federation continued the welfare work of its predecessor ELFS, and continued to be constantly in need of funds. Its bill for babies' milk alone ran to around sixty pounds per week. In December 1916, it held an exhibition of its work at Caxton Hall, the red brick and pink sandstone building in Westminster which hosted many suffrage meetings and events. Moreover, it reached out to others fighting for votes for all, and planned to convene a joint suffrage conference as its committee felt that 'it was bad for the suffrage movement to be disintegrated.'[174] For Israel Zangwill, 'In the Workers' Suffrage Federation and its manifold activities there is fortunately more organising ability, a more humane ideal than is likely to be discovered in the most up-to-date Cabinet.'[175]

Meanwhile, that Cabinet was badly neglecting the pensions of the men it had sent to war.

Pursuing Pensions

In the same month that Minnie Lansbury left her teaching job, a report to the House of Commons revealed that of forty-five thousand soldiers discharged from the Army due to permanent invalidity, over a third were receiving no pension; and of forty-one thousand soldiers' widows, just over half were receiving a pension. Even those who did get pension payments had to wait weeks or even months for the money to arrive. Minnie and the League of Rights demanded that irreparably wounded soldiers be kept on the Army payroll until their pensions were in place,[176] but the government was not listening.

The obvious and terrible suffering of men who had answered their country's call and suffered the consequences led even until-then-tame MPs to revolt. Some formed a backbench pensions committee, and

---

[173] *Woman's Dreadnought*, 22nd July 1916.

[174] WSF Committee minutes, 19th June 1916.

[175] Quoted in Pankhurst, 1932/1987, p.429.

[176] Pankhurst, 1932/77, pp.351-2.

under pressure of this and extra-parliamentary campaigning, the government brought in legislation to create War Pensions Committees. But still progress was slow. The *Herald* complained in August that while the public wanted full and adequate pensions for injured soldiers and the dependents of dead soldiers, the government just set up 'committee after committee … whose business has been to produce schemes needing miles of regulations and red tape to administer.' The following month, the paper added that, 'The parsimonious spirit shown in the allocation of pensions is little short of a disgrace. Millions have been poured out, with both hands, to the exploiters of the war; while a few shillings have been denied to those who have sacrificed everything.'[177]

Nationally, nearly three hundred local War Pensions Committees were to be set up. In London, there would be forty-six local sub-committees in the twenty-nine boroughs, overseen by a central London War Pensions Committee consisting of seven charity nominees, five labour members nominated by trade unions and the Labour Party, and thirteen others appointed by the London County Council. Poplar was one of the boroughs big enough and needy enough to warrant two local sub-committees: Poplar (A), dealing with Bow and Bromley; and Poplar (B), dealing with Poplar itself. The local sub-committees were charged with making sure that pensions were paid; making additional grants, for example for healthcare or training; and helping disabled ex-soldiers to find work.

George Lansbury became a member of the Poplar (A) War Pensions Committee, but was soon disillusioned, writing that, 'These committees have very little power, very little money, and are hedged around with a whole mass of rules and regulations, all designed to secure that a minimum rather than a maximum allowance shall be granted to any of those who need succour or help.' George wanted to 'sweep away all the Pensions Committees, all the Charity Commissioners' and give directly to soldiers, sailors and their dependents what they needed.[178] His daughter-in-law Minnie may well have shared his sentiment, but she was less inclined to demagogy and more to getting stuck in and making the War Pensions Committee a fighting ground for the rights and maintenance of those in need. In doing so, she would not only give practical support to the victims of a war that she opposed, but would also engage Poplar's working-class population in struggle for its interests

[177] *The Herald*, 12th August and 9th September 1916.

[178] *The Herald*, 22nd July 1916.

as a class, strengthening the labour movement for its battles during and after the war.

Poplar's War Pensions Committee would be 'the organisation with which [Minnie Lansbury's] name will always be associated by thousands of East Londoners,'[179] but when it first formed, she was not a member. Although the local committees were based in boroughs, their members were appointed by the London County Council, which did not feel obliged to pick people who lived in the area they would serve. So it was that Minnie Lansbury first became a member of the nearby Hackney War Pensions Committee in November 1916. The Committee ran offices in Homerton High Street and in Aspland Hall, opening their doors to pension applicants for two hours over lunchtime on Mondays, Wednesdays and Fridays. Minnie was one of two labour representatives on the Committee, sitting alongside nominees from the London War Pensions Committee, the Borough Council, the Soldiers' and Sailors' Families' Association and the Soldiers' and Sailors' Help Society.

Discontent at London's local committees not being drawn from their local areas spread even as far as Parliament, which in March 1917 debated a proposal that borough councils rather than the LCC appoint their local committee. Liberal MP James Daniel-Kiley asked rhetorically, 'Can you imagine that in a great working-class district it is not possible to find more suitable people than the people who have been selected? … we venture to think locally that we could do it quite as well and very much better.'[180] Although MPs voted down the proposal, the London War Pensions Committee may have noted their and others' concerns and made some changes to address them. Before long, Minnie Lansbury was appointed to the Poplar (A) War Pensions Committee. This Committee carried out its work from the Parish Hall on Avenue Road, Bow, which was later renamed in honour of the first Chair of the Committee, Reverend Henry Kitcat. It is still named Kitcat Terrace, and the old Parish Hall still stands at the end of this short street.

Poplar (A) War Pensions Committee functioned with an administration budget of just £176 for the ten months from May 1917. £85 of this was for staff wages, £46 for office expenses, £11 for stationery and printing, £26 for postage, telegrams and telephone, and £8 for miscellaneous spending. While the London War Pensions Committee scrutinised this expenditure, it paid its own chief officer, Secretary Mrs.

---

[179] *The Herald*, 7th January 1922.

[180] House of Commons Hansard, 20th March 1917, vol.92, p.122.

H.F. Wood, the generous figure of five hundred pounds per year, more than six times the salary of local sub-committee assistants. Even this, though, seemed insignificant compared with the two thousand pounds paid annually to the President of the Board of Pensions, established in late 1916.[181] At least some people were doing well out of the war.

Reverend Kitcat later recalled of Minnie Lansbury that 'often at the expense of her strength she laboured … to help the whole staff of the office in carrying out their duties' and that she had a 'wonderful comprehension of the ever-changing regulations by which the Pensions Committee was governed.' Committee Secretary Harry Gibbs agreed, telling how Minnie 'carried out her duties in a manner which surprised everyone, her ready grasp of the difficulties which inevitably present themselves on such committees, being very remarkable.' Reverend Kitcat was soon confident enough of Minnie's abilities to stand aside as chair and support Minnie's unanimous election as his successor. Minnie Lansbury was clearly competent, conscientious and clever. But just as important as her talent was the cause in which she chose to deploy it. Kitcat remarked that Minnie's efforts were not just to administer effectively but 'above all to do all that could be done for the thousands of ex-Service men.' Sylvia Pankhurst wrote that to all her work, Minnie 'brought the determination – rare among the holders of such office – to fight to get the greatest possible advantages for the workers concerned. She made no pretence of impartiality between the Government and the applicant. She regarded herself as the advocate of the applicant, and fought, as a lawyer does, to get the best possible terms for her client. Therefore the people, especially the women, knew her as their friend.'[182] When Minnie Lansbury held public office as a working-class representative, her approach was to fight for the class she represented, not to defer to the protocols of the office or to the class which sought to co-opt her into distributing crumbs.

Sylvia also recalled that Minnie carried out the majority of the work of the *Herald* Pensions Campaign. Her father-in-law's newspaper championed the work of the League of Rights and the labour representatives on the War Pensions Committees and decided to supplement their work with an upfront campaign to expose the miscarriages of justice and the unfairness of the system and to demand

---

[181] London War Pensions Committee agenda, 19th July 1917; minutes, 7th June 1917; *The Herald*, 25th November 1916.

[182] *Daily Herald, Workers' Dreadnought*, 7th January 1922.

better. Its issue of 30th September 1916 launched its pensions campaign, announcing that it was opening an office at its headquarters at 21 Tudor Street in the City of London to receive letters and visits from discharged soldiers and dependents who were not receiving their proper pensions or allowances. A week later, the paper reported that, 'The first post after publication brought responses, and each day since they have been coming.' From then on, a regular column, 'The Herald Searchlight on the Pensions Scandals', listed examples of impoverished victims of the war, alongside reports, analysis and calls for change.

Minnie Lansbury was providing practical support to the victims of war through her work in the *Herald* campaign, the League of Rights and the Poplar War Pensions Committee. She was doing so in a particular political framework: involving working-class people in their own struggles for justice, revealing the politics behind the suffering, fighting as a representative for working-class interests, helping to build a movement.

Arrested for Peace

Two years into the war, the patriotism and enthusiasm that had greeted its start was beginning to wane. As more and more working-class people experienced the deprivation, fear and bereavement brought by war, and as the promises of a swift victory proved illusory, opponents of the war – including Minnie Lansbury – found that they could more easily speak out and receive a hearing. But they still received hostility as well.

In April 1916, what the *East London Advertiser* described as 'Misguided women from East London' (almost certainly the WSF, among them Minnie and Sylvia) held a demonstration for peace in Trafalgar Square. War supporters charged the plinth, tore up peace flags and placards and doused the protesters with flour and ochre. The *Advertiser* reported that there were 'screams from the women and loud yells and cheers from the crowd' and declared that the peace protesters were 'asking for trouble'.[183] But the peace campaign continued and the following month the WSF noted that 'Soldiers are writing constantly saying they are very grateful to us for wanting to stop the War.' They organised a peace memorial (what we would now call a petition), and 'Mrs. [Minnie] Lansbury said she was going to canvass Bromley members & take 100 to [an anti-conscription meeting on 1st June at]

[183] 15th April 1916.

the Portman Rooms.' The meeting turned out to be 'smaller than hoped for but very enthusiastic.'[184]

Later that year, war weariness was growing. Raymond Postgate wrote that:

> [B]y the end of 1916 the mood of 1914 had disappeared. There was a universal sourness ... the army was tired, sick and angry – parts were near to mutiny ... strikes were reappearing even in essential war industries ... the workers at home and soldiers in the army ... were both becoming steadily more disquieted by the never-ending suffering.[185]

When Germany and its allies suggested peace talks on 12th December 1916, the WSF called a peace meeting for the following Sunday at the East India Dock Gates, the huge entrance to the busy trading wharves. Campaigners distributed their posters on the East End's walls, and despite worries about violence from 'jingoes' (keen supporters of the war) and a thick black fog over the weekend, a crowd of around two hundred people assembled on the Sunday to advocate the ending of the military conflict.

Among the protesters were Edgar and Minnie Lansbury, as described by Sylvia Pankhurst: '[Minnie] hanging to his arm, her Puck-like glance seeming to convey to me, as she caught my eye, that she was here at his side to stir up, in kindly, affectionate spirit, her big, good-natured lazy-bones.'[186] Minnie and Edgar were comrades as well as spouses. Both were political activists in their own right, and they carried on their day-to-day political work in different places – Edgar in Poplar's council chamber, Minnie in the League of Rights and the War Pensions Committee's offices. But they enjoyed a shared political outlook and often found themselves protesting and campaigning alongside each other.

Not everyone was at the Dock Gates on that Sunday to call for peace, and the fear of violence from the jingoes proved well-founded. A small group of war supporters – described by Sylvia as a 'bare half-dozen elderly well-dressed men' backed by 'a gang of irresponsible lads barely above school age' – were intent on causing mischief. Elderly campaigner Miss Bennett mounted a chair to call the crowd together, but when the

---

[184] Minutes, WSF Members' Meeting, 15th May and 19th June 1916.

[185] 1951, p.162.

[186] Pankhurst, 1932/1987, p.431.

ILP's Tom Attlee (Clement's older brother) got up on the chair to address the crowd, he got through less than two minutes of his speech before, as several newspapers reported, 'a determined rush was made by the crowd'. Then, 'Miss Sylvia Pankhurst endeavoured to stay the rush, and was raised to the soap box by her friends.'[187] The police had thus far stood by and watched, but now decided to act – not by stopping the attackers, but by ordering the peace meeting to disperse and imposing their order 'with knees and fists'.[188]

The peace campaigners reconvened around the corner on the East India Dock Road, the area's major thoroughfare with its shops, wide pavements and traffic to and from the docks. Sylvia 'clung to some iron railings, and from this precarious position she attempted an address.'[189] This was too much for the constabulary, who arrested several anti-war attendees, among them Edgar and Minnie. The WSF described the scene: 'Mr. Edgar Lansbury was waiting for his wife amongst a crowd of 150 persons when he was arrested. Mrs. Minnie Lansbury came up to see her husband being dragged off by the coat collar and because she ran alongside, she was also arrested.'[190]

In court the following morning, Sylvia, Minnie, Edgar and fellow peace protesters Charlotte Drake and Melvina Walker faced charges of obstructing the highway, with Melvina facing an additional charge of using insulting words, her case to be heard a few days later. The police gave evidence that the accused had refused to stop their meeting, that the crowd had blocked the traffic and that several members of the audience had been knocked down. Edgar told the court that when a man had asked him if he was 'playing the German game', he had replied by asking the man what sort of game he thought he was playing. The peaceniks stood before magistrate Mr. Leycester, who you may remember had dealt severely with Edgar and his sister before the war. On this occasion, though, he judged that 'so far as Mrs. Lansbury was concerned he was in doubt if she ever obstructed the police' and also discharged Edgar, as he thought 'he had been unnecessarily arrested.'[191]

[187] *Nottingham Evening Post* and others, 16th December 1916.

[188] Pankhurst, 1932/1987, p.432.

[189] *Nottingham Evening Post* and others, 16th December 1916.

[190] WSF report, 1st January 1916 – 31st March 1917.

[191] *Birmingham Mail*, 18th December 1916; *East London Advertiser*, 23rd December 1916.

Leycester was not so kind, though, to Sylvia and Charlotte, binding them over to keep the peace and then fining them two pounds each when they refused to be bound over. This ought to have resulted in them being imprisoned for seven days, but the authorities did not pursue the matter. Sylvia recalled that, 'The affair fizzled out quietly. The Government did not want us to be going to prison then. They remembered too well the growth of the Suffragette movement under the stimulous [sic] of imprisonment.'[192]

Minnie and the WSF continued their campaigning against the war over Christmas and into the new year, collecting signatures on a petition for peace by negotiation, hosting a peace conference at the Women's Hall on 14th January, and calling a demonstration in April 1917 that was attended by three thousand people.[193] The WSF's annual conference over Whitsun weekend re-elected Minnie Lansbury as Honorary Assistant Secretary and appointed her to its Finance Committee.

Refusing War

Once conscription came into force in March 1916, men of qualifying age (eighteen to forty-one) – soon to include Minnie Lansbury's husband Edgar – could claim exemption by applying to a local Military Service Tribunal and if they received no mercy there, to the Appeals Tribunal. Some applied on the basis of their family, business, public service or other responsibilities; others sought exemption because of an 'objection [that] genuinely rests on religious or moral convictions'. The latter were known as 'Conscientious Objectors' (COs), and were rarely granted absolute exemption, instead being required to carry out non-combatant duties such as road-making or ambulance work, or if they refused that as well, facing court martial and prison.

Labour MP Philip Snowden described the tribunals' treatment of Conscientious Objectors in dramatic terms: 'Never since the days of Judge Jeffries and the Bloody Assize has such a travesty of justice been seen.'[194] Hostility to the COs raged outside the tribunals too, with preachers and newspapers denouncing them, jingoes pinning white feathers to them and frequently physically assaulting them. There were

[192] Pankhurst, 1932/1987, p.432.

[193] WSF report, 1st January 1916 – 31st March 1917.

[194] Speech to No Conscription Fellowship conference, 8th April 1916, cited in Pankhurst, 1932/1987, p.293.

around sixteen thousand Conscientious Objectors; at least seventy dying as a result of their imprisonment.

In East London's tribunals, socialists fought for exemptions. Historian Julia Bush notes that 'At every tribunal it seems to have been more difficult to sustain an objection on socialist grounds than one based on business or family responsibilities, or even on religious faith.'[195] The *East London Advertiser* carried weekly sneering reports of the area's tribunals, in which the Chair – in Poplar's case, Mayor and prominent freemason Alfred Warren – laughed as he dismissed men's pleas for exemption and sent them to war. The paper claimed that public opinion was steadily hardening against Conscientious Objectors, or, as it preferred to call them, 'conscience shirkers'.[196]

In Poplar, unlike some other East End districts, socialist applicants were generally allowed to speak at their tribunal hearings, and some were asked to prove the sincerity of their political views by producing their membership card of a socialist organisation. More men applied for exemption in Poplar than in neighbouring boroughs such as Stepney, but with Labour holding only four Tribunal seats (Joe Banks, Sam March, Charlie Sumner and David Adams) out of thirteen, still the tribunal refused to exempt the majority of socialist applicants. The Borough Council refused the nominations of Labour's George Lansbury and A.A. Watts, and Sylvia Pankhurst refused her own nomination, explaining that, 'By no means would I have served. I would not share part or lot in the odious work of Conscription.'[197]

Nonetheless, as Bush describes, the Labour tribunal members' 'presence was constantly felt, as they cross-examined applicants to help them put their cases in the most favourable light. Disputes arose mainly between political opponents on the tribunal.'[198] One such case arose when Minnie's husband Edgar applied to the Poplar tribunal for exemption.

Once Parliament added married men to the scope of conscription, Edgar matched the criteria for the call-up to a war that he actively opposed. Minnie and her husband would now face a long personal and political battle to stop him being taken away to kill or be killed for a

---

[195] Bush, 1984, p.62.

[196] 29th April, 27th May 1916.

[197] Pankhurst, 1932/1987, p.289.

[198] 1984, p.61.

cause that he did not support. Edgar could have reasonably expected that his application for exemption would succeed, as he was a member of Poplar Borough Council and it was standard practice elsewhere to exempt councillors. But after hearing Edgar's case in September 1917, the Tribunal was deadlocked at four votes in favour and four against, and the Chairman cast his vote in favour of sending Edgar to war. It seemed that his political opponents had found a way to remove Edgar from the political battlefield by sending him to the military one.

By this time, the Poplar tribunal had dealt with over ten thousand cases, and five hundred had appealed the outcome.[199] Edgar was not going to accept going to war, so in September 1917 he joined the numbers of those appealing. He attached to his appeal his statement to the local tribunal and additional statements from his father and from Robert Williams of the Transport Workers' Federation. He explained his case as follows:

> That the Local Tribunal did not give due consideration to the grounds upon which I based my appeal, but devoted itself to a consideration of irrelevant matter. … I am a member of the Poplar Borough Council and an active worker in the Socialist and Political Labour movement of Poplar and East London. This brings me into conflict with my colleagues on the Borough Council. The Tribunal was composed of a majority of my opponents whom I consider to be not the best qualified people to consider my application.[200]

It would be several months before the Appeals Tribunal reached its conclusion on Edgar's case. His mother Bessie wrote to her friend Mrs. Sewell in January 1918 that, 'Poor Edgar is appearing again today at Guildhall, I am anxious how he is getting on.'[201] But the Appeals Tribunal eventually recognised the justice of Edgar's case – and perhaps the bias of his political opponents – and granted his exemption.

There must have been great relief at Minnie and Edgar's home, among the Lansburys and among the Glassmans. By now, it was 1918, and revolution had twice transformed the country that Isaac and Annie Glassman had fled.

---

[199] *East London Advertiser*, 24th November 1917.

[200] Edgar Lansbury's appeal, 13th September 1917, LANSBURY 7, 369.

[201] Letter, Bessie Lansbury to Mrs. Sewell, 29th January 1918, LANSBURY 7.

Chapter 4 – Revolutionary Dawn

The Jews and the War

By 1914, the position of Minnie's family and other Jewish immigrants in British society was improving, albeit slowly. However, the outbreak of war threatened to throw back this fragile progress, as patriotism reached fever pitch and old antisemitic suspicions of disloyalty revived.

As the National Register came into force in 1915, the *East London Observer* spat out its view that, 'there is a strong local feeling that the "Jew boys", as they are termed, who hang about street corners and public houses, the cheap foreign restaurants and similar places, ought to be made to do something for the country they honour with their presence.'[202] In fact, Jews who had not become naturalised British citizens were not allowed to join the British armed forces, even voluntarily. And while lots of naturalised British Jews did enlist, there were good reasons why many did not. They had not fled the antisemitic tyranny of the Russian Tsar's regime just to fight for its ally! Many Jews opposed the war on internationalist, political or religious grounds.

The arrival of conscription in 1916 put Jews in an even more difficult position, as British men were forced to go to war while unnaturalised immigrant Jews could take their jobs or buy their businesses. Intemperate language peppered the pages of the East End's local newspapers, the *East London Advertiser* railing against 'alien shirkers', 'job snatchers' and the 'East End alien scandal'.[203] The *Herald* tried to dampen the discord and promote unity, its editorial arguing that conscription was an injustice that created further injustices. It appealed to English and Jewish people to see each other's point of view, while admitting that in the circumstances, 'it is idle to expect the people concerned to consider the matter in the cold light of the abstract principles of justice.'[204] Those Jews who were naturalised citizens and sought exemption from conscription faced an even more harsh reception at the tribunals than other objectors. Historian Julia Bush records that 'There is no shortage of evidence that the East London tribunals were prejudiced against Jewish applicants because

---

[202] 3rd July 1915.

[203] 24th June, 14th October and 6th May 1916.

[204] 15th July 1916.

they were Jewish and "foreign", as well as because they did not want to fight.'[205]

In June 1916, the government allowed 'friendly aliens' (immigrants from countries that were Britain's allies in the war) to enlist, while threatening that if not enough did so, it would deport those who did not. The Anglo-Jewish establishment backed the government's approach, Chief Rabbi J.H. Hertz describing Jews who applied for exemption as 'laggards'.[206] And rather like mainstream Labour leaders, the *Jewish Chronicle* had opposed the war until it started, when it abruptly began cheerleading the military campaign.

In August, the Foreign Jews' Protection Committee – newly formed by Jewish trade unions, socialist and anarchist groups – issued an 'emphatic protest' against official Anglo-Jewry's backing of the government, accusing it of overlooking the feelings and views of Jews concerned about the deplorable position of their fellow Jews in Russia. The campaigners asked rhetorically how enlistment could be considered voluntary while the threat of deportation loomed, and explained that deportation to Russia would mean delivery to a regime that still savagely oppressed their people. They appealed to the British labour movement to defend the right to asylum and to support their cause.

While the TUC and the national Labour Party failed to oppose the enlist-or-be-deported threat, East London's labour movement did offer support to its Jewish residents. The Workers' Suffrage Federation's anti-war campaign had brought it into contact with Jews who had fled Russia, and in 1916, it published a pamphlet, *Execution of an East London Boy*, consisting of letters from a young Jewish East Ender who had enlisted, suffered shellshock and been sentenced to death for desertion.

In 1917, the Jews' fear of deportation to Tsarist Russia took a dramatic turn, as in February, revolution overthrew the Tsar, and then in October, the Bolsheviks led a second revolution and took Russia out of the war. Considerable numbers of Jews returned to Russia from Britain, with no deportation order required, feeling safe to do so following the revolution.

---

[205] 1984, p.173.

[206] East London Advertiser, 14th October 1916.

Greeting the New Dawn

Minnie Lansbury and other East London Jews and socialists welcomed Russia's revolution in February 1917, which overthrew the Tsar and set up a provisional government that was unelected and supposed to be temporary, and that was dominated by remnants of the old state machine. On Saturday 17th March,[207] over seven thousand people packed into the five-thousand-capacity Great Assembly Hall on Mile End Road to listen to speeches in Russian and Yiddish cheering the downfall of the Tsar.

The excitement extended beyond the East End, as two weeks later the Albert Hall hosted what George Lansbury called 'one of the biggest and most enthusiastic' public meetings in England's history. Calling the revolution 'the dawn of a new day', he wrote that at the Albert Hall meeting, 'It seemed as if all the long pent-up feelings of horror and shame of war and intense longing for peace were at last let loose.'[208]

Rallying turned to organising as Minnie's husband Edgar joined over a thousand delegates from trade unions, trades councils, local Labour parties, peace groups and women's groups at a conference in Leeds on 3rd June. The conference set up a Council of Workers' and Soldiers' Delegates (CWSD), seeking to replicate in Britain the soviets which were challenging Russia's provisional government over its failure to bring about sufficiently radical and democratic change. The newly-formed Council invited the Workers' Suffrage Federation to send two delegates. Minnie's commitment to building a revolutionary movement saw the WSF Committee meeting on 13th July elect her to this role alongside Sylvia Pankhurst. A week later, though, there was some doubt as to whether Minnie would be able to attend the CWSD meeting, so the WSF appointed Norah Smyth as a reserve.

The CWSD's London meeting was scheduled for 28th July, but although hundreds of delegates attended on this Saturday, a pro-war mob broke up the event. While some other regional conferences were successful, others were blocked by local authorities or, like London's, by opposition disruption. As the year went on, opinions about the revolution's progress diverged among its British supporters, and the Council of Workers' and Soldiers' Delegates fizzled out.

---

[207] by the Gregorian calendar used in the UK; Russia still used the Julian calendar.

[208] 1928, p.186.

Minnie, Sylvia and Norah were among many suffragettes inspired by the revolution. In contrast, Emmeline Pankhurst travelled to Russia in the summer of 1917 to lobby the provisional government to stay in the war, and when in October the Bolsheviks took power and withdrew Russia from the war, prioritised campaigning against them. The gulf between the left and right wings of the women's suffrage movement had grown wider than ever. Those differences were not just about how militant their tactics were but about their political and class allegiances.

For the British government, the February revolution was even more reason for Russian Jews to either join up or go home. In May 1917, it legislated for the conscription of citizens of Allied states into the British army. Russian Jewish men of military age would now have to enlist or be deported, with no passage provided for their families. With Russia's provisional government agreeing that Britain could conscript its nationals, it is little wonder that many Russian Jews and socialists thought that the revolution had not yet gone far enough.

The *East London Observer* delighted in issuing a 'WARNING TO JEW SHIRKERS: Three Months for Evading Military Service'[209] and ran a weekly report on 'The Alien Problem'. During May, London's police pre-empted the Bill becoming law by rounding up over a thousand Jewish men and boys, physically beating them and their families in the process. Although the pretext was to enforce conscription, only four were handed to the military authorities and only nine charged in court as absentees; the rest were released.[210] Even though the new Military Service Act had removed the main grievance against the Russian Jews, hostility to immigrants and specifically to Jews not only continued but increased. In September 1917, two to three thousand Jews and gentiles fought a pitched battle in Blythe Street and Teesdale Street, Bethnal Green. Persecution of 'foreign' Jews was more prevalent than ever during the final year of the war.

It was in this threatening atmosphere that Minnie Lansbury's father Isaac Glassman sought to prove the British citizenship that he had obtained four years previously. He contacted the Home Office asking for evidence, to protect himself and his family from the hostility being meted out to foreigners or perhaps even from deportation. The Home Office replied to his legal representative that it would be sufficient for

---

[209] 5th May 1917.

[210] *Woman's Dreadnought*, 26th May 1917.

Isaac to state that a certificate of naturalisation had been granted to him on 6th May 1913.[211]

While many Jews did return to post-revolution Russia, others did not want to. Some, such as the Glassmans, had made their home in Britain. Others feared that Russia might still be a hostile host to them. As revolution toppled the Tsar, Russian writer Maxim Gorky explained in *The Herald*[212] the persistence of antisemitism, arguing that antisemites scapegoated Jews for military failures and war distress, used examples of 'bad Jews' to suggest that all Jews were bad and portrayed all Jews as rich when over ninety per cent were poor.

Despite the hostility, those Jews who remained in Britain became further integrated into British society and into the labour movement. Julia Bush argues that 'the foreign-ness of the ghetto could not outlive the original generation of immigrants' and described a new generation of Jews born in Britain and speaking English – Jews like Minnie and her siblings. For this new generation, 'the existence of separate Yiddish-speaking trade unions and political parties gradually became an anachronism. The war speeded up the process of change. In 1918 Jews began, for the first time, to enter the foreground of East London Labour politics.'[213]

Having attended a non-Jewish school and teacher training college, been active in an English trade union, fought for the vote alongside English women, married a gentile, and organised and supported the families of English soldiers, Minnie Lansbury was one of the pioneers of this integration.

Food Fights

As Russian workers overthrew their Tsar, British workers faced a worsening food crisis.

The flour that Isaac Glassman delivered from his business in Chicksand Street had risen in price during the war, and with wheat imports from the USA disrupted by the military conflict, flour supplies were so depleted that the government advised people to eat less bread and even to make pastry with potatoes. Fifteen-year-old Samuel Iles

---

[211] Letter, Home Office to Isaac Glassman, held by family.

[212] 10th February 1917.

[213] 1984, p.190.

started working as a carman for Isaac on 1st November 1916, and on his first day in his new job found himself in possession of a commodity much in demand and saw his chance to make some money on the side. Sent to deliver forty bags of flour to a baker in Old Ford Road, Iles had delivered only thirty of them, later telling the court that 'Me and another fellow took them round to Deptford and sold them to a baker.' The baker was forty-eight-year-old Charles Brall, whose shop was Brall Conrad at 98 Church Street, a five-mile diversion from its intended destination. Brall claimed that he had no idea that the flour was stolen until the police called after he had bought it. He said that a man [Iles] had called at his shop, telling him that his employer, Mr. Glassman, was hard pressed for money and would sell him ten bags of flour for just five pounds. Seeing the van parked outside with Mr. Glassman's name and address on it, Brall bought the flour. He saw it as a bargain but was not suspicious of its legality.

Brall and Iles were both charged with being concerned in stealing and receiving ten bags of flour, value eleven pounds.[214] Iles confessed and was sentenced to two years' probation for stealing the flour but acquitted on the charge of receiving, and Brall was found not guilty on both charges.

Some retailers were quick to take advantage of the food crisis, over-charging for potatoes, oatmeal, peas, swede and other produce. A few found themselves prosecuted for overcharging or for refusing to sell potatoes or sugar unless the buyer bought something else as well. But the government ignored calls to take control of the supply of food, preferring to urge working-class people to abstain from eating bread while making 'no serious attempt to check the luxurious indulgence of the rich,' according to the *The Call*, newspaper of the British Socialist Party, which had formed shortly before the war through the Social Democratic Federation coming together with some ILP members. The paper complained that 'The ruling class has permitted food manipulators, flour factors, profit-mongers of all descriptions to make millions in profits out of the people's necessities.'[215]

Minnie Lansbury involved herself in tackling the food crisis, in the first place by gathering information. When the Food Controller asked for an information committee to be set up, Minnie successfully proposed

[214] *Illustrated Police News*, 18th November 1915; Sessions Rolls, London County Court.

[215] 3rd May 1917.

that the WSF get such a committee together. And while the WSF demanded that the price of milk be fixed at five pence per quart (quarter of a gallon, or two pints), Minnie had checked and reported that instead, it had been fixed at seven pence per quart if bought in a shop and eight pence if delivered to your home.[216] The WSF asked for representatives on the Poplar Food Central Committee and sent a deputation to see Mayor Alfred Warren, telling him that 'thousands of women have had to stand in this recent bitter weather for hours in a long queue, in the hope of obtaining a small supply of potatoes.'[217]

But Minnie also relished more direct action against the food shortages, as shown in this handwritten note by Sylvia Pankhurst, probably written for, but then not included in, her book *The Home Front*:

> Minnie Lansbury burst in, exultantly announcing 'a riot in the Roman!' A crowd of women had threatened to storm a fish and chip shop for potatoes. A policeman attempting to stop them had been swept aside and 'they tore off all his buttons!', her black eyes twinkled with merriment. To save further disturbance the policeman had compelled the fishmonger to bring out his store of potatoes and sell them at three halfpence a pound from a table outside his door.[218]

Minnie was also the main national contact person for the League of Rights for Soldiers' and Sailors' Wives and Relatives, the *Woman's Dreadnought* directing readers who wanted to know more about its work to write to Minnie at 400 Old Ford Road. The League continued its work battling for support for servicemen's dependents, but Minnie and its other leaders knew that it had to consolidate and step up its work, so they planned a conference in March 1917. As Poplar socialist A.A. Watts wrote, 'The League has been very active since its formation, but its field is too limited, and we feel that it should be placed on a wider and more stable basis ... There is not the slightest doubt such an organisation is needed ... who is to champion the cause of the wives and children, mothers and fathers? We have had hundreds of cases to deal with.'[219]

The conference took place on 24th March, with one hundred and fifty-four delegates representing eighty-nine London bodies: trade

---

[216] WSF Committee minutes, 5th May and 23rd November 1917.

[217] IISH 38.

[218] File 67, IISH, undated.

[219] *The Call*, 22nd March 1917.

unions, trades councils, labour representation committees and socialist groups. It passed resolutions demanding full pensions for all who needed them, and unanimously voted to set up a central organisation to safeguard the interests of servicemen and their dependents and a provisional committee to draft a constitution. The *Herald* reported that the conference 'was a great success and shows that the forces at work on behalf [of] our broken soldiers and sailors are widening, deepening, and gathering in strength.' It highlighted the contributions of women delegates, who showed a great understanding of the subject and 'a magnificent determination that put a fine fighting spirit into the proceedings.'[220]

House of Hope

Minnie Lansbury's experiences in fighting for war pensions had seen her become a champion of the victims of a war that she opposed. She had become, as historian of 'Poplarism' Noreen Branson wrote, 'well known among the war disabled and bereaved for her work on the local War Pensions Committee which, among other matters, had responsibility for some 500 war orphans in the borough.'[221] Minnie was so committed to this work that she literally took it home with her.

From their first married home in Mornington Road, Minnie and Edgar had moved to the next street along, and now lived at Wellington Cottage, 6 Wellington Road. The *Daily Herald* later described their home as 'pretty',[222] and Poplar Labour Councillor Thomas Blacketer spoke of it as 'the well-known centre of her great public activities':

> To the many poor people of this wide East End district, No.6 was a House of Hope. Here flocked every morning, between the hours of nine and half past ten, the men and women and little children broken by the terrible conditions under which they live.
>
> They knew they were always sure of sympathy and assistance in their trouble from Minnie Lansbury, and no needy one was ever turned empty away.[223]

---

[220] 31st March 1917.

[221] 1979, p.18.

[222] 7th January 1922.

[223] *Daily Herald*, 2nd January 1922.

Sylvia Pankhurst visited Minnie at the new house and noted her efforts at furnishing it on a budget:

> She showed us a splendid bedroom suit[e] with a magnificent wardrobe and told us she had procured it by selling her old one as everything sold for much more than one gave for it now.[224]

During 1917, Minnie and Edgar did manage to take a break from their labours, in Cornwall. They accompanied their friends Francis and Hilda Meynell on a holiday, to help Francis to recuperate following his spell in military hospital brought about by his deliberately making himself too ill to fight in the war.[225]

They also had some help at Wellington Cottage, as Lucy Cole became their housekeeper. Like Minnie and Edgar, Lucy was a suffragette, an 'ardent Labour supporter' and attended rallies at Hyde Park. Lucy was the same age as Minnie, and went on to live a very long life before dying aged 104 in 1993.[226] It is unclear whether Lucy lived with the Lansburys in Wellington Cottage, as she does not appear on the electoral register. Before the days of mass-produced household appliances, with Edgar running the timber yard and sitting on the local council and with Minnie's work with war pensioners – and with so many daily visitors – housework would certainly have been onerous enough to need additional help. It seems that they were not going to follow Edgar's parents' example and have Minnie sacrifice her political activism in order to keep house. They had the choice of dropping Minnie's (or even Edgar's!) political activity or hiring domestic help, and chose the latter. But the fact that they could afford to make this choice indicates that Minnie and Edgar were better off than many working-class families. The labour and feminist movements had their own internal inequalities, and although Minnie and Edgar were nothing like the wealthy suffragettes led by Emmeline and Christabel Pankhurst, they did have a reliable and independent income.

Votes for All

In October 1916, the government – under pressure to grant votes to the fighting men, fearful of a post-war return to suffragette militancy and

---

[224] Handwritten note, Sylvia Pankhurst collection, File 69, 456, undated, IISH.

[225] Meynell, 1971, p.103.

[226] Taylor, 2001, p.111.

unable to forge a consensus in Parliament – commissioned a Speaker's Conference to draw up proposals for extending voting rights to more people. When it did so in late January 1917, it accepted the right of women to vote, but proposed a higher qualifying age for women than for men and that even those women who qualified by their age must also meet a property qualification. Minnie and three other WSF officers wrote to the local newspaper outlining their dissatisfaction with this, explaining that 'The working class widow left with a little family to bring up needs the protection of the vote more if possible than anyone else. In the majority of cases she is a lodger, not an occupier, and would be unable to qualify under the proposed terms.'[227]

The Workers' Suffrage Federation was keen to strengthen its fight for votes for all adult women and men, and wanted to unite with others with the same aim. It had helped to bring together a National Council for Adult Suffrage, but Sylvia Pankhurst was concerned that its Committee was 'very wobbly' and that the WSF 'must not compromise with our friends'. With a National Council meeting scheduled for Saturday 3rd March 1917, the WSF elected Minnie Lansbury and two other delegates to represent it and ensure that the WSF's allies shared its strong stance. But although London Labour Council for Adult Suffrage (LLCAS) agreed with the WSF, the National Council for Adult Suffrage supported the Speaker's Conference proposals and ended the LLCAS's affiliation to it because it did not agree.[228]

Meanwhile, Sylvia had an idea for local campaigning in East London, and Minnie had an idea to make it more effective. In April 1917, Sylvia proposed to the WSF that it hold a 'model election', with every man and woman having a vote. It would be a vote about the right to vote: for or against adult suffrage, the Speaker's Conference report, provision for referenda, and proportional representation. The idea was that rather than just lobbying for votes for all to be introduced at a later date, they could put it into practice and show how well it could work. The Committee agreed, and Sylvia suggested that they hold public meetings to 'work it up' and get people to campaign as they would in an official election. They could hold the vote across the whole area or in one specific district. The WSF set up sub-committees to oversee aspects of the work, and elected Minnie as Secretary of the Hospitality Committee.

[227] *East London Advertiser*, 3rd February.

[228] Sylvia Pankhurst papers, IISH, file 215.

They decided to run the poll in the northern wards of Bow and Bromley constituency. While Sylvia had initially proposed setting up voting booths in shops, at the next month's Committee meeting Minnie successfully proposed that 'it would be better to take a poll, canvassing each house'. By the end of a wet and warm June, the canvassers were out in force. The *East London Advertiser* enthused that they were 'busy calling at the houses in the chosen area', fulfilling Sylvia's earlier stated hope that their action might prompt some press coverage. The *Advertiser* reported that 'preparations … [were] exciting much interest' and that 'The experiment … should be of practical value not only from an educational, but also from a statistical point of view'. Another local paper, the *East London Observer*, commented that by giving every woman and man in the area a vote, the WSF was 'taking time by the forelock',[229] a phrase used more often then than now, meaning that they were taking an opportunity when it presented itself.

Later that summer, adult suffrage campaigners held simultaneous processions from south, east and west London to a rally in Trafalgar Square, which their opponents tried but failed to disrupt.

Agitating, Educating, Organising?

Minnie's activity in the WSF did not stop at suffrage campaigning. Possibly because of her previous job as a teacher, the Federation nominated her to represent it in various initiatives on the issue of education. However, there is little evidence that Minnie pursued these to any fruitful conclusion, perhaps because of the pressure of her other responsibilities.

When in June 1917, Mrs. Bouvier proposed that the WSF 'take some steps to prevent the militarism being taught in the schools,' Minnie proposed that they call in an expert organisation such as the Women Teachers' Franchise Union (WTFU) to help them to prepare a memorial (a petition or statement for supporters to sign) and was delegated to do this and report back. But at the following month's Committee meeting she reported that she had been too busy to do so and promised to write to the WTFU before the next general meeting. There is no record of this issue thereafter: it seems to have been quietly dropped.

In August, the WSF Committee elected Minnie and Mrs. Lagsding to represent it at a conference called by the Education Committee (of what,

---

[229] 30th June 1917.

the minutes do not specify). The following month, it appointed Minnie to represent it on the Central Council of the Workers' Educational Association (WEA), a body promoting and organising study for working-class people. The WEA had invited the WSF to affiliate in May 1917, and Minnie had seconded Mrs. Boyce's proposal that the WSF accept and affiliate. In November, the WEA Executive accepted the affiliation, but there is no record of Minnie attending the Central Council, nor of the WSF sending any other representative in her place. Minnie was not listed as a Central Council member in the WEA's 1918 Annual Report, and neither was the WSF listed among the new affiliates. Perhaps they had lost enthusiasm for it, perhaps they had other priorities, perhaps they struggled with the affiliation fee of two pounds and two shillings.

Minnie continued her campaigning and organising work, in June hosting a WSF meeting at the Gravel Pit Hall on the corner of Valette Street and Morning Lane in Hackney.[230] And as she had done previously, Minnie proposed firm action when the WSF faced organisational or financial difficulties. In April 1917, Sylvia reported to the Committee her concerns about Provincial Organiser Miss Stephens, whose 'expenses were large & the returns small'. The Finance Committee was recommending that branches fund Miss Stephens to work for them for a week at a time, but Minnie proposed that if this was not working well after a few weeks, Miss Stephens be asked to find other work, a euphemism for removing her from her post. The next month, Miss Stephens was duly relieved of her post, and having proposed that, Minnie went on to propose that a Mrs. Holloway also be asked to find other work. It may sound rather brutal for a socialist to be proposing the sacking of staff. However, the WSF had few resources to sustain its paid workers and unpaid volunteers, and if they were not effective, then the WSF's difficult campaigns and struggles would become even more difficult.

Minnie was a member of the Finance Committee, as was Edgar until he resigned as Honorary Treasurer in August 1917, 'owing to greater pressure of his own business, as so many of his men had gone [to war].' He had just issued his latest appeal for donations and subscriptions, explaining that 'each week we find we are spending more money than we receive.' The *East London Advertiser* described the appeal as 'piteous' and delighted in the prospect of the WSF going under: 'If the Old Ford

---

[230] *Woman's Dreadnought*, 2nd June 1917.

Federation agitates for a German-made peace, its bankruptcy will be not only inevitable, but the most beautiful business failure on record.[231] Not to be outdone in its venom against anti-war socialists, the *East London Observer* called them 'peace cranks', 'fanatics' and 'irresponsible nobodies', and cheered on pro-war crowds who violently broke up peace meetings and demonstrations.[232]

Fleeing the Air Raids

Hostility to peace campaigners resumed with a vengeance in summer 1917 when the German air force renewed its bombing raids, now using fixed-wing aircraft during daylight hours. The raids created a terror among the population of the East End that would separate Minnie's family.

The Reverend William Lax, who became Poplar's Mayor towards the end of the war, later described the raids:

> Zeppelins, Taubes, or Gothas hovered like devouring hawks above the humble roofs. Fear of these horrid visitants accounted for the nightly thronging of dug-outs, tunnels, basements – indeed, anywhere out of danger – by thousands of terrified women pushing rickety prams containing children, blankets, pillows, and food, and strong men carrying sick and infirm folk. [233]

The first night air raid had come as May 1915 passed into June. A boy at the time, eighty years later Cyril Demarne described how, as the raids became more intense, he and others 'took to sheltering in the Blackwall Tunnel where the wind howled gale force on cold, winter nights.' In June 1917, the month when Minnie was campaigning in the WSF's suffrage election in Bow, daylight raids began to hit London. Demarne recalled that 'Policemen on bicycles, carrying sandwich boards bearing the notice 'Air raid – take cover' came riding through the streets blowing their whistles.'[234] Then, on Wednesday 13th June, just before noon, a large squadron of Taube aeroplanes attacked London. Women working at a jam factory were killed, as were women working in the blending

---

[231] 25th August 1917.

[232] 15th September and 21st April 1917.

[233] 1927, p.197.

[234] Ramsey 1997, p.76.

department of a tea factory. Eighteen children perished when a bomb fell through the roof of their school. In all, ninety-seven people died in the raid and over four hundred were injured.

Perhaps it was this raid which prompted Minnie's mother-in-law Bessie Lansbury to move away from London. Or perhaps she was persuaded by the ongoing bombardment that left many dead and six hundred East Enders homeless and forced into the workhouse. By the turn of 1918, Bessie had moved to a house named The Firs on Broadway in Farnham Common, a village in Buckinghamshire three miles north of Slough and nearly thirty miles from Bow.

Writing to her friend Mrs. Sewell in January 1918, Bessie revealed the disruption to her family life. She had not seen Edgar since moving there, whereas while she was still living in London, he had called in to their home in Bow Road nearly every evening with Minnie. Bessie hoped that he would visit that weekend 'and that he doesn't mind humping his swag on the floor if necessary.' Her daughter Annie had stayed at the Lansbury family home at 39 Bow Road and was 'doing as she pleases'. At least Bessie had got her to put clean curtains up.[235]

Edgar wrote to his mother,[236] hoping that the move was completely over and that she was settling in to the new house. The raids, he wrote, must have been a very trying time for them. Edgar and Minnie were also 'very thankful to be out of the raid' and were writing from their holiday in Morfa Bychan, a village in North Wales' Llyn Peninsula famed for the beach and the dunes at Black Rock Sands. Edgar wrote that:

> We are now having good weather and everything looks splendid. This is the real place for a quiet holiday. Unless we walk at least 2 miles we can't spend a halfpenny, with the best will in the world to spend pounds we can't work up the will to walk the distance. Minnie says that this inability to spend money is my one worry … it is!

In the absence of shopping, Minnie and Edgar – and their friend Will Yoxley, who would be joining them the following week for a few days – could live off the fruits of the land:

> This is a great place for mushrooms & blackberries. You can gather stacks of mushrooms a couple of fields from here & when I remember that we pay 1s/9d per lb in London, I feel very small.

---

[235] Letter, 29th January 1918, LANSBURY 7.

[236] Letter, undated, LANSBURY 7/389.

Although long holidays or travelling abroad during the war were frowned upon as unpatriotic, people who could afford to do so still took short vacations in Britain. Middle-class families holidayed every summer, working-class families less regularly, often taking day trips instead.[237]

One reason that it was easier and more affordable for Edgar and Minnie than for others to go on holiday was that they did not have children. We can not be sure why this was. On the basis of her chosen career as an infants' teacher, her welfare work with children and her close relationship with her nieces and nephews,[238] we can be confident that Minnie liked children, although this would not necessarily mean that she wanted her own. We know that Edgar was fertile, as he had children with his second wife later in his life, but maybe Minnie was not. Or perhaps they were using contraception: although its use was still controversial, Marie Stopes published her book *Married Love* in 1918 and opened her first clinic in 1921, so birth control was becoming more accessible.

Representing the Workers

Into 1918, Minnie Lansbury was still active in fighting for pensions and in the Workers' Suffrage Federation, although as the year went on, her relationship with the latter would change.

In January, the WSF elected Minnie and fellow activist Melvina Walker to the housing committee of the Women's Labour League. The League had been founded in 1906 independent of but affiliated to the Labour Party, but with the coming of women's votes, it would become the women's section of the Labour Party. As the WSF's cash crisis got worse, Minnie remained conscientious and practical, putting forward proposals to keep the Federation afloat. At a special meeting of its Finance Committee on 26th January, she proposed that 'if in a fortnight's time we considered our financial embarrassment likely to be permanent we should shut down one or two departments.' But she also promised to try to get four pounds to pay for a speaker to help to publicise the upcoming demonstration about food and to pay a Miss Beamish for some typing. She also agreed to personally advance 'a sum of money' to the WSF's restaurant to allow it to start with some money in hand.

[237] Ugolini, 2013.

[238] evidenced in her death notices.

Minnie was by now the Chair of the Poplar 'A' War Pensions Committee, which elected as its Honorary Secretary one Mr. A Chapman, who had been severely disabled in the war. For the *Herald*, this appointment was an example for others to follow, as 'Men who have been through the mill can be relied on to see justice done much better than many of the well-to-do people who desire to perpetuate what is called the "human touch" in relation to discharged soldiers and sailors.'[239] Much provision for war pensioners was still in the hands of well-meaning, wealthy nominees of charities. Poplar's committee was shifting the balance towards those directly affected, like Mr. Chapman, supported by those who lived among them, like Minnie.

Also by 1918, men returning from war could expect a say in the government of the country. After the deliberations of the Speaker's Conference, seismic changes to the voting franchise – although not the full, unqualified adult suffrage that Minnie and other socialists wanted – came into force on 6th February 1918. The Representation of the People Act gave the vote to virtually all men aged twenty-one and over, the least propertied forty per cent of whom had previously been excluded. It also gave the vote to those women aged at least thirty who occupied land or premises of a yearly value of five pounds or a dwelling house, or who were married to a man registered as a local government elector. In 1912, Britain had 7.7 million voters, all male; at the end of 1918, it had 21.4 million male and female voters. Aged twenty-nine, Minnie Lansbury was not one of them. The government hoped that the inclusion only of older, propertied women 'would provide conservative ballast within the new mass electorate, reinforcing the stability of a society threatened by war and the spectre of Bolshevism.'[240] Revolutionary Russia had granted the vote to all women the previous summer.

The Act also changed the law to allow people who received help from the Guardians of the Poor to vote for them. Elected Boards of Guardians had existed in each local area since the 1834 Poor Law (Amendment) Act, and were charged with providing for the destitute, but in a way that punished them for their destitution. Part of this punishment was to be barred from voting for the Boards. The Poplar Borough Municipal Alliance, sponsor of Tory and Liberal candidates in local politics, was horrified by the removal of this bar, still complaining years later that

[239] 16th March 1918.

[240] Julia Bush, *BBC History*, February 2018.

'The almsgiver ... became the vote asker; the receivers of alms ... became the vote givers', as if the wealthy ratepayers' wealth came from their own endeavours rather than from the labours of the working class, some of whose members fell from time to time into destitution. The PBMA regretted that Poplar's local electorate was now 'composed to a large extent of those who, under sound principles of local government, would not have the right to vote.'[241]

The *East London Advertiser* was concerned at the various political parties' responses to the expansion of the voting franchise. As it reported, 'So far the Labour Party is the only one that seems to be alive to the changed situation since prewar times.' In particular, Labour was 'showing a lively appreciation' of the entry of women into the electorate.[242] Until now, the Labour Party – as distinct from the broader labour movement – had not figured centrally in Minnie Lansbury's political activity. Her husband was a Labour councillor and her father-in-law a former Labour MP, but her day-to-day political activity was centred on the War Pensions Committee, the League of Rights and the Workers' Suffrage Federation. This was soon to change.

The Labour Party had been founded in 1906 to promote the election of workers' representatives to Parliament, after enough socialists and trade unionists had concluded that relying on favours from the Liberal Party was never going to achieve real improvements for working-class people. The Labour Party formed as a coalition of trade unions and socialist societies (primarily the Fabian Society to the right and the Independent Labour Party to the left), with no individual members and little local activity. Although it had been a step forward in the political development of the working class as an independent actor in its struggle against exploitation, it was focused not on radical social change but on winning seats in Parliament, and those who won those seats quickly disappointed the labour movement.

By 1918, matured by the experience of the war and the widening of the voting franchise, and in the wake of revolution in Russia, the Labour Party was about to radically change itself into the party in which Minnie Lansbury and others could involve themselves. In February 1918 – the same month in which Parliament passed the Representation of the People Act – the Labour Party adopted a new constitution. It allowed individuals to become members, enhanced the role of local party

[241] PBMA, 1925, pp.7,6.

[242] 16th February 1918.

branches, and bound its candidates more closely to the Party's political programme. It also introduced Clause IV part 4, which set out the party's aim 'To secure for the workers by hand or by brain the full fruits of their industry and the most equitable distribution thereof that may be possible upon the basis of the common ownership of the means of production, distribution and exchange, and the best obtainable system of popular administration and control of each industry or service.' This clause grounded the Party in a commitment to dispossessing the capitalist class and placing society's productive wealth in the hands of the producers. However, it aspired to do this *for* the workers rather than *with* the workers. As Ralph Miliband later argued, Labour 'had finally done with its own brand of Liberalism' but had replaced it not with socialism but with 'Labourism'.[243]

The reconstitution of Labour inspired activists in London to set about building the newly-empowered local parties with newly-admitted individual members. Labour activists had very good reason to build their forces, as the needs of working-class Londoners were not being met by the paternalists of 'higher' classes: in the East End where the Lansburys lived and worked, poverty, poor health, inadequate housing and insecure, poorly-paid employment still dominated working-class lives, and only direct representation could challenge this. Labour organising gained a new impetus in July 1918, when the Party declared the end of the wartime political truce, expecting the war to end soon and finally accepting that military war had not suspended class war. The employers had continued – in some ways, stepped up – their exploitation and oppression of workers, and Labour had a duty to defend and represent the working class.

Poplar Labour Representation Committee's affiliated membership had grown by three thousand people to 13,550 in the first six months of the year. By September, Labour Party organising in Bow and Bromley was 'proceeding apace' with 'members joining in good numbers'. Labour held public meetings and delivered a recruitment leaflet through every door in the area. It especially wanted women to join Labour's efforts, noting that thirteen thousand women had joined the local electoral roll.[244]

It was to organising local Labour women that Minnie Lansbury now gave her attention, helping to form the Poplar Women's Labour Party, and parting ways with the Workers' Suffrage Federation.[245]

[243] Miliband 1961/2009, p.61.

[244] Bush, 1984, p.86; *Herald*, 29th and 8th September 1918.

The Parting of Ways

Minnie Lansbury's enthusiasm for building the newly-reconstituted Labour Party was not shared by her friend and fellow suffragette leader Sylvia Pankhurst. In April 1918, Sylvia told the WSF's General Members' Meeting that 'it was well for the WSF to be on the local Labour Party to start with, though the time might come when we could not continue in the Party.'

The WSF Conference in May re-elected Minnie as Honorary Assistant Secretary and Sylvia as Honorary Secretary. It also changed the organisation's name to the Workers' Socialist Federation, reaffirmed its opposition to the war, supported self-determination for the people of India and of Ireland (ie. the right to become countries fully independent of Britain if their people wished), and pledged itself 'to work for the abolition of the capitalist system as the paramount question of immediate importance.' The WSF at this point did not see its implacable opposition to capitalism as counterposed to supporting candidates in Parliamentary elections. On the contrary, it 'urge[d] British workers to return as many international socialists as possible to Parliament at the next election.'[246] But while Minnie Lansbury maintained this political approach, Sylvia and other WSF leaders changed direction over the following six months.

The organisational break between the WSF and Labour in the East End came in September 1918. When Poplar Trades Council held a meeting in Victoria Park, the WSF took over its lorry and used it as its own platform. The Trades Council and the local Labour Party expelled the WSF. It seems unlikely that an incident of this scale would be the sole reason for the organisations to separate, and more likely that it was a culmination of a relationship already deteriorating.

Minnie remained with the Labour Party. For Sylvia, Minnie 'stayed to tinker with the system; to try to ameliorate its cruel hardships, after we took our hands from such tasks and set our faces towards revolution.'[247] However, there is no evidence that Minnie saw her involvement in the Labour Party as a rejection of revolutionary struggle. As we have seen, the WSF itself had embraced Parliamentary electoral activity as part of its revolutionary approach at its conference earlier that

---

[245] *Workers' Dreadnought*, 7th January 1922.

[246] *Workers' Dreadnought*, 1st June 1918.

[247] *Workers' Dreadnought*, 7th January 1922.

same year, and Minnie remained a leading member of the WSF as it developed its revolutionary stance. Why would the WSF now counterpose electoral activity and revolutionary struggle? Sylvia's own words reveal that it was she, rather than Minnie, who was changing political direction. Minnie's political work continued that of the League of Rights and the East London Suffragettes – she had 'stayed', while Sylvia and 'taken [her] hands away from such tasks.'

It may seem counterintuitive that Sylvia Pankhurst, lifelong warrior for women's right to vote in Parliamentary elections, would, now that most women finally had the vote, advise them not to use it. But she did just that. Sylvia refused an invitation to stand as a Labour Parliamentary candidate in Sheffield, then in December, on the eve of the first general election with near-universal suffrage, she and the WSF Committee issued a statement placing on record 'its belief that Parliament is an out-of-date re-actionary body, which should be abolished as soon as possible' and that the part the WSF would play in the general election taking place that month would be 'merely to make propaganda for the overthrow of Parliament.' Describing the new Russian system of government by workers' councils (soviets), it concluded that 'The Workers' Socialist Federation wants that Revolution here; therefore, it is promoting no Parliamentary candidatures.' Despite the apparent contradiction, there is a line of logic to Sylvia's political direction: that the Russian Revolution had shown forms of democracy more advanced than Parliament and that now the Parliamentary vote had been largely won, socialists could fight for that advanced democracy to supersede it.

Minnie had to choose between two camps, both of which were very much part of her political and personal life. On the one hand, Sylvia Pankhurst and other friends in the WSF, her comrades for several years, whose revolutionary outlook she shared and had helped to develop but which was now taking a new path. On the other hand, the emerging force of the Labour Party, in which her husband and father-in-law were heavily involved, which seemed to offer a more immediate prospect of social change to benefit the working class and in which revolutionary socialists freely participated. Minnie chose the latter.

Chapter 5 – Military Peace, Class War

The War's End

It was by now apparent that the war was nearing its end and that the government would call a general election soon. Although not knowing exactly when, Labour prepared itself, for the first time selecting candidates to contest all five seats in Tower Hamlets – the area east of the City of London that included Whitechapel and Poplar and which now constitutes a borough.

After four years of bereavement and loss, of separation and distress, of fear of bombs from the air and telegrams from the front, the war finally ended on 11th November 1918. What a relief this must have been to Minnie, Edgar, the Glassmans, Lansburys and everyone else in the East End and beyond. The *East London Advertiser* described the scenes:

> When the sound of the syrens on the river and the report of the maroons were heard, the first thought of thousands was obviously that of air raids, but it was quickly realised that this time the 'warnings' were those of joy and not of peril. Therefore instead of scuttling for raid shelters people rushed into the streets. Flags appeared as if by magic … The excitement was almost indescribable …

> It was a day which will not easily be forgotten by anyone. The joy and relief of thousands at the lifting of the great weight of dread and anxiety which has sat upon them for four years thus found expression. As for the alien population, to whom possible air raids have proved a constant nightmare, the remark of one old lady must have been typical of many. 'Thank God,' she exclaimed, 'I shall now be able to go to bed with my clothes off!'

Just three days after the Armistice, on 14th November, the government announced that there would be a general election exactly one month later. It appeared to be a manoeuvre to hastily cash in on the upbeat mood of victory and peace before concerns about poverty, inequality and social conditions could come back to the fore, and it would take place before many servicemen could return home from the war. A Labour leaflet asked rhetorically. 'WHY a General Election when many soldiers cannot vote? *The government is trying to snatch a vote of confidence before the fighting men have a chance to examine reconstruction plans and say what they want*' (italics original).

Nevertheless, Labour swung into electoral action, promising the soldiers and sailors a speedy discharge, a generous gratuity, no exploitation of pensioners, immediate employment, trade union wages, full employment maintenance, and full provision for disabled men, women and orphans. Labour pledged to 'GET JUSTICE for the soldiers and sailors.'[248]

The Labour Party's manifesto promised steep progressive taxation, nationalisation of some industries and state regulation of others. Although it was titled 'Labour and the New Social Order', its policies outlined less a new social order and more the best version of the old one. Nevertheless, it was a bold and important step forward for Labour which, if implemented, would significantly benefit working-class people.

The partners in the existing coalition government – the Conservatives and the faction of the Liberals led by David Lloyd George – had spent the last summer of the war in secret talks to continue their coalition into peacetime. They endorsed over three hundred Tories, more than one hundred Liberals, and a handful of pro-war renegade Labour MPs as their preferred candidates, giving each of them a 'coupon' to identify them as such: this gave rise to the tag 'the coupon election'.

The 1918 general election was the first to be held on a single day. It was the first in which nearly all adult men were entitled to vote, and the first in which women voted, although these did not include Minnie Lansbury, still two months short of her thirtieth birthday. Only seventeen women stood as candidates, and the only one elected – Constance Markiewicz – did not take her seat. She was one of seventy-three successful Sinn Fein candidates in an election which saw Irish voters rally behind the call for the country's independence, all of whom refused to sit in the British Parliament because they did not recognise its legitimacy.

The coalition's tactics gave it the result it wanted: a landslide victory bringing to power a Conservative-dominated government with a Liberal Prime Minister, Lloyd George. Labour came second, with over two million votes, but its twenty per cent of the vote translated into only eight per cent of the seats. None of the fifty-seven seats it won were in London's East End. Popular though he was – despite his anti-war views – George Lansbury again lost the election for the Bow and Bromley constituency to Reginald Blair, this time by 7,248 votes to 8,109. Blair

---

[248] Labour Party advertisements in the *East London Advertiser*, 7th December 1918 – italics and capitals in the original.

was a company chairman, a member of several private members' clubs and lived not in Bow or Bromley but in Harrow Weald. In South Poplar constituency, Liberal Sir Alfred Yeo won with nearly twice the number of votes of Labour's Sam March. Yeo was a self-made businessman – a seller of musical instruments – who had served on Poplar Council for twenty-five years, including as Mayor in 1903-04, and had been the MP since 1914. He is still memorialised today by the Yeo Society, whose website describes him as 'a man of strong personality and of picturesque appearance, with his white hair and flowing white moustache … a promoter of manly sports … a good judge of brass bands.'

Despite its electoral defeat, Labour was getting stronger, and it went into 1919 on a class-war footing in both industrial struggles and the three sets of local elections that approached.

A Land Fit for Heroes?

Working-class East London was battered by war, exploited by profiteers, and hungry for change. It had witnessed the nation's resources mobilised for war and now wanted them mobilised for peace, reconstruction, and a fundamental shift in power from the wealthy to improve the lives of the workers, the wounded and their families. Although few explicitly called for Russian-style revolution, most were unwilling to accept a continuation of poverty, disease, slum housing and gross inequality.

Instead of the 'land fit for heroes' promised by Prime Minister David Lloyd George, there were rising prices and little support for those disabled or bereaved by war. Former soldiers unable to find work sold matches or busked in the street in the hope of collecting pennies. Casual working returned to East London's docks as men returning from the front found themselves competing for work with men who had started working there during the war. When the Czech journalist and science fiction writer Karel Čapek visited the area, his liberal political outlook and slight distaste for the common people showed in his description of it:

> The horrible thing in East London is not what can be seen and smelt, but its unbounded and unredeemable extent … miles and miles of grimy houses, hopeless streets, Jewish shops, a superfluity of children, gin palaces and Christian shelters … the quarters inhabited by navvies, Jews, Cockneys and stevedores from the docks, poverty-stricken and down-trodden people –

> everything equally dull, grimy, bare and unending, intersected
> by dirty channels of deafening traffic, and the whole way equally
> cheerless.[249]

Čapek's quote describes the misery but not the resistance. Minnie Lansbury and others continued to fight for working-class interests and in particular pension rights. The end of the war did not mean the end of the War Pensions Committees, nor of Minnie's involvement with Poplar's. The *Herald* advised its readers of their rights, telling widows and ex-servicemen to go to their local War Pensions Committee to claim what was owed to them. With government parsimony and the impending closure of the National Relief Fund, Minnie – along with the other Committee members and staff – was kept very busy. Minnie worked hard to support individuals in need, but also to change the political system that made them needy.

The Labour Party of which Minnie was a member continued to grow, boosted by the large new electorate, the experience of wartime organising, and the disarray of the Liberals, who were now fractured into two parts, one led by Lloyd George in coalition with the Conservatives, the other a rump led by Herbert Asquith. Although Labour had lost the general election, it was at least now the main opposition party, and its support in the country far exceeded its Parliamentary representation in both quantity and quality.

London's Elections

It was a confident and belligerent Labour Party – at least at rank-and-file level – that prepared for the elections to the London County Council (LCC) in March 1919. Like Minnie, the LCC had been conceived in 1888 and born in 1889. It covered the whole of the area that we now call 'inner London', embracing twenty-eight metropolitan boroughs, one hundred and seventeen square miles and over four million people. The LCC consisted of two representatives elected by each Parliamentary constituency except for the City of London, which had four. It was responsible for issues and services that crossed borough boundaries, such as licensing, bridges and the fire brigade.

London Labour kicked off its LCC election campaign in January 1919, its Secretary, Herbert Morrison, declaring that 'Political Labour must fight for predominance in Local government no less than in Parliament

---

[249] *Letters from England*, 1925, quoted in Ramsey, 1997, p.235.

… Housing, transit, education, electricity, public health – these and all the other important spheres of municipal work are either to be inspired by Socialist and Labour ideals or they are to be damned by capitalistic interests.'[250]

In Minnie's home borough of Poplar, Labour activists fought hard for their candidates – canvassing for Susan Lawrence and Sam March in South Poplar, and Ted Cruse and Charlie Sumner in Bow and Bromley. For the LCC's first eighteen years, the 'Progressives' – unofficially allied with the Liberal Party – had held a majority, until the 'Municipal Reform' group – established by Conservatives – ousted them and took control in 1907. Labour had held only a handful of seats, but in 1919 it made a breakthrough. Across London, one-third of electors cast their votes for Labour, although the first-past-the-post electoral system meant that it won only fifteen of the 124 seats. They included all four candidates in the borough of Poplar.

In the spirit of their coalition in government, the Progressives and the Municipal Reformers had combined in an electoral pact for the LCC. The *East London Advertiser* had printed glowing descriptions of the Municipal Reform candidates in the Poplar seats, and now blamed the coalition partners for their defeat, arguing that 'both the Conservatives and Liberals failed to support their candidates, with the result that the Labour and Socialist candidates were returned in both divisions.'[251] The *Advertiser* found it hard to accept that newly-enfranchised working-class people had voted Labour because they supported its programme and liked its candidates.

The LCC election was swiftly followed by another vote, this time for the Boards of Guardians. Until now, the Boards had been elected and dominated largely by men of property. Minnie's father-in-law George Lansbury saw a nefarious motive behind the successful candidatures of local traders and clergymen:

> [T]he Board was made up of those who reckoned to make a bit out of the poor, and who could play into each other's hands. You see, the slum owner and agent could be depended upon to create conditions which produce disease: the doctor would then get the job of attending the sick, the chemist would be needed to supply drugs, the parson to pray, and when, between them all, the victims died, the undertaker was on hand to bury them.[252]

---

[250] *The Herald*, 18th January 1919.

[251] 15th March 1919.

By 1919, though, the propertied men were not so interested, and several Labour candidates were elected to the Poplar Board of Guardians without opposition. Others faced a vote on Saturday 5th April, and pledged to voters that if elected, they would pursue a sympathetic policy of 'outdoor relief' on an adequate scale, meaning that they would pay relief money to people without sending them to the spartan dungeons known as workhouses. They also pledged generous treatment for the aged; pensions for widows with children; good infirmaries; and education for workhouse children. And they promised to appoint women Relieving Officers (the officials who decided the fate of people who applied for relief) and employ all Board staff on conditions agreed with the trade unions. Enough of them won enough votes for Labour to now command a majority on the Poplar Board of Guardians for the first time, holding fifteen of the twenty-four seats. Minnie Lansbury's husband Edgar would join the Board in a by-election the following year, and the work of the Guardians would have a huge impact on her political activity in Poplar.

Across London, Labour won 135 of the 757 seats on the local Boards. The *Daily Herald* declared the result 'a "sign of the times" of rather more significance than the coupon election that returned a bogus House of Commons.'[253] George Lansbury added in his usual passionate and dramatic style that, 'Organised Labour is at last coming into its own. After long years of struggle our hope and aspirations for a united industrial and political fighting organisation looks like being realised … The old policy of the Charity Organisation Society and other kindred organisations for helping the poor by starving the poor seems very cheap and small these days.' He advised the newly-elected Labour Guardians to 'Shun the workhouse as you would hell itself. Don't send anyone in whom you can possibly keep outside.' He also urged a healthy disrespect for legal niceties, in comments that foreshadowed the next few years in Poplar, events in which his daughter-in-law Minnie would play a key role:

> Don't be afraid of the law or of your ignorance of the law. Make up your mind what you want to do, and go for it … We are going to get great changes in the law in the near future.[254]

---

[252] 1928, pp.134-5.

[253] 8th April 1919.

[254] *Daily Herald*, 12th April 1919.

Within a short time, the new Poplar Guardians were arranging better treatment for workhouse inmates and increasing support to paupers outside the workhouse. While the Ministry of Health recommended that Guardians pay twenty-five shillings (£1.25) per week to a destitute couple, Poplar's Guardians paid thirty-three shillings (£1.65) and unlike other Boards, gave an extra allowance for rent. The Poplar Guardians' spending rose because at last they were looking after the poor rather than the wealth of the ratepayers. The Municipal Alliance, representing those wealthy ratepayers, was indignant, and cautioned against electing 'the same class of men' to Poplar's Borough Council in November as had been elected to its Board of Guardians in April.[255]

The Board looked at its finances and, like a more assertive Oliver Twist, asked for more. Boards of Guardians' work was funded by their local borough councils with money raised by local rates, so the poorer the area, the greater the demand for the Guardians' help but the less their ability to raise funds to pay for them. The system was not fair, so the Poplar Board asked the Ministry of Health 'whether any steps can be taken to relieve the excessive burden of rates which falls upon the poorer parishes and [Poor Law] unions'[256] but received no positive response. They wanted the 'equalisation of rates', a redistributive demand which would grow more and more urgent and attract increasing support over the following two years, eventually leading Minnie Lansbury, her husband and others to court and to prison.

Striking Back

While the working class made gains in the political arena, it also exploded into action on the industrial front. Workers were appalled by impoverished social conditions and unimpressed by the ineffectiveness of their representation in Parliament. They knew that to improve their lot, they would have to take militant action, and so 1919 became the year in which they not only voted Labour in local elections but also took more strike action than in any year since records had begun nearly thirty years earlier.

Strikes hit and won in the cotton mills, railways and shipyards. Engineers, miners and even the police walked out. Trade unions had gained strength from defending workers during the war and now had

---

[255] *East London Advertiser*, 27th September 1919.

[256] *News and Chronicle*, 29th July 1919.

eight million members, twice the number they had in 1915. Ralph Miliband argues that 'The core of that membership was made up of a deeply class conscious, highly militant segment of the working class' but that their leaders did not match that militancy: 'Again and again, pressure from the rank and file for resolute action was deflected and neutralized.'[257]

The miners' union called off strikes when the government promised a commission on coal industry ownership, only to see the union's demand for nationalisation rejected when the commission reported after the momentum of the strikes had waned. From 27th September, the National Union of Railwaymen (NUR), together with members of the smaller union ASLEF, which organised those who drove trains and who fired their engines, brought the country to a halt for nine days and defeated government plans to cut wages, replacing those plans with a levelling-up of pay and guaranteed working hours.

In Minnie Lansbury's home borough of Poplar, where thousands worked on the railway services that carried people to and from their daily business and goods to and from the docks, labour movement activists were strikers and organisers, not just candidates. Their drive for public office was part of the struggle of their community, whether for jobs, wages or pensions.

A divide was showing in the labour movement, between those willing to carry out militant action, whether on the political or the industrial front, and those urging caution and respect for the sovereignty of Parliament. This was not a divide between revolutionaries and reformists but between supporters of 'direct action' and 'constitutionalism'. Minnie Lansbury, despite having avoided direct action when she was younger, now embraced it. She was no longer a school teacher in fear of losing her job, she had been arrested on an anti-war protest, and she spent her days helping and campaigning alongside people whose sufferings were not being alleviated by polite lobbying. She had witnessed on the one hand deputations making fine arguments to no avail and on the other, angry women on the Roman Road get the potatoes they needed by taking direct action to get them. Poplar's labour movement had a long experience of direct action – whether in workplace struggles or for the vote – and it would soon take that experience into the council chamber. It would be carried there by a local working class angry about the desperate social conditions imposed on it by a prosperous elite.

---

[257] 1961/2009, p.65.

One million workers were unemployed, over a third of whom were returning servicemen. They faced not just joblessness but rising demands on what little money they had. Prices had more than doubled during the war and following a short respite during spring 1919, they began to rise still further. By the autumn, the cost of living was more than double its level before the war, with the prices of some food essentials even more inflated – eggs sold at four times their pre-war rate, sugar at three-and-a-half times.[258] Local price tribunals were supposed to keep rises in check but lacked the power to do so. Working-class people came to the conclusion that the promised reconstruction was a sham. In Poplar, the stage was set for them to elect a council that would challenge the system.

Storming the Council Chamber

Throughout the summer of 1919, Labour in the East End poured out publicity and put its speakers on street corners. Labour's growing support included many East End Jews, who were still being targeted by antisemites and by the government. A new Aliens Restriction Act came into force in April, and hundreds of Jews were deported to Russia as 'alien undesirables' and 'known Bolsheviks'. Historian Julia Bush argues that when George Lansbury spoke at a protest against the British government's support for the Polish regime that was facilitating pogroms of Jews, 'his presence epitomised the new relationship which had developed between organised Jewish workers and the Labour Party.'[259]

Throughout the summer, Labour built towards the borough council elections in November. In Poplar, Minnie Lansbury was amongst its campaigners, her husband Edgar and father-in-law George among its candidates. The *Daily Herald* reported on Labour's 'enthusiastic meetings, hard work and great expectations.'[260] The Dickensian theme continued with the *Herald*'s repeated reference to the Tory and Liberal councils' regimes as 'Boodle and Bumble': Lord Boodle was an aristocratic right-wing politician in Dickens' *Bleak House*, Mr. Bumble the cruel and pompous beadle of Oliver Twist's workhouse. Labour's campaign championed working-class interests against privilege and profiteering.

---

[258] *Labour Gazette*, cited in *Daily Herald*, 21st October 1919.

[259] Bush, 1984, p.208.

[260] 1st November 1919.

The Poplar Borough Municipal Alliance's campaign to retain power in the council was run by Sir Alfred Warren, the wartime Mayor of Poplar who was now Conservative MP for Leytonstone. True to form, the PBMA's campaign claimed that if elected, Labour would usher in a regime of 'waste'. Labour responded boldly that 'We believe that nothing can be more wasteful or more shameful than to rear a sickly and poverty-stricken people; and no so-called saving which bears hardly upon the people deserves the support of honest men and women.'[261]

Labour's candidates for Poplar Borough Council included four women while the PBMA stood only one. Labour's Jane March had been a health visitor; Nellie Cressall a laundrette worker and ELFS activist; Jennie Mackay the first woman member of what would become the National Union of General Municipal Workers (forerunner of today's GMB); and Julia Scurr active in the Irish community and as a suffragette. All were listed in their nominations as 'married women', and three of them – Jane, Nellie and Julia – were, like Minnie, married to Poplar Labour candidates. Although all were socialist women in their own right, with records and politics ample for their candidatures, it appears that either Poplar Labour was willing to promote the wives of its male figures more readily than other women or that it was easier for wives to get involved. Although four women candidates may seem a small number, Poplar Labour was ahead of comrades in other East London boroughs, who mustered only five women candidates between them. Bush argues that women, now forty per cent of the electorate, were 'by far the largest group of new, inexperienced voters, and the most lacking in political traditions and education.'[262]

Apart from its gender imbalance, Poplar's line-up of Labour candidates looked very much like its electorate. The male candidates comprised twenty-seven manual workers – dockers, rail workers, engineers and labourers – plus clerical workers, trade union officials, a journalist, a school teacher, a grocer and the two Lansbury timber merchants. The Municipal Alliance, in contrast, stood just four manual workers, alongside traders, managers and professionals. For Bush, 'in the post-war climate of heightened class-consciousness, when Labour's election appeal was based firmly on its pledge to defend workers against profiteers, class differences between candidates took on a new importance.'[263]

[261] *Daily Herald*, 31st October 1919.

[262] 1984, p.233.

Thus it was that on a cold and dismal Saturday 1st November, Poplar's newly-confident and newly-enfranchised working-class voters swept their own people into the council chamber. Labour won in thirteen of the borough's fourteen wards, increasing Labour's representation from just ten to an overwhelming thirty-nine of the forty-two council seats. Edgar topped the poll in Bow North ward, with a few more votes than his successful fellow Labour candidates and around four times as many as his Municipal Alliance opponents. The Municipal Alliance won only in Bow South ward, where their two candidates – a solicitor and a manufacturer – were elected alongside Reverend Kitcat, who stood as an independent with Municipal Alliance support.

Similar Labour waves crashed through the doors of Town Halls across London. Thirty-nine per cent of votes went to Labour, giving the party a majority on twelve of the twenty-eight borough councils, making it the largest party on a further two, and piling up a total of 572 of the 1,362 seats on offer. The *Daily Herald* lauded 'a mighty and a smashing victory. Bumble and Boodle have had their notice to quit. Coupon and Cashit [the coalition government] will get theirs as soon as they dare face the test … Labour now has a splendid opportunity of putting into practice the principles for which it stands: better education, better housing, better sanitation; in fact, better everything that concerns our everyday life.'[264]

Two days after the election, the new Labour-led Poplar Borough Council met, began putting that into practice, and added Minnie Lansbury to its ranks.

Alderman Mrs. Minnie Lansbury

At its first meeting, Poplar's new Borough Council appointed four aldermen: Minnie Lansbury, Susan Lawrence, Robert Hopwood and John Scurr. Literally meaning 'man of high rank', the (unpaid) post of alderman on a borough council had been created by the Municipal Reform Act in 1835 and would continue to exist until scrapped by the 1972 Local Government Act. Aldermen carried out a similar role to the councillors themselves, but with a few additional responsibilities. Their six-year term of office meant that some of the previous council's appointed aldermen remained in place, so the Municipal Alliance's

[263] 1984, p.220.

[264] 3rd and 4th November 1919.

Minnie (inner horseshoe-shaped table, fourth from left) at a meeting of
Poplar Borough Council in the Town Hall on Newby Place

pitifully depleted force on Poplar council was bolstered by the
continuing presence of Aldermen Lax, Knightbridge and Brandy.

Poplar's council had chosen four long-standing local Labour activists
for the role – all, reported the *Daily Herald*, were 'well-known and tried
workers of Poplar', noting in particular that Minnie Lansbury had
'served a long apprenticeship on care committees, food control and
pension committees.' Later, the *Herald* reported that Minnie's selection
as an alderman was 'regarded as a reward for the work she had already
put in on behalf of the Bow and Bromley Labour Party,'[265] and the
Women's Freedom League congratulated its former member in the pages
of its newspaper *The Vote*.[266] Perhaps the *Daily Herald* was trying to
justify its appointment of another Lansbury to a council which already
included Edgar and George. However, Minnie's appointment was not
just a reward for her hard work but the addition of a capable and
effective comrade to the council. Many considered Minnie to be the
sharpest intellect on the council,[267] and writer Oscar Tapper later named

[265] 4th November 1919; 7th January 1922.

[266] 14th November 1919.

[267] Told to me by Chris Sumner, who recalled his parents – Charlie Sumner's
son and daughter-in-law – often saying so.

Minnie along with five of her colleagues as councillors of notable 'calibre'.[268] Their faith in Minnie would be justified by her time in office: her eventual successor, Muriel Lester, wrote of Minnie's 'grasp of affairs, her whole-time devotion, her vivacious and wonderful knack of getting things done.'[269]

Poplar Borough Council had chosen two Labour women and two Labour men as its new aldermen. Susan Lawrence came from a very different background from the other Labour representatives: she had been a Conservative when first elected to the LCC in 1910 but, disgusted by the Tory-led LCC's treatment of school cleaners, she joined the Labour Party and in 1913 was re-elected under her new political flag. Robert Hopwood was a toolmaker who had worked for Bryant and May matchmakers before the war and was the secretary of the Bow branch of the Amalgamated Society of Engineers. John Scurr (Julia's husband) was a *Daily Herald* journalist, of Irish descent but born in Australia, who had been active in Poplar's labour movement for over twenty years. Minnie was in good company.

While the labour movement celebrated having a new council made up almost entirely of working-class people, the Poplar Borough Municipal Alliance was horrified, later asking rhetorically (and patronisingly), 'All may be estimable in the spheres which they adorn, but who would ever think of entrusting to them alone the expenditure of more than half a millions sterling annually?'. The PBMA condemned the Labour councillors for 'lack of appreciation of the value of money' and declared that in Poplar, 'The masters there have become the servants and the servants have become the masters.'[270]

That first council meeting elected George Lansbury as Mayor. George donned the Mayoral insignia round his neck but placed the official clothing on a chair, and once the cheers quietened, outlined Poplar Labour's plans to win significant change for working-class Poplar. After the meeting, a triumphant procession made its way around the borough, with an Irish fife and drum band, the councillors and five hundred of their supporters. Celebrations continued a few days later at Bow and Bromley Labour Party's meeting at Bow Baths Hall, with speeches, square dancing, live music, a large attendance and plenty of enthusiasm.

---

[268] Tapper, 1960, p.59.

[269] Lester, 1937.

[270] PBMA, 1925.

Poplar's labour movement was saluting the new self-assertion of the working class which had propelled its representatives into office. Achieving this after years of opposition and disenfranchisement was not enough, though. Now they had to do something with it.

The *Daily Herald* called for London Labour borough councillors to meet together and work out a common programme, but by the time that the London Labour Party held an aggregate meeting of its councillors and aldermen on 6th December, Poplar already had a month of action under its belt, with Alderman Minnie Lansbury taking a leading role.

Making a Change

The first Poplar Labour council meeting voted to hold all its meetings at seven o'clock in the evening, as the previous practice of daytime meetings prevented working people from attending. For a council now comprising mainly workers, this was an important move towards making council business more democratic and accessible. With a similar aim, the council also made its halls available to local people to hire for social, political and industrial meetings, on the signed request of twenty residents.

With the new council's working-class composition, the *Daily Herald* compared it with Russia's revolutionary system of government:

> People sometimes talk of the word "Soviet" as something too terrible to contemplate, yet it is true that thinking of a Soviet as a Council of people who earn their living by useful toil, some of the new councils, especially Poplar, may be considered a Soviet, for all its members are workers except a very small minority.[271]

But the soviets in Russia had taken state power, while London's municipal councils still laboured under the yoke of capitalism and its Tory-Liberal coalition government. So, what could they do with the limited powers they had? This question has vexed Labour in local government for as long as both have existed, and still does today.

The first thing they needed to do was to improve the lives of the working-class people who had elected them. The London Labour Party's chairman William Barefoot had declared during the election campaign that 'Too long have our Borough Councils been the preserves of vested interests. Too long has public health been sacrificed to the interests of

---

[271] 3rd November 1919.

property.'[272] But when he continued that 'Too long has London waited for the effective social services which will make possible for the people a full, free and healthy life,' he seemed to be suggesting that good council services were all that were needed for working-class liberation. Herbert Morrison, London Labour Party Secretary and newly-appointed Alderman of Poplar's neighbouring borough of Hackney, asked himself the same question that Poplar's councillors did: 'what sort of success would we make of the job now that we had it to do?' His answer was to improve Labour Party organisation, train and educate Labour's inexperienced councillors, and give the people 'a progressive, public-spirited and enlightened administration.'[273]

Edgar Lansbury offered a different view from Barefoot's and Morrison's, later recalling his and others' conviction that these improvements were sticking plasters on a gushing wound: they were helpful but they were not enough. He wrote that:

> all forms of activity in connection with local government were grouped in one category – palliatives – suitable for employment by Socialists only as accompaniments to vigorous action for the overthrow of Capitalism. The sin against the holy ghost was to make palliatives an end in themselves … But it is safe to say that not a single Socialist or Communist would find a seat on a local Council … unless, besides advocating Socialism, he stood for such palliatives as slum-clearance and re-housing, a reasonable standard of maintenance for the destitute, etc.[274]

There were already two wings of the Labour Party: one that wanted to fight capitalism, the other that wanted to administer it. Before Britain had even had a Labour government, these two wings now had a chance to put their theories into practice in local government. It was a year since the war had ended, and working-class people's demands and expectations for social change were running high. Those demands and expectations had carried Minnie and her comrades into the council chamber, and now they could either disappoint them as most Labour Party and trade union leaders had done, or mobilise them to push those demands and realise those expectations. It is impossible to properly discuss what Labour can achieve in local government without

[272] Chairman's address to LLP Special Conference, 29th September 1919, ACC/2417/A/006, Folio 99.

[273] 'Herbert Morrison: an autobiography', 1960, p.81.

[274] 1934, pp.187-8.

considering the working-class consciousness and mobilisation around it, but it is also impossible for Labour to succeed in local government if it bows before the authority of capitalism and its national government. Minnie's – and Poplar Labour council's – first two years in office would demonstrate this dramatically.

Now they were in office, it was time to make a change.

Improving Poplar's Housing[275]

Poplar Borough Council allocated its members to various committees to focus on specific policy areas. Minnie joined the Special Housing Committee, the Assessment Committee, and the Public Health and Housing and Maternity and Child Welfare Committee. The latter was an unwieldy name (which we will call the Public Health Committee for short) for a body presiding over essential provision for residents' welfare, and Minnie took a particularly active role in it. Minnie did not sit on any of the same council committees as her husband Edgar: they were comrades and partners, but even now Minnie had joined Edgar on the Council, they continued to take on different areas of work. While this does suggest a level of independence, it is also notable that Minnie's committees were those most associated with the stereotypical women's role in caring, while Edgar took responsibility for a traditionally masculine sphere as chair of the Finance Committee.

Poplar people had elected Labour councillors to make radical improvements to their desperate conditions of life, in a borough where an average of sixty-six people lived on each acre of land. In one part of the borough – Bromley – that figure was a shocking and unhealthy one hundred per acre.[276] Just ten days into their term, Minnie and her fellow Public Health Committee members agreed a drastic overhaul of Poplar's slum-standard living quarters. The Council would appoint seven new Assistant Sanitary Inspectors to examine all housing in the borough and identify homes not fit for habitation. Armed with new legal powers,[277] the Council would order the landlords to bring the homes up to standard, and if they failed to do so by a set deadline, the Council would

---

[275] Sources in this and following sections are minutes and *East London Advertiser* reports of the relevant Council and Committee meeting unless otherwise stated.

[276] Medical Officer of Health report, 1919.

[277] under the Housing and Town Planning Act 1919.

do the work itself and send the landlord the bill. It also set up a bureau at which tenants could get expert advice about their legal rights and so arm themselves against abusive landlords.[278]

We can see the unhealthy conditions in which Poplar residents were made to live from the figures that Council officers presented to Minnie and her committee colleagues. In the four weeks to 25th October, Poplar had seen twenty-eight deaths from respiratory diseases, nine from consumption (tuberculosis) and seventeen from diarrhoea. Eighteen infants had died. There had been 156 notifications of infectious diseases, one third of them scarlet fever and a quarter diptheria and croup. The Medical Officer for Health had overseen the disinfection and fumigation of premises, bedding and clothing of over three hundred households. Nearly four hundred 'verminous persons' – all bar six of them children – had had their clothes disinfected and their bodies cleaned of their unwelcome parasites.

Under the previous regime, the Public Health Committee had issued an average 275 Statutory Notices each month: legally-binding orders to address sanitary defects, overcrowding and infringements of byelaws. Now that Minnie and her comrades were at the helm, that number rose dramatically: over the following ten months, their committee issued an average of 768 notices per month, with the figure rising steadily as it uncovered and tackled more abuses. Court proceedings tackled landlords' failure to repair defective roofs, toilets without a water supply, smoke nuisance, unpaved yards, and inadequate cleansing.[279]

Each month, the housing inspectors reported back on the squalor that they found. In March 1920, they told of one street on which forty-eight of the fifty-one houses were infested with vermin, and another on which many of the houses were dilapidated. Councillor Charles Key urged the Public Health Committee to take 'more drastic action in connection with the housing of the people' and showed his impatience with the Council's Works Committee: 'They were still without any definite scheme and he warned them that they had little time to spare if they did not want to disappoint the people of the borough by their lack of performance.' The bolder Labour councillors were already openly chivvying their colleagues to deliver change.

Two weeks later, Edgar Lansbury joined Key in taking the Works Committee to task, and this time forced the issue to a vote. The

---

[278] London Labour Party Executive report, 1919-20.

[279] Medical Officer of Health report, 1919 and 1920.

committee intended to repair some houses but not those owned by substantial landlords, whom they planned to compel through legal action to make the repairs themselves. Lansbury and Key, though, feared that this would delay the repairs being carried out, with Key arguing that 'It was absolutely necessary for the dignity of the Council that the work should be done.' They lost the vote but had made their point. Poplar's Labour Council was capable of maintaining its unity while openly debating when they disagreed: not for them the imposed 'unity' of secret caucusing and pretend agreement.

This ability to both debate and unite was a strong feature of Poplar Labour, and one which would help it through the difficult times to come, during which the more left-wing and militant councillors, such as Minnie and Edgar Lansbury, would be able to convince their colleagues and carry them into battle.

A Healthy Committee

Poplar's Public Health Committee considered reports from food inspectors about prices, contamination and permits; funded convalescent homes; and in summer 1920, tackled a smallpox outbreak by promoting vaccination. It also appointed Minnie Lansbury – along with fellow councillor Jane March and the Medical Officer – to represent it at a conference about care for mentally ill and disabled people on 28th November 1919, which attracted over a thousand delegates from local authorities, boards of guardians, educational and public health bodies.[280] Presided over by government representatives and officials and with discussion 'considerably curtailed', we can imagine that Minnie would have found it frustrating, but at least, according to the report, written in the language of the time, 'The keen interest shewn by the delegates proved that real concern is now being felt all over the country for the welfare of the mentally defective.'

The councillors, and Minnie in particular, also turned their attention to improving care for Poplar's mothers and babies. Minnie's wartime work with the Mothers' Arms, the ELFS clinics and milk provision had given her the experience to tackle this issue head-on. The war had also prompted the government to consider infant welfare, and it did so by passing the responsibility to local councils. The 1918 Maternity and

---

[280] 'News and Notes' in *Studies in Mental Inefficiency*, vol.1 no.1, 15th January 1920.

Child Welfare Act empowered councils to supply milk to babies and their mothers at cost price or less, and Poplar decided to supply it for free to those with less than a certain income. By February 1920, the council was spending five hundred pounds per week providing this milk, with all applications checked to prevent abuse by 'a committee of lady members' which included Minnie. This put Minnie in a position of policing applicants, checking that those who came to her and her colleagues were sufficiently poor to qualify for the Council's handouts.

Poplar's Public Health Committee set up a new dental clinic, and new maternity centres at Wick Lane, Smeed Road and Manier Road, in the hall under the arch in Quickett Street and in the Mission Hall at Allanmouth Road. The committee also produced handbills and posters advertising the milk provision. The socialist councillors were not content to simply make decisions, but also pursued their implementation: within ten days, the Council insisted that inefficient distribution of these handbills be put right.

The Council also responded to a call from Poplar women to do what it could to get the price of milk and other commodities reduced. It called a conference with other London councils and sent a deputation to the Prime Minister: after a fractious meeting, Lloyd George took no action to cut prices.

Poplar Council took over the running of the Infant Welfare Clinic and Centre in the Isle of Dogs, the dockland area at the southern tip of the borough tucked in the bend of the river. Run until then as a charitable endeavour, the centre's management could at last see a public authority willing to take responsibility for the care of its babies and toddlers. So they asked the Council to take over, stating that they were pleased with the work of their clinic and centre over the last fourteen years but were struggling to raise funds and believed that improvements could be made. Public Health Committee representatives visited the clinic and centre and reported back that they were 'impressed by the evident confidence of the mothers and the affection for those who have been carrying on the work.' On the Committee's recommendation, the Council took over the provision, including its staff, and immediately began expanding it, including appointing more health visitors.[281]

---

[281] Letter, K. Wintour, Hon Sec, The Infant Welfare Association, to Dr Alexander, Medical Officer for Health, Poplar Borough Council, 25th February 1902; Public Health etc Committee minutes, 22nd March 1920, report to Poplar Borough Council.

As its transformation of these services progressed through 1920, the Public Health Committee included Minnie Lansbury among its four representatives to the General Council of the Association of Maternity and Infant Welfare Centres. By the end of the year, Poplar Borough recorded its lowest ever infant mortality rate. Eighty-one of every thousand Poplar babies died before they could reach their first birthday, but the number had fallen significantly, and would continue to do so over the following years, reaching the figure of sixty by 1923.[282] The political work of Minnie Lansbury and her comrades was literally saving lives.

Battling the White Plague[283]

Minnie Lansbury, with others, drove Poplar Council's ambitious and effective drive against the 'white plague', tuberculosis (TB). At a time before widespread use of vaccinations and antibiotics, TB was one of the UK's most urgent health problems, as the bacteria that caused it thrived and circulated easily in the country's overcrowded and unsanitary cities. This issue was close to home for Minnie, as her brother Louis would die from TB in the early 1920s, so he would probably already have been ill by the time that Minnie became an alderman. Indeed, he may have been unwell for a few years, as there is no record of him fighting in the war despite becoming eligible for conscription in 1916.

In the month before Labour swept to power, the Poplar Dispensary for the Prevention of Consumption (the popular name for tuberculosis) had 764 attendances, confirming thirty-six definite new cases of TB and identifying a further fifty-eight suspected cases. The TB Dispensary had opened in 1911, and was located at Alexandra House, 135 Bow Road, opposite the Thames Magistrates' Court and near to both of Minnie and Edgar's marital homes. With a waiting room, nurse's room, medical officer's consulting room, dispensary, bacteriological laboratory, and committee room, it was equipped with state-of-the-art medical facilities including X-ray apparatus, and provided living accommodation for the caretaker and his wife. The dispensary set itself the bold aim of eradicating consumption, particularly in Poplar. Before his death that

---

[282] Poplar Borough Council, 1925.

[283] All information from reports of the Medical Officer of Health for Poplar unless otherwise stated.

year, King Edward VII had delivered a speech to the effect that if consumption were preventable then it ought to be prevented, which prompted a flurry of legislation and charitable efforts against the killer disease, including donations to the Poplar dispensary.

Following the start of the war, Poplar Borough Council committed itself to pay half the dispensary's costs, up to a cap of twelve hundred pounds per year.[284] Armed with this semi-stable financing, the dispensary made itself the borough's hub for collecting data, distributing information and tackling the disease. Its priority was to educate local people, teaching parents the value of fresh air, sunlight and health precautions for children. This was an uphill struggle while the East End's living conditions continued to be so poor, but the local political establishment preferred to target their efforts at Poplar people's behaviour rather than at changing the conditions in which they were made to live. The Poplar dispensary sent physicians and nurses to visit homes and give advice, and arranged for the Medical Officer to examine people who had come into contact with an infected person. It provided its services free of charge to those who were not already under the care of a medical practitioner.

The dispensary's management knew that it was falling short of what was necessary and possible in the fight against tuberculosis, and just as the Maternity and Child Welfare Centre's management had, they saw the election of a Labour council as an opportunity to take the dispensary's work out of the precarious philanthropic sector and into the hands of a solid and committed public body. In January 1920, its chairman offered the dispensary as a gift to the borough. Minnie and two colleagues met with the Dispensary's Committee, and when they reported to the Public Health Committee it gladly accepted the offer and set up a sub-committee to oversee the takeover, which Minnie joined. The full council endorsed this, with the Municipal Alliance opposition councillors raising no objection to a measure that they could have, but had not, carried out at any time during the dispensary's sixteen years of existence while the borough was under their rule.

The Ministry of Health approved the takeover, but with typical government parsimony, expressed concern about the estimated costs. Minnie and the Council set about expanding the dispensary's work, opening a branch dispensary in the busy Poplar High Street to serve the

---

[284] Agreement dated 20th October 1914, cited in letter, Evans-Thorpe to Skeggs, 8th January 1920.

southern part of the borough, establishing open-air schools for children at risk, and starting a new scheme co-operating with School Medical Officers to give infected children milk and meals at school and regular examinations at the dispensary. The Council also increased dispensary staff's pay and numbers, although it seems incongruous that a socialist council increased the pay of the highest-paid staff by more than that of the lower-paid. Chief physician Dr Smith saw his comfortable £700 annual salary increased in increments to £900, while health visitors saw theirs rise from a rather more modest £200 to a still-modest £250, a lower rise in percentage terms as well as in cash terms. Socialists had debated extensively the issue of unequal wages, and had generally concluded that it was utopian to try to equalise wages under a capitalist system with a labour market. However, when pay rises were in the gift of socialists, it would surely have been possible to at least not widen inequalities as this particular pay award did.

The takeover completed, the Council began negotiating to relocate the dispensary across Bow Road to 1 Wellington Road, a move that would eventually take place in 1924. The Council thought Alexandra House's location to be unsuitably noisy, with the Bow Road traffic on one side and a recently-extended engineering works on the other side. Wellington Road, where Minnie and Edgar lived, was comparatively quiet.[285]

Poplar Borough Council established a permanent TB Care Committee, to which it appointed Minnie and six other councillors, together with representatives from the local War Pensions Committee, Invalid Children's Aid Association, Public Health Department and the LCC's School Care Committee. The committee met fortnightly, arranged both care and after-care, and organised the looking-after of children whose mothers were in hospital.

Minnie Lansbury applied her energy, commitment and socialist politics to the fight against tuberculosis. Her politics told her that this fight was not just a medical one but a social one. Poplar's people needed not just treatment but dramatic improvement in their conditions of life.

In 1918, one in every four hundred Poplar borough residents died of tuberculosis. In 1920, the first full year of the Labour council, that figure had fallen to one in every six hundred and twenty-five. As the years went on, it continued to fall.[286]

---

[285] www.soundsurvey.org.uk

[286] Report of the Medical Officer for Health, 1923.

Building Homes

As well as bringing substandard housing up to standard, Poplar's new Labour council also got to work getting new housing built. Minnie was a member of the Special Housing Committee, which within a month of being elected presented its plans to the council: it would buy land for building new housing, whether through negotiating with the current owner or through compulsory acquisition. It invited tenders for the construction work, applied to the LCC for a loan towards the £100,000 cost of three housing schemes, and as early as 30th January 1920, Mayor George Lansbury was ceremonially cutting the first turf of the Chapel House Street development. A photograph shows George wearing a suit, a bowler hat and an open-mouthed grin, holding a spade loaded with earth and backed by two dozen men, some in work clothes and flat caps, others in long coats and bowlers.

Chapel House Street was a road without houses, running between East Ferry and West Ferry Roads across the Isle of Dogs towards the disused ground where Millwall Football Club had played its home games until it had moved south of the river in 1910. Inspired by the garden cities movement in which Minnie had shown an interest during her WSF days, the new estate's houses had gardens, chestnut paling fences and front hedges. The Council provided a fruit tree for each garden, planted by unemployed ex-servicemen for wages. Inside, the houses boasted electric lighting, gas heating stoves, three or four bedrooms, a living room and a bathroom, described by an Isle of Dogs history website as 'quite remarkable for council housing at the time – a bathroom with a fixed bath!'[287]

As well as the one hundred and eighteen houses at Chapel House Street, the Special Housing Committee ordered the building of fifteen similar homes on the site of the old Grove Park Asylum in Bow, and nine tenements at St Leonard's Road. The Ministry of Health approved these three schemes, although it tutted at how little the Council proposed to charge for rent. However, the Ministry refused Poplar's plans for thirty tenements in Bow Road and fifty to sixty houses at Kingfield Street on the Isle of Dogs. Faced with this obstruction of its efforts to provide decent housing for its slum-dwelling residents, the committee resolved to press its case.

The Kingfield estate would eventually receive its first tenants in 1924. Meanwhile, Poplar's Labour council was already getting a taste of the

---

[287] www.islandhistory.wordpress.com

hindrance from the central authorities that would intensify over the next few years, as the Ministry adopted for developments that it had helped to fund a policy that would force councils to charge rents that socialist councillors thought were too high for poor and working-class tenants. In July 1920, Deptford Borough Council – another newly-Labour authority – called a conference of councils to discuss mounting a united protest against the Ministry's rent policy. Minnie represented Poplar at this conference, along with George Lansbury and Sam March, a popular comrade who had served on Poplar Borough Council since 1903 and was General Secretary of the National Union of Vehicle Workers. She followed up the conference by taking part in a deputation to the Minister and a recall conference in October. Meanwhile in Poplar, the Special Housing Committee referred its local dispute with the Ministry over rents to arbitration. With the Ministry wanting Poplar to charge twenty-two shillings (£2.10) per week for its new homes in Bow, and the Council charging eighteen shillings, the arbitration committee eventually split the difference and set the rent at twenty shillings.

One external veto of a decision of the Special Housing Committee does seem to have been justified. The committee meeting in May 1920, at which Minnie was present, decided to name two of the streets in its new development after the Council's own members: Lansbury Avenue and Key Road. The LCC, though, would not allow this lionising of living, elected, political representatives, and the Council agreed to name them Thermopylae Gate and Macquarrie Way instead, after ships associated with the district. This episode reflects poorly on the Labour councillors involved, especially Minnie Lansbury and Committee chair Charles Key, who had a personal interest. It was probably due diligence, then, that councillors expressed concerns that favouritism be avoided in the allocation of the new housing at Chapel House Street. The Council stressed that it wanted to prioritise housing large families and reuniting families forced apart by their current inadequate accommodation. The first one hundred and twenty tenants to move into Poplar's new council housing were mostly labourers, dockers and industrial workers, plus a dozen clerical workers – including a Labour Party secretary and a trade union secretary – and the remainder widows, relief claimants, under-employed and unemployed people. They included a number of families with nine or ten members, but also five husband-and-wife couples.[288]

---

[288] www.islandhistory.wordpress.com

Labour members of the Special Housing Committee were divided on the issue of including war service on the application form for Chapel House Street housing, voting by six votes to five to not include it. Unfortunately, the record does not show which councillors voted which way, but it is notable that their unity of purpose did not prevent them from airing different views.

As Minnie and the Special Housing Committee ordered the building of modern, well-equipped, new housing, it also ordered the demolition of Poplar's slums. In June 1920, it condemned the housing in Lower North Street, which ran between the East India Dock Road and Poplar's second main road, the High Street, on a site where 257 people lived in fifty-three houses, for 'the closeness, narrowness and bad arrangement or bad conditions of the buildings … the want of light, air, ventilation or proper conveniences, or other sanitary defects in such buildings are dangerous or prejudicial to the health of the inhabitants.' The neighbouring, smaller slum in the Sophia Street area met the same fate.

Poplar's Labour council was improving the living conditions of Poplar's residents in a way that its Municipal Alliance predecessors had never bothered to do.

Struggling to Work

Poplar's working-class residents continued to suffer from exploitation in the workplace, unemployment out of it, and a constant struggle to keep out of poverty whether they had a job or not. Just as Minnie and other Labour councillors took office, the government withdrew the 'unemployment donation'. A payment to jobless civilians and ex-servicemen, the donation had been introduced after the war to help smooth the transition from wartime to peacetime employment, but although it was always meant to be temporary, its withdrawal came at a time of intense poverty. At its meeting on 27th November, Poplar Borough Council recorded its 'emphatic protest' and called two Town's Meetings in December: one at Poplar Town Hall and the other at Bow Baths Hall. Poplar's Town Hall had been built in 1870, and could fit thousands into its seventy-foot-long main hall into which light flowed through fourteen tall windows.

The Council appointed its representatives to two committees which aimed to prevent the fleecing of working-class consumers – the Profiteering Act Committee and the Food Control Committee – which brought together representatives of the Council and of local working-class organisations. Minnie joined fellow councillors and nominees of Poplar Trades and Labour Council on the latter of these: a body charged with ensuring that people got the food that they needed at a price they could afford.

Town's Meetings carried some formal authority: they were meetings of residents for the purpose of governing the town or area. But meetings and committees alone would not raise the rights and living standards of the working class, so Poplar Council also offered its support to workers in struggle. After appointing their committee members – and passing a resolution opposing cuts to local bus routes – Minnie and the other councillors listened to a deputation from the Police Union, who were fighting for the reinstatement of members sacked during their strike earlier in 1919. The Mayors of thirteen London boroughs went to see the Home Secretary and when he refused to agree to the policemen's reinstatement, the Mayors declared that their councils would not pay their contribution (called a precept) to the Metropolitan Police. Perhaps if they had seen this threat through, they might have won, but the other councils withdrew their threat and Poplar reluctantly followed suit. The government successfully defeated the police's strike, refused to re-employ their activists and neutralised their union, leaving the police with the subservient federation that it still has today and ending any rebellion within its ranks against the government or the political status quo.

Minnie's fellow alderman John Scurr explained that 'Poplar did not feel disposed to enter alone upon a legal fight which they could not win'. The Council would make sure that the next time it used the tactic of withholding precepts, it would be in a position to win, preferably alongside other Labour councils but alone if necessary. That would happen less than two years later: until then, Poplar Council kept its powder dry, while continuing to build its fighting forces. Meanwhile, when police officers wrote to the Council about their campaign for a rise in their pension, it was Minnie who proposed that they support the campaign, provided that national government met the cost of the pension rise.

John Scurr and Minnie Lansbury worked together to press the case for better wages and more secure employment for Poplar's dock and waterside workers, proposing to Poplar Council in January 1920 that it offer evidence to the Industrial Court's inquiry into their union federation's claim for a standard minimum daily wage of sixteen shillings

(80p). Seconding this proposal, Minnie 'said the low wages had been brought home to the committee dealing with the milk supply.' Health and home depended on conditions at work.

If Poplar's Labour council were to support workers' struggles with credibility, it had to improve the lot of its own workforce. It did so, hoping not just to benefit its own employees but to exert upward pressure on the meagre wages and conditions given by other local employers. Within a few months, the Council had granted May Day as a paid holiday to all its employees (with a substitute day off for those whose work had to be done on the day), had doubled the pre-war salaries of technical and clerical staff at its Electricity Undertaking, and had added a halfpenny an hour to the wages of its rammermen, who operated the machines which packed down hardcore in preparation for laying pavements. The pay rises were conditional on trade union membership. Why, they reasoned, should someone benefit from the efforts of a collective they refused to join?

When London Labour's Municipal Conference in May 1920 agreed a minimum wage of four pounds per week for council workers, Poplar was one of several (although not all) Labour councils to implement it for male employees and the only one to enforce it for women as well.

Meanwhile, each Poplar councillor took a seat on the management committee of a local group of London County Council schools, Minnie (and Edgar) being allocated to Bow and Bromley no.1 group, which comprised Atley Road, Fairfield Road and Smeed Road schools. This was a role for which she had relevant experience as well as political expertise. And in July 1920, the Council agreed to request that Minnie and eleven of her fellow councillors be appointed as magistrates, due to 'the inadequate representation of Labour on the Bench'. I could find no evidence of the request being agreed. While this may have deprived the area of more compassionate judges, it saved Minnie from being drawn further into the role of administering a system with which she would surely not have been comfortable.

Minnie's council work even looked beyond the UK, as she helped Reverend Kitcat with his efforts to raise money across London for distressed and starving children overseas. But it was firmly rooted in Poplar, and in its community as much as in its council chamber. A later socialist writer, Michael Lavalette, explained that:

> The women councillors ... operated an open door policy in their homes. From morning to night local women would bring them

their problems. Minnie, in particular, was an energetic representative, solving all manner of issues for local families. She became a vociferous, militant community leader who local people could trust to take up their cause – no matter how small or trivial it may have seemed to someone on the outside.[289]

Communism Coming?

George Lansbury had only recently become Mayor of Poplar, but at the start of 1920, the Council temporarily excused him from his duties so that he could visit Bolshevik Russia. On his return, he reported to Poplar Borough Council's March meeting that the last council meeting he had attended was the Moscow Soviet, at which he 'was delighted to find the municipal work carried on in much the same manner as the L.C.C., there being reports from all departments: Public Health, Education, Housing, Food Control, Co-operation etc.' George had addressed the Soviet and congratulated its members on 'the efficient manner in which they carried on their work.'

During his visit, George Lansbury had secured a newsprint consignment worth £25,000. He explained that this was a commercial necessity due to British paper suppliers' hostility to the *Daily Herald*, ' and that the paper was bought at cost price with a Soviet loan to be 'very gradually repaid'.[290] Unlike the subsequent episode in which Minnie and her family helped to sell Russian diamonds, this deal received little opprobrium other than the general tutting from anti-socialists about George's Russian trip.

The British government, along with others, was militarily supporting attempts to overthrow the Russian government, and the British labour movement was campaigning to stop Britain's hostile intervention. In July 1918, while Minnie was still involved in the Workers' Socialist Federation, the WSF had initiated the People's Russian Information Bureau and had published and handed out Lenin's 'Appeal to the Toiling Masses' to the toiling masses of the East End. Sailors looking forward to the end of one war were not keen to be despatched to another, especially against a country which had overthrown its previous tyrannical regime and put workers in charge, and began refusing to board ships to attack Russia.[291] At the start of 1919, British socialists and trade unionists formed the Hands Off Russia campaign.

[289] Lavalette, 2006, p.13.

[290] Morgan, 2006, p.107.

As workers rose up through 1919 and beyond, they continued to fight against Britain's war against Russia as well as for their own jobs, wages and rights. And while the labour movement's leaders urged caution and constitutionalism, its socialist grassroots advocated – and took – direct action. Labour Party leader J.R. Clynes argued that if Labour took unconstitutional action against a Conservative and/or Liberal government then a future Labour government could expect the same in reverse. As Ralph Miliband explained, 'What Clynes was asking was that Labour should deliberately forbear to use its power over urgent issues in the expectation that is opponents, in grateful memory of that forbearance, would also behave nicely when Labour came to office. It was a remarkable view … of the manner in which traditional elites acquit themselves in politics when their power, property and privileges and threatened.'[292] The same argument would resurface when Minnie and her fellow councillors took municipal direct action against the unfair local government funding system in 1921, and is still deployed today when socialists advocate defiance. But back in 1920, Poplar dock workers were about to demonstrate in practice the effectiveness of direct action.

On 10th May, the steam-powered cargo vessel SS Jolly George was waiting in Poplar's East India Dock to be loaded with weapons to take to Poland to be fired at Russia's Red Army. But local dockers' union leader (and Poplar Labour councillor) Dave Adams led his fellow dockers in refusing to load the ship, the coal trimmers refused to load the coal needed to fuel the ship, and it did not sail to war. Future Communist Party General Secretary Harry Pollitt wrote that, 'The strike on the Jolly George has given a new inspiration to the whole working-class movement. On May 15th the munitions are unloaded onto the dock side, and on the side of one case is a very familiar sticky-back, "Hands Off Russia!". It is very small, but that day it was big enough to be read all over the world.'[293]

Plodding in the wake of workers' action, the Trades Union Congress and the Labour Party set up a Council of Action and called peace demonstrations around the country in August, and the government finally pulled Britain out of the military assault on Bolshevik Russia.

[291] See Simon Webb, '1919: Britain's year of revolution', 2016, Pen and Sword History.

[292] 1961/2009, p.72.

[293] Harry Pollitt, 'A War Was Stopped', 1925, p.10.

That same month, Britain got its own Communist Party, and Minnie Lansbury became a member.

Launched too late to prevent the loss of the potential of 1919's working-class upsurge, the Communist Party of Great Britain (CPGB) was instead a response to that loss of potential, as well as a move to follow Russia's revolutionary road. The delay in forming the CPGB is partly attributable to the torturous negotiations between its component factions, which had spun out for over a year by the time of the founding congress. Sylvia Pankhurst found herself unable to remain a member of the Communist Party, refusing to hand over control of the *Workers' Dreadnought* and disagreeing with the CPGB's policy of seeking affiliation to the Labour Party. But she saw Minnie's membership as 'moving back in our [WSF's] direction', writing that Minnie 'had lately joined the Parliamentary Communist Party – the half-way house toward the revolutionary standpoint which we hold.'[294] Sylvia was now beyond even the revolutionary left of the labour movement, and engaged in a polemical exchange with Lenin in which he argued for the CPGB to seek affiliation to the Labour Party and she argued against.[295]

While remaining a Labour Party member, Minnie joined the Communist Party as soon as it formed, and would consistently fight for the Party in the East End for what remained of her life.[296] Her husband Edgar joined too, as did his sisters Nellie, Annie, Violet and Daisy, and Daisy's husband Raymond Postgate. Family patriarch George Lansbury did not, though, maintaining that although revolution was justified in Russia, it was not necessary in Britain.

When George refused the £75,000 chocolate-coated donation from the Bolsheviks to the *Daily Herald*, the money made its way to other activities sympathetic to Russia, which according to one newspaper meant channelling 'red money' to 'Soviet missionaries to go up and down the country spreading Bolshevism,' including 'street corner orator types' and 'taproom talkers … men with plenty to say to the British worker in his hours of leisure, so that he could imbibe Bolshevist principles with his beer.'[297] How outraged the newspaper was that

---

[294] *Workers' Dreadnought*, 7th January 1922.

[295] Lenin's 'Left-wing Communism: an infantile disorder' was in part a response to Sylvia Pankhurst.

[296] *The Communist*, 7th January 1922.

[297] *Edinburgh Evening News*, 23rd September 1920.

working-class people could hold strong political opinions, want to overthrow their oppressors and dare to talk to their fellows about it over a drink!

Some of the money went to *The Communist*, the newspaper of the newly-founded CPGB, which appointed Francis Meynell as its editor after he had resigned from the *Daily Herald* under the shadow of the chocolate jewels scandal. Still, Meynell and his wife Hilda had the consolation of gorging themselves on the chocolates in retrieving the gems.[298]

And the *Daily Herald*? It carried on in its sackcloth and ashes, and went on to play a key role in the historic battle waged by Minnie, Edgar, George and their fellow Poplar councillors against the unfair rating system. But its meagre money would run out in 1922 and it would survive only by being taken over by the TUC and made to toe the official labour movement line. There was no bourgeois outrage about 'TUC gold' – but then again, the TUC was not foreign, Jewish, nor a particular threat to the capitalist status quo.

Roads to the Year's End

While Minnie and the Communist Party were laying out the revolutionary road to socialism, Minnie and the borough council were laying roads in Poplar. The first decade of the twentieth century had seen a rapid expansion in motor traffic on London's roads, and the standard of road surfacing needed to catch up. The days of gas-lit, wood-surfaced roads were drawing to a close, with asphalt and tarmacadam surfaces needed to bear the weight of modern traffic. A new feature of the city, particularly of its deprived, working-class districts, the new roads did not yet have traffic lights or road markings, but they moved life forward.

Desperate levels of post-war unemployment meant that there were plenty of men available to do the work, men who needed paid work to stave off destitution. Socialists advocated 'public works', such as road laying, to provide jobs and meet public need. Poplar had already tried to create jobs for the jobless in the areas of its work in which Minnie was involved. The Special Housing Committee lost an argument with the Ministry of Health that new flats be built by directly-employed labour and was compelled to use a contractor instead. And the Public Health Committee called on the LCC to repair and clean its dilapidated

[298] *The Communist*, 12th February 1921.

school buildings, emphasising that this would create jobs as well as improving the comfort and safety of schoolchildren.

The government, perhaps fearful of a return of 1919's militancy, partially acquiesced to pressure for public works. The 1920 Roads Act allowed the Ministry of Transport to give grants to county councils to fund improvements to trunk roads and bridges, but government and LCC hands held tight to the purse strings. By mid-1920, Poplar Council had spent £105,406 on paving roads, with the government's Road Board contributing only half the cost. The Council sent a deputation to the Transport Minister to ask for more. By November, they had asked for a loan from the LCC for street works, been refused, protested, and had the loan granted. The Council was learning in practice that the central authorities do not fund improvements to working-class areas unless those areas put up a fight. It would put that lesson to very effective use.

Despite these troubles, George Lansbury summed up his year as Mayor as 'not a bad effort for a council which was suspected of Bolshevik tendencies,' raising laughter from his colleagues. For the Poplar Borough Municipal Alliance, though, that same record was 'a carnival of extravagance' and would be for several years to come.[299]

As he ended his term as Mayor, George Lansbury confessed to his fellow councillors that his wife Bessie was still excluded from political activity by her domestic burden, even during her year as Mayoress. He explained her absence from public functions as being due to their 'large household for the work of which, in the absence of servants, she was responsible.' Free of the burden of children and with help at home, Bessie Lansbury's daughter-in-law Minnie was able to continue her political and municipal work into 1921. Sam March became the new Mayor, and Minnie Lansbury took an increasingly influential role in driving the Council along a radical, confrontational and effective road.

---

[299] 1925.

Chapter 6 - Defying the Law

New Year, New Struggles

The work being too much for a single committee, Poplar Borough Council went into 1921 with both a Public Health and Housing Committee and a new, separate Maternity and Child Welfare Committee. Minnie Lansbury continued to serve on both. Through the former, she was soon campaigning against measles, a contagious, infectious disease which had killed thirty-three people in Poplar the previous year.[300]

1921 was the year in which the war victors announced heavy reparations on Germany; Adolf Hitler became leader of the German Nazi Party; Ireland was divided in two; and Albert Einstein won the Nobel Prize for Physics. It was also the year in which the British economy plunged into crisis. The country's imports and exports fell by nearly half, so dockside Poplar hurt even more than elsewhere. Employers were keen to preserve their profits and their positions, so they set about ensuring that workers would bear the cost of the economic crash. Beginning in late 1920, they cut prices, wages and jobs. As Poplar Council lifted people out of poverty, so the bust of capitalism's boom-and-bust cycle threw them back into it.

The Council held Town's Meetings about unemployment in Poplar and Bromley in October 1920, each attended by so many people that they overflowed. At each, the Mayor and councillors spelt out the case for government action against joblessness, urged people to join their campaign, and explained how capitalism caused this crisis. Minnie Lansbury was not one of the councillors on the platform: she was still not a public speaker, although some of her fellow women councillors were, Julia Scurr and Susan Lawrence often featuring on platforms at meetings. The Town's Meetings voted for resolutions calling on the government to provide grants to enable the workers without jobs to do the work that needed doing, enough money to live on ('full maintenance') for those for whom there was no work and adequate allowances for those who could not work through disability.

Ex-servicemen and their families still needed financial support from the government, which in spring 1921 reorganised the local War Pensions Committees on which Minnie still served. In London, it

---

[300] Medical Officer's Report, 1920.

transferred responsibility from the LCC to the borough councils, establishing one War Pensions Committee in each borough. Minnie changed from being a member of the Poplar 'A' committee to being a representative of the two local Soldiers' and Sailors' dependents' charities – the Help Society and the Families Association – on the Poplar War Pensions Committee.

It seems odd that Minnie now represented the Soldiers' and Sailors' Families Association (SSFA), which she had previously thought so inadequate as to set up a rival organisation, the League of Rights – and which the *Daily Herald* had once labelled 'Middle-class Busybodies'.[301] But by now, the League of Rights had run its course, seemingly not meeting after 1919. The SSFA, among others, was now carrying out some of the League's functions, but as a charity with the Queen as its patron, it remained a mainstream, establishment group. It had been willing to challenge the government on occasion (for example, for unmarried mothers' eligibility for pensions) and its local branches had a degree of autonomy that allowed Poplar's to cooperate with the local labour movement. By 1921, Minnie Lansbury was not just a representative but the President of the local SSFA.[302] As much as this may be evidence of Bow and Poplar SSFA branches moving closer to Minnie's standpoint, it could equally suggest that she had moved closer to theirs, becoming more 'establishment' and charity-minded. Perhaps they met somewhere in the middle.

The demands on Poplar's council grew while its ability to fund them did not. The labour movement had long declared the local government funding system to be grossly unfair. Each council had to fund the services it provided through taxing its locality, which it did through a property tax known as the rates. Poorer boroughs had considerably more need for services but considerably less local wealth to tax. This inequity still exists today, but at least it is now relieved to an extent by (albeit rapidly decreasing) government grants and at least local councils are no longer responsible for funding the maintenance of the poor and unemployed. In London after the First World War, West London's five wealthy boroughs had five thousand paupers to support and fifteen million pounds worth of property on which to charge rates, while East London's five poor boroughs had a rateable value of just four million pounds but eighty-six-and-a-half thousand paupers to look after. With

---

[301] 3rd July 1915.

[302] Daily Herald, 4th January 1922.

a quarter of the resources and seventeen times the burden, Poplar and its neighbours were stretched fifty times as thinly as the West Enders.

Moreover, there was an inequality at work that was peculiar to London. Other large cities funded poor relief across the whole urban area, with everyone paying into a central pot whether they lived in a rich or a poor part of the city. Only in London was the funding divided into smaller areas, and as those tended to be either rich or poor, the burden fell dramatically more heavily on poor areas like Poplar.

Patching a bursting dam, Poplar's council continued with its job-creating, road-laying schemes. Near the end of 1920, the government committed itself to providing grants for such schemes, and Poplar drew up a plan costing £31,000, which was approved by Liberal Minister of Labour Thomas Macnamara with no conditions attached. But Macnamara's word turned out to be unreliable as a month later, the government refused the grant on the basis of Poplar's failure to meet two conditions which it had not previously mentioned. It insisted that the Council recruit the scheme's workers through Labour Exchanges, although Poplar had none, and it demanded that ex-servicemen get the work ahead of others, whereas Poplar had prioritised men with large and/or young families regardless of whether they had fought in the war or laboured at home.

Already struggling with insufficient resources, the non-payment of the expected £31,000 – the equivalent in purchasing power of £1.27 million in 2018 – would tip Poplar Borough Council's precarious finances over the edge unless the Council took drastic action. So it did.

Deciding to Defy

Whatever Poplar Borough Council was going to do about the crisis it faced and the unfair rating system that caused that crisis, it was not going to do it behind closed doors. Instead, it was going to inform Poplar's people of the problem and involve them in battling for a solution.

At the start of 1921, the Council issued a leaflet explaining how the funding system was driving up the rates. London Labour Party Secretary Herbert Morrison liked the leaflet so much that he circulated it to all London's Labour councillors, explaining that 'It states a smashing case and should be of interest to Labour Parties in other Boroughs.' But Morrison also urged, in BLOCK CAPITALS no less, that these leaflets

SHOULD BE PUBLISHED BY LABOUR PARTIES NOT BY BOROUGH COUNCILS 'AT THE EXPENSE OF THE RATEPAYERS'.[303] Morrison was very concerned for Labour councils to be seen as respectable and efficient, not confrontational or profligate. He saw councils as administrative rather than campaigning bodies.

As well as being London Labour's Secretary, Herbert Morrison was also now Mayor of Poplar's neighbouring borough of Hackney. He would lead it along a very different road from Poplar's, and the friction between the two borough councils and their leaders would grow as 1921 wore on. Poplar set itself on a course to collide with the government and the entire municipal funding system, and when people had to take sides, Morrison would find it unconscionable to take Poplar's.

Poplar Borough Council now had a stark choice to make. It was on the verge of bankruptcy. It could choose to submit to a funding system it knew to be unfair, by cutting services, increasing rates or abandoning the improvements it was making. Or it could choose to defy that system.

Like many Labour councillors before and since, Minnie Lansbury and her comrades had involved themselves in the labour movement because they wanted to change society for the better. The people who elected them to the council wanted and expected their conditions of life to improve as a result. They came up against a system that claimed to be democratic but which stopped them carrying out their democratic mandate. With a few notable exceptions, most Labour councillors in the century since then have chosen to submit to the system. Minnie and the Poplar councillors chose instead to defy it.

But how exactly would they do that? Minnie and others drew on their long experience of labour movement democracy and community activism to mobilise the local movement to determine their strategy in a participatory and democratic way. Minnie had been active in her trade union when she was a school teacher; she and other Poplar councillors had been involved in the local suffragette organisation that was democratic and grassroots-led in a way that others were not. Minnie had helped to set up and organise the League of Rights and the WSF, and had worked very effectively on the local War Pensions Committee. Her fellow councillors had similar experience – Susan Lawrence on the School Care Committee, Nellie Cressall on the Food Control Committee, several of the men in the National Union of Railwaymen, Julia Scurr in strike support, her husband John Scurr in the United Irish

---

[303] LLP Municipal Circular no.65, 14th January 1921, ACC/2417/A/7, Folio 480.

League, and more. From this work, they had gained a commitment to participatory democracy, a knowledge of how to organise it, and between them, a substantial network of local comradeship and support. They had also learned through bitter experience that sticking to lawful means of protest meant accepting limits on what they could achieve.

Poplar's Labour Party called its members and affiliates together to decide how it was going to confront its financial crisis. In the absence of Mayor Sam March, George Lansbury had a dramatic strategy to propose, an idea originally thought up by Councillor Charlie Sumner.[304] A long-standing and popular local labour movement figure, Sumner had for decades represented Poplar's working class in various capacities while also working at a furnace in Pearce's chemical factory. Thinking back to the aborted action in solidarity with sacked police strikers, he suggested that Poplar refuse to collect and hand over that portion of the rates – known as the precepts – levied by cross-London bodies. These precepts were substantial, growing and unaffordable. The London County Council demanded twenty-five per cent more than in the previous year, the Metropolitan Police thirty-two per cent more, and the Metropolitan Water Board a massive fifty-four per cent more; increased demands from the Metropolitan Asylums Board had helped to push up the Board of Guardians' bill by forty-two per cent.[305]

The Poplar Labour Party meeting considered this proposed action carefully and in detail, with a lot of discussion, some of it 'quite heated',[306] and agreed to set off on its confrontational course. It immediately began building support. Poplar Labour wrote to other London Labour Parties inviting them to send two delegates each to a conference in Poplar's Council Chamber on Saturday 26th February, at which they would explain their decision to refuse to levy the precepts.[307]

Charlie Sumner told the London County Council, on which he represented Bow and Bromley, what Poplar planned to do, declaring that his borough 'was out to fight and would give the L.C.C. hell.' He made his declaration of war in a fiery debate at the LCC meeting on Tuesday 15th March, during which Labour members tore into the Municipal Reform (Tory) LCC leadership for failing to build new

---

[304] E. Lansbury, 1934, p.72.

[305] Key, 1925.

[306] Tapper, 1960, p.59.

[307] Bethnal Green Borough Council Labour Group minutes, 2nd March 1921.

houses. Sumner 'contrasted the success achieved in Poplar with the apathy of the L.C.C.' and when Lord Eustace argued that it was 'bad business' to proceed with a housing scheme in Beacontree, Labour's Harry Gosling retorted that, 'It is not a question of commerce, but of humanity.' While Minnie Lansbury and her council colleagues made every effort to improve their borough's health and housing, the LCC demanded money but did nothing. It had even failed to clear the twelve Poplar slum areas that it was supposed to.[308]

Poplar Labour now needed to get Poplar Borough Council to adopt its fighting strategy, surely a formality given Labour's huge majority. In the event, not only did every Labour councillor vote to refuse to collect and pay the precepts, but the two Municipal Alliance councillors present did too! The only vote against was that of Reverend Kitcat, and even he expressed sympathy with the Council's predicament and support for its demands, opposing only because he could not support breaking the law. Charles Key proposed the deletion of the precepts, Charlie Sumner seconded, and Edgar Lansbury was one of several councillors who made the case for defying the law and expressed his hope that other councils would follow suit.

With the decision taken in front of a crowded public gallery at its meeting on Tuesday 22nd March, the Council would now have to deal with the consequences of its actions. Poplar's Town Clerk, J. Buteaux Skeggs, had written a letter cautioning the Council that it would lose loans and grants, that its creditors would take it to court and that it would be unable to pay its workers' wages. Skeggs' letter was read to the council meeting, but the Council pressed ahead anyway. Minnie and her colleagues were, reported the *Daily Herald* the next day, 'fully prepared' for the authorities taking legal action, 'and will fight on in order that this question, vital to all the poorer boroughs in the Metropolitan area, may be ventilated.'

The immediate reaction of the cross-London bodies appeared to be one of astonishment that Poplar Council had carried out its threat to withhold their monies. All four – the London County Council, Metropolitan Asylum Board, Metropolitan Water Board and Metropolitan Police – avoided answering questions as to their intentions, Colonel Karalake, chairman of the Water Board, responding with incredulity, 'I know a lot of these Poplar people, and I don't think they could be so silly.' While the Police Receiver refused to comment on

---

[308] *Daily Herald*, 16th and 21st March 1921.

the suggestion that the force may be withdrawn from Poplar, the General Secretary of the National Union of Police and Prison Officers, J.H. Hayes, assured Poplar that the union 'would be placed at the Council's disposal to safeguard the interests of the ratepayers.' The Dockers' Union also volunteered to help police the borough should the Met withdraw.[309] This was working-class struggle organised well: prepared for possible hostile action and ready to take matters into its own hands. This was possible because of the democratic, participatory nature of Poplar's labour movement and its experience of struggle.

The Council explained its strategy to Poplar's people through Town's Meetings and in a statement delivered to every local household and lodger. Five days after the Council voted for defiance, Poplar's jobless marched through the borough, accompanied by banners and an Irish band, collecting money for the Mayor's fund to relieve distress, assisted by the local 'Pearly King'. 'All through the slums we marched,' wrote the *Daily Herald*'s reporter the next day, 'and the meaner the streets the more generous were the onlookers ... Hardly a soul allowed a collector to pass without giving at least a copper.' He added that, 'With so much poverty in a normally poor borough, there is little wonder that Poplar cannot pay its rates.'

Poplar Council affirmed its stance on 31st March when it set its rate for the quarter at four shillings and fourpence in the pound – considerably lower than the more than six shillings it would have been with the precepts included. But although the vote was again nearly unanimous, below the surface some councillors were more nervous than others, and Minnie Lansbury would play an important role in maintaining the Council's steadfast approach when others wavered. Sam March explained, with a hint of irony, that 'there are a few members who favour opposition to the demands of the outside authorities, but think that this opposition could be expressed in a way better than that of actual resistance,' while assuring supporters that the majority 'certainly' preferred the strategy of defiance.

Holding the Line

When, at the end of June, Poplar Borough Council was again required to set its quarterly rate, Labour councillor James Jones, a railway worker and churchwarden, expressed concern 'not about the refusal to pay the

---

[309] *Daily Herald*, 24th March and 1st April 1921.

central authorities the money owing to them, but on the wisdom of omitting to collect the money.' He worried that Poplar's tenants would have to pay eventually and would struggle to meet bills that included hefty arrears.

When Minnie Lansbury spoke in response, she shot down Jones' objections, asking rhetorically what the use was of taking the action they were taking if people would end up having to pay anyway. She was not planning on Poplar people paying off a backlog of rate demands but on getting those rate demands scrapped. Jones' proposal to collect but not hand over the precepts was met with 'indignation' by his fellow Labour councillors, and those like Minnie who spoke against persuaded him to drop the suggestion. The Council agreed to set the rate for the quarter with the precepts excluded, with just one vote against – that of Councillor Walter Cowl of the Municipal Alliance.

Sylvia Pankhurst later wrote that Minnie 'was in the forefront of the struggle to induce the more backward elements on the Council to fall into line.'[310] Sylvia also laid down a challenge to those councillors elsewhere who declared themselves revolutionaries: 'Now, Communist Borough Councillors, let us see what you can do.'[311] Minnie and Edgar Lansbury were the only Communist Party members on Poplar Council, and they were leading a mobilisation to defy the law and challenge the foundation of the unfair council funding system. Their neighbouring borough of Bethnal Green had a Communist Mayor, Joe Vaughan, yet was not joining Poplar in its defiant action, despite Poplar asking other councils to follow its lead. Would Poplar have to continue fighting alone?

As a Communist, Minnie was also a republican, which brought her into conflict with some council colleagues when King George V visited Poplar. On Friday 8th July 1921, Poplar would finally see the official opening of its new dock. Its construction had started before the war, paused during it, completed following it, and it would now be officially declared open by the King after whom it was named. The Council arranged for a large banner to be displayed on the riverside, stating that 'Poplar Council expect this day the King will do his duty by calling on His Majesty's Government to find work or full maintenance for the unemployed of the nation.' Alderman John Scurr wanted to go a step further than this and proposed to the Council that it present the King

[310] *Workers' Dreadnought*, 7th January 1922.

[311] *Workers' Dreadnought*, 16th July 1921.

with a sealed memorial drawing his Royal attention to 'the intolerable burdens from which the Borough is suffering, as a consequence of the present acute unemployment.' Charles Key supported Scurr's proposal, declaring himself 'a loyal subject of the King'. But Minnie and Edgar Lansbury opposed it, saying that they were 'nothing of the sort'. After some debate, Scurr withdrew his proposal.

The London County Council (LCC) and the Metropolitan Asylums Board (MAB) duly obtained their court order on 7th July. The court instructed Poplar Council to pay,[312] but with no sign of the Council doing so, the LCC and MAB tried a tactic to divide the councillors. Representatives of the two bodies called on some of the Poplar councillors and told them how sensible they were, how there were other sensible councillors too, and that 'when the time comes to obey the court a large number will give in.' One councillor asked his visitor whether they had spoken to the Lansburys in this way. 'Oh no,' came the reply, 'we don't talk to them, only to you sensible people.' Rather than being divided, the councillors were made more resolute by this, as well as being rather amused. The further they carried their protest, the more determined they became to see it through.[313]

Summer Manoeuvres

It was a remarkably hot and dry summer in Britain in 1921, so much so that it features in the top five hottest and driest of the century. The drought drove up the price of milk and made the living conditions of those in poverty even more difficult. As the heatwave went on, so did the legal proceedings against Poplar's councillors. When Labour councillor John Suckling resigned, the Municipal Alliance used the platform provided by the consequent Poplar East by-election to call Poplar Labour 'bolshies', 'wasters' and 'law breakers', and urged voters to teach them a lesson. Voters did exactly that, although not in the way that the Municipal Alliance wanted them to. They elected Labour candidate William Lyons by over a thousand votes to just four hundred, delivering a lesson that Poplar's people would stand up for their rebellious representatives.[314]

---

[312] For details of the legal process, see Booth, 2009.

[313] *Daily Herald*, 21st July 1921.

[314] *Daily Herald*, 23rd July 1921.

Those representatives were continuing their municipal work as well as clashing with the courts. On Thursday 28th July, the Maternity and Child Welfare Committee reported to the full council meeting on its supply of free milk during the previous two months and, lest anyone accuse it of profligacy, also reported on its action to obtain payment from those who had claimed under false information. It is easy to imagine, though, that some people whose income just exceeded the level to qualify for free milk might still have been struggling financially and have felt justified in misleading the committee to get the milk they needed.

At the same council meeting, the four Municipal Alliance councillors proposed that the Council levy and pay the precepts. They spoke about the 'sanctity of law' and of their commitment to upholding it, but Minnie and the Labour majority took a different view of the law, George Lansbury summarising it thus: 'Ultimately it was a question of two kinds of contempt: Contempt of court, and contempt of the people.'[315] The opposition councillors made their proposal, knowing full well that it would be defeated, because the very next day the councillors were due in court to answer the writs against them, and despite having supported the action at the outset, they now wanted to extricate themselves from the threat of prison. The council meeting had been packed with supporters of the council majority, and the next day they packed the Lord Chief Justice's court as well, having marched the five miles from Poplar to the Strand.

The Labour councillors did not hope to win in court, as they knew that their actions were illegal. For them, the court room was another platform to explain their case, another backdrop for mobilising their supporters, for pressing their fight for work or full maintenance for all. Several of them spoke in court, but Minnie did not. Their solicitor – W.H. (known as Harry) Thompson – shared the councillors' approach, having himself been to prison for his socialist beliefs, as a conscientious objector to the war. Lawyer Owen Parsons later described Thompson as a man who 'believed in using his great skill and knowledge and courage as a lawyer, in the interests of the oppressed against the rich and powerful.'[316]

Cheered by the gallery on their arrival in court, the councillors put their case in terms not of judicial detail but of their borough's suffering

---

[315] *Daily Herald*, 30th July 1921.

[316] Allen and Flynn, 2007, p.11.

under its impossibly high rates. George Lansbury later wrote, 'What the judges though of us it is hard to say. What we thought of them is more easy. We knew they lived a life apart from us altogether and therefore could not know what such rates meant for our poor people.'[317]

It was now legally decided that if the councillors did not pay the money then they would be detained in prison for contempt of court. In mid-August, Harry Thompson received the list of thirty names of those who would be sent to prison, five women and twenty-five men who would become known as the 'Fighting Thirty'. The list included Alderman Mrs. Minnie Lansbury, but did not include a dozen other Labour councillors who fully supported the refusal to levy the precepts. It was never made clear why some names were included and others not. The *Daily Herald* attributed it 'entirely to the hurry-up, make-haste methods of the London County Council, which gave itself time neither to prepare its case properly nor to issue its so-called writs.'[318]

Meanwhile, the government made some minor concessions that it hoped would persuade the councillors to abandon their resistance. It set up a Royal Commission on local government in London, and it re-established the Metropolitan Common Poor Fund on its pre-war basis. This would benefit Poplar by less than fifty thousand pounds, nowhere near enough to employ, feed or clothe its poor, but enough for the *East London Observer* to acknowledge that the council had gained results through direct action.[319]

After the courts ordered Poplar Borough Council to pay up, some unscrupulous landlords used this as a pretext to demand that their tenants pay up too. On some streets – including Wellington Road, where Minnie and Edgar lived – some tenants found themselves served with a week's notice to quit if they did not pay the full rates including the precepts. Poplar's council quickly issued a notice advising tenants that their landlords had no legal right to charge them for rates which the Council had not levied, and agreed to fund tenants' legal costs even though they knew that such a payment might be unlawful: the councillors were more concerned that it was right. The landlords were made to withdraw their threats and repay those tenants who had handed over the money.[320]

---

[317] 1935, p.116.

[318] 17th August 1921.

[319] 13th August 1921.

The judges had given the councillors the month of August to reconsider their position, but instead of reconsidering, they redoubled their efforts to mobilise support for their stand. In the final ten days of the month, twelve Town's Meetings took place, in schools and parish rooms as well as in the large meeting halls. An Old English Fair ran for a week on Poplar's recreation ground and raised money and morale. Opening at two o'clock each afternoon and running into the evenings, thousands of people joined the fun, enjoying roundabouts, a joy wheel and a cake walk, and children winning prizes including pencils and bracelets on a miniature punching machine.[321]

The councillors declared their readiness for prison. Mayor Sam March pronounced that they were 'all ready to go if they want us. The women are of the same frame of mind. They are not upset about it at all.' Julia Scurr confirmed this, saying that 'We will just go. That is all.' She reminded people that some of the thirty had been in prison before, for their part in the fight for votes for women.[322] Although Minnie was not one of those ex-prisoners, any anxiety she had about prison was tempered by her commitment to seeing through the fight that she had embarked on. And at least she did not have the worries that some of her colleagues had about losing their wages or their jobs, or about how their children would be looked after. The councillors' local supporters were already planning to resolve these worries, but prison was nonetheless a daunting prospect for Minnie and the others, reflecting that their choice to not back down was a brave and principled one.

Before prison, there was one major demonstration to come, and some Council business to be done.

Preparing for Prison

The last Sunday of August saw nearly ten thousand people carrying over seventy trade union banners demonstrating at Tower Hill against unemployment and in support of the Poplar rebellion. Marchers carried banners declaring that 'Poplar Council are still determined to go to prison to secure equalisation of the rates for the poor boroughs' and placards stating that 'Poplar has 12,000 unemployed' and 'Poplar is

---

[320] *Daily Herald*, 11th and 24th August 1921.

[321] *Daily Herald*, 24th August 1921.

[322] *Aberdeen Journal*, 25th August 1921.

backing its Borough Council'. All thirty of the councillors threatened with prison, including Minnie, were present. A contingent of four thousand from Poplar were joined by thousands more from Bethnal Green, Stepney, Shoreditch and elsewhere. The protesters included the diverse ethnicities of the local population, as the *Daily Herald* described in the language of the time: 'Black and yellow men from the Docks district joined themselves to the whites, and all were manifesting equal interest.' Councillor Wooster addressed the crowd and set out the need for practical action: 'The poor people of Poplar don't want mere sympathy, for sympathy without relief is like mustard without beef.'[323]

Then on the Wednesday, the final day of the month, Minnie joined her colleagues at the final Poplar Borough Council meeting before she and the majority of its members were due to be imprisoned. The arrest warrants would come into force the following day and they had municipal affairs to put in order. They began their business half an hour after the scheduled 7pm start, delayed by supporters and the press mobbing the councillors, the former cheering them on and the latter taking photos and filming them. Every daily newspaper had sent a reporter.[324] The council meeting then elected Charles Key – who was not one of the thirty – as Deputy Mayor; appointed those who were not to be arrested to the council's various committees; resolved that council workers' wages not be reduced during the next four months; and granted 'leave of absence' to Minnie and her twenty-nine fellow councillors who would be away until further notice. More photos followed the meeting, the councillors and supporters sang The Red Flag, and then they all made their way the two hundred yards from the Municipal Chambers on Poplar High Street to the Town Hall on Newby Place, where a huge crowd was eagerly awaiting their attendance at a Town's Meeting:

> [T]he big building was crowded, until it was literally impossible for another person to obtain admission.
>
> In the hall every alleyway was packed, and those lucky enough to obtain seats were almost swamped by the onrush of enthusiasts.
>
> In the gallery men and women were huddled to such a state of discomfort as would not have been tolerated by the most enthusiastic 'movie' first-nighter. But the utmost good humour

---

[323] *Daily Herald*, 29th August 1921.

[324] Historians' Group of the Communist Party, 1953.

prevailed, the demonstrators realising that their temporary inconvenience was slight compared with the ordeal which the 30 they had come to support were prepared to undergo. Crowds even gathered on the window-sills and on the balcony.

Even more people – some six or seven thousand – were unable to squeeze into the hall and filled the street outside: 'Every point of vantage was seized. Men clung to railings, and every foot-hold on adjoining buildings was eagerly utilised.'[325] The adjoining buildings were the All Saints' Institute (social club) to one side and a row of houses to the other, the whole scene overlooked by the grand All Saints' Church and its sizeable graveyard and gardens.

For the next two hours, the crowd of Poplar people listened to their councillors, loudly showed their support, and unanimously carried a resolution endorsing their action. The councillors issued a statement:

Thirty of us, members of the Poplar Borough Council, have been committed to prison. This has been done because we have refused to levy a rate on the people of our Borough to meet the demand of the L.C.C. and other central authorities. We have taken this action deliberately, and we shall continue to take the same course until the Government deals properly with the question of unemployment, providing work, or a full maintenance for all, and carries into effect the long-promised and much overdue reform of the equalisation of rates.

Poplar's ex-servicemen felt a strong loyalty and support towards one councillor in particular: Minnie Lansbury, who had campaigned so persistently for their and their families' rights, and had helped so many of them to get the financial support which the government had promised to them but made it so hard for them to actually get. Now the ex-servicemen championed their champion, guarding Minnie's house at 6 Wellington Road from the night her arrest warrant came into force until her actual arrest five days later. They insisted that in this war, Minnie Lansbury was not going to be taken away without 'a demonstration being made in her favour'. One said, 'Sending these women to prison; it's a shame,' and called on former servicemen in London's other boroughs to call on their councils to do what Poplar's was doing. As she faced being taken from her home and into detention, this act of solidarity will undoubtedly have boosted Minnie's morale and reassured her that when the authorities took her away from Poplar, they could not take away her support.

[325] *Daily Herald*, 1st September 1921.

The thirty councillors each gave an eve-of-imprisonment quote to the *Daily Herald*. Minnie said, 'I wish the Government joy in its effort to get this money from the people of Poplar. Poplar will pay its share of London's rates when Westminster, Kensington, and the City do the same!'

Arrests Begin

Arrests began on Thursday 1st September. The Sheriff would not complete his task of finding and arresting the thirty councillors until exactly a week later, giving the Council and its supporters seven days of opportunity to mobilise and advertise their campaign. Some were away at TUC Congress, some were out when the Sheriff called, but otherwise, the order in which they were taken seems to have been arbitrary. On the first day, the Sheriff's officials drove to the houses of several of the male councillors – although not the Lansburys – arrested them and drove them to Brixton prison. It was a slow and cautious drive through Poplar as supporters thronged around, 'men sat on the luggage-carriers, [so as] not to run over the hundreds of small children who were greatly infected by the excitement, and skipped about dangerously near the front wheels.' Once clear of the Poplar crowds, the Sheriff's car pulled over at a hostelry in Aldgate to allow the councillors their last drink as free men.[326] The Sheriff would not have been in the habit of doing this for his detainees, so perhaps this was a show of sympathy, or maybe an indication that he did not consider them to be real villains.

The whole proceeding had an air of street theatre about it, and cinema newsreel producer Topical Budget broadcast a report from Poplar very much in this vein. The reel has survived, preserved by the British Film Institute with a musical accompaniment of a pianist playing a jaunty Red Flag. It comprises clips of the councillors preparing for arrest, alternating with title cards carrying captions. After showing 'Poplar's Benevolent "Bolshie" Boss' – George Lansbury – and then John and Julia Scurr, a frame displayed the words 'Mrs. Alderman "Minnie" Lansbury gathers a nosegay for Holloway'. (Perhaps the film-makers thought that 'Minnie' was a nickname rather than her given name.) The film then cuts to footage of Minnie in the garden picking flowers. The garden seems to have been a place of relaxation for Minnie, as several family photographs show her happy

---

[326] *Eastern Post and City Chronicle*, 3rd September 1921.

and easy-going with friends and pets in garden settings. The Topical Budget newsreel is, to my knowledge, the only film of Minnie Lansbury, and despite being a short clip, shows a lot of the person she was. She looks content and quietly confident in front of the camera, and her face then breaks into a smile as though she just could not help herself. She comes across as defiant but delightful.

Arrests of the male councillors continued over the next few days. George Lansbury, impatient to proceed to prison, contacted the Sheriff's office to make an appointment to be arrested at his home on Bow Road at half past eleven on Saturday morning. His son Edgar, together with councillors Dave Adams and Albert Baker, joined him there to be arrested too, while Susan Lawrence and Minnie were present to see them off. The Sheriff's officer drove the men away, accompanied by cheering crowds and a dockers' band.

Minnie had now been separated from her husband. He was in Brixton prison and she would soon be in Holloway. But while she was still at liberty, Minnie could still campaign. The following evening, the first public meeting since the arrests had begun took place at Bromley Public Hall. It was filled with people an hour before it was due to start, with the crowd spreading down the stairs. There was 'tumultuous cheering when Alderman Minnie Lansbury and the prospective "Brixtonians" mounted the platform.'[327]

Minnie also sent a letter to *The Times*, which had published repeated attacks on its twin bêtes noires of Poplar Council and communism. *The Times* was contemptuous of councillors whom it accused of seeking martyrdom, and of 'a revolutionary movement for the equalisation of wealth or, as London generally sees it, for the equalisation of poverty'. The newspaper outlined how it saw the situation: 'the Socialists of the East End turn hungry eyes upon such boroughs as that of Westminster. They desire that while the richer or more effectively managed districts should provide the money, the socialist prodigals of the poorer ones should have the spending of it.'[328] This was how the conservative political establishment saw working-class rebellion: as the undeserving lower orders greedily demanding what was not theirs. It was the opposite of the reality in which the labours of those working-class people generated the wealth which the wealthy so jealously guarded. Responding with a strident and articulate defence of her and her fellow councillors' actions,

---

[327] *Daily Herald*, 5th September 1921.

[328] 3rd September 1921.

Minnie wrote what later writer Oliver Tapper described as a 'most poignant' letter[329] to the Editor of *The Times*:

> Sir, - While I realize that "martyr" is in your mouth a fit word of abuse, I think you have misjudged its application even according to your standards.
>
> My colleagues of the Poplar Borough Council, and I with them, are normal human beings with a normal hatred of the inhuman conditions of imprisonment to which we are being subjected. We have taken every ordinary course open to us in the processes of the law, and not a few extraordinary; we have employed the most skilful legal aid; and we have appeared in Court after Court precisely to have our action vindicated and to avoid going to gaol. The only step we have not taken, and will not take, is to leave 12,000 unemployed people to starve – for that is the real alternative. The levying of a further 9s. 2d. per annum (the amount of our liabilities to the authorities who are gaoling us) on a rate which already amounts to 19s. 2d. per annum in the pound is a sheer impossibility. Remember that vast numbers of the ratepayers are themselves only partially employed on casual dock labour.
>
> I will not discuss the theory of equalization of rates; but here are data as to its practice as it would affect Poplar. If the rates were equalized over London they would amount to 16s. 5d. per annum. Poplar has already levied at a yearly rate of 19s. 2d., which is 2s. 8d. per annum more than its fair share. We are now sent to gaol with almost every circumstance of ignominy and with felon's conditions for refusing or rather for being unable, to levy the rate of an additional 9s. 2d.
>
> To-morrow I and my women colleagues are to be arrested at 3 o'clock at the Poplar Town Hall. If we said the word, the people of Poplar would prevent our arrest by anything less than a machine-gun corps. Is it because we have managed to prevent riot and bloodshed and have hidden our better sense of wrong behind smiles that you level at us a word which you have so succeeded in debasing?
>
> Faithfully yours,
>
> MINNIE LANSBURY, Alderman, Poplar Borough Council, Sept. 4

---

[329] Tapper, 1960.

Minnie and Susan had made the appointment for the Sheriff's officer to arrest the five women councillors while they had been at George Lansbury's house awaiting his arrest on Saturday morning. The *Taunton Courier*,[330] which saw the unfolding events in Poplar as 'COMMUNISM RAMPANT', reported that Susan Lawrence had initiated the conversation with the Sheriff's officer, which then proceeded as follows:

> Sheriff's Officer: What time shall we say? – Mrs. Edgar Lansbury: Three in the afternoon.
>
> Officer: That is a bit late. Very well, then: three o'clock. (Aside): They are having it all their own way.

Of course, 'having it all their own way' would have meant not being arrested and imprisoned at all, but at least Minnie and the others were asserting themselves and making every move available to help their campaign. They were undoubtedly helped in this by the authorities' failure to arrest them swiftly and decisively, perhaps through ineptness, perhaps feeling rather overawed by the huge demonstrations of popular support.

If Minnie suggested an arrest time that was 'a bit late', it was probably to enable her to visit Edgar in Brixton prison in Monday morning, for that is what she did. Minnie took the opportunity to spend her last few hours at liberty seeing her husband, travelling to Brixton with her mother-in-law Bessie who visited her husband George. Speaking with Edgar and George through heavy wire gratings, the two women found that the festival atmosphere of the previous day had been replaced by the grim reality of incarceration. Prison operated a system of 'divisions', where the standard of your incarceration depended on the reason you were in prison. Established practice was that people detained for contempt of court were put in the first division, along with political prisoners and those convicted of libel, where they could have expected newspapers, their own food and their cells to be cleaned for them. However, Poplar's rebel councillors found themselves placed in the second division, alongside those convicted of criminal offences. They were allowed only two visits and one letter per week and no newspapers. Minnie and Bessie were 'indignant' at the treatment of their husbands and comrades, and Minnie dispatched a telegram to Home Secretary Edward Shortt:

---

[330] 7th September 1921.

Have this morning visited my husband, Edgar Lansbury, and his father, George Lansbury, in Brixton Gaol. Protest most emphatically against disgraceful treatment of them and their colleagues of Poplar Borough Council. George Lansbury called you 'liar' to your face when you declared there was equal law for rich and poor. I presume this is your method of rebutting the charge.

Remember that Hooley was allowed freedom in prison to continue his affairs and remember Stead was allowed political treatment.[331] My husband and colleagues are now being starved physically and mentally for no other purpose than to serve your political spite.

Minnie made similar points in an interview that she gave to the press after visiting Brixton, adding that:

They went in on Saturday at lunchtime, and until this morning had eaten only two pieces of bread each, half the size of my hand. They could not touch the rest of the food although both of them are plain livers and accustomed to few luxuries. Mr. George Lansbury is looking ghastly, and two or three of the others, including Scurr and O'Callaghan, are already in the infirmary. They think that they ought to be treated as political prisoners. …

I want to make it quite clear that the Councillors are not whining at their treatment. They are prepared to suffer for their principles, but they object to being made the victims of political spite.[332]

She added that she would no longer try to keep the unemployed under control and regretted having done so until this point. Why should she hold them back when the government was not holding back in the mistreatment of the Poplar rebels? Minnie Lansbury was clearly a determined, angry, direct and articulate political campaigner. She would now take that spirit and intellect to prison.

---

[331] Ernest Terah Tooley was a financial fraudster who had spent a month in Brixton prison in 1911 for contempt of court; W.T. Stead, editor of the *Pall Mall Gazette*, had been allowed to edit the newspaper from prison in 1885.

[332] *Gloucester Citizen*; *Yorkshire Post*, 6th September 1921.

To Holloway[333]

Word was out in the newspapers and around Poplar that the women councillors were to be arrested at three o'clock. By two o'clock, the Town Hall in Newby Place was already packed with supporters and even more were gathering outside. A detachment of police on horses joined them. Photographs show hundreds, maybe thousands, of men in flat caps and women in bonnets, some holding placards and trade union banners. Supporters stood on brick columns and film camera crews stood on ledges.

The best photograph of all, at least for the subject of this book, captures Minnie Lansbury arriving at Newby Place. She is stepping forward with a sprightly gait, wearing a loose top and skirt in her usual style, plus a less usual hat, and carrying her coat, while a man in a suit and trilby walks a couple of paces behind her carrying her suitcase, packed for prison, on his shoulder. Minnie's way is lined on both sides with rows of standing supporters, watched over by other supporters sitting on the high wall behind them. Several are reaching out their hands towards her, and one woman has stepped out from the ranks to

Minnie arriving at Poplar Town Hall to be arrested

---

[333] All references in this section from the *Daily Herald*, 6th September 1921 unless otherwise stated.

Minnie and the other women councillors address their supporters from the balcony of Poplar Town Hall

grasp her by the right hand and wish her on her way. It is an image full of action, of determination, but mostly, of comradeship.

The arrest plan had changed, with Minnie Lansbury and Susan Lawrence going to the Town Hall while Jennie Mackay, Julia Scurr and Nellie Cressall were arrested at home and then brought to join them. So it was Minnie and Susan who spoke to those crammed into the Town Hall. Minnie Lansbury had finally become a public speaker, on the day that she also became a prisoner!

When Minnie stood up to speak, an 'appreciative ratepayer' presented her with a bouquet of roses. Minnie then 'roused the meeting to indignation' by telling them of the conditions at Brixton prison. She added that the only reading matter available to the Poplar prisoners was the novels of (conservative Victorian popular author) Mrs. Henry Wood and that, she thought, was 'torture in itself'.[334] As we have already seen, Minnie was by all surviving accounts a cheerful and friendly person, and she now retained her sense of humour even in such a grim situation as this.

The growing crowds outside the Town Hall kept up their

[334] *The Times*, 6th September 1921.

demonstration of support. They were entertained by a band and by local speakers, who encouraged support for an upcoming 'Red Week' to 'enforce the justice of their cause'. One newspaper reported that, 'The women alternately cheered and cried, but the men for the most part were dour and sullen to a degree that caused uneasiness among their leaders, who occasionally saw the necessity of urging calmness.'[335]

When the Sheriff's officer arrived with Jennie, Julia and Nellie, the five women councillors met in a private room and had tea. After their discussion, Minnie asked permission for the councillors to address the crowd from the Town Hall balcony. The 'immense crowd' that had accompanied the three arrested at their homes had swelled the numbers already swarming inside and outside the Town Hall. The throng now numbered several thousand, and their champions appeared on the balcony, which was above the main entrance and boasted six caryatides: the women councillors stood alongside these stone carvings of women as they gave their brief speeches. Minnie told them that 'We are going with a good heart. We will go on to the finish whatever happens.'[336]

The *Daily Herald* published parting messages from the five. Jennie Mackay reassured supporters that 'our cause is just and right'. Susan Lawrence urged London and the whole country to take up the fight. Julia Scurr pressed people to join the Tenants' Defence League, while Nellie Cressall reminded them that if and when necessary, the councillors would call on them to refuse to pay their rent. Minnie Lansbury said:

> My call is to the women of Poplar, and the womenfolk of the whole country, to rally to our cause. Our prisoners are being treated not as political offenders; they are treated worse than murderers, except that they are allowed to wear their own clothes. The treatment is scandalous, and shows clearly the attitude of the Government and the authorities to those who really fight for the poor.

Finally, the women got into the Sheriff's car to be driven to prison. But the show was not yet over. A photograph shows the councillors greeting supporters from the vehicle, Minnie leaning out of the side window with a confident smile, while the other four kneel and stand in the open back section. Another shows Julia Scurr addressing the crowd with pointed finger from the back of the car, behind her a *Daily Herald* placard calling

[335] *Nottingham Journal*, 6th September 1921.

[336] *Nottingham Journal*, 6th September 1921.

Minnie (left, leaning our of car window) and the other women councillors leave Poplar in the Sheriff's car to be taken to Holloway prison

for a 'No-Rent Strike'. The car's eventual departure was accompanied by 'wild cheering from the crowd,' the car's progress through the borough a 'triumphal procession' escorted by trade union banners and a band: 'All along East India Dock-road crowds were packed in serried rows, cheering and eager to congratulate the prisoners on their self-sacrificing stand for justice.' The parade of supporters was over a mile long and completely blocked the traffic on the East India Dock Road, 'the windows in the houses of which were filled with people cheering and waving handkerchiefs.' The women councillors cheerfully waved at their supporters, stood up in the car and 'kept up a running fire of pleasantries.' It seems that the only person not cheering was the Sheriff's Officer, who 'looked anything but comfortable.'[337] He had, though, been persuaded to make at least one contribution to the collection being taken to support the unemployed.[338]

In a 'great culminating scene' as the car crossed the boundary from the borough of Poplar into Stepney, a crowd now numbering ten thousand 'formed a vast solid phalanx in the great traffic artery in front of the Eastern Hotel.' Bands played 'They are jolly good fellows', personal friends 'surged round the car for the final farewells,' and the car drove

---

[337] *Nottingham Journal*, 6th September 1921.

[338] *Gloucester Citizen*, 6th September 1921.

away, Minnie and her companions waving and their supporters singing their pledge to keep the Red Flag flying. The *Daily Herald* commented that, 'With all the bouquets and the cheering, applauding crowds it might have been a wedding party. It was symbolical, for the multitude were speeding on their journey women who had wedded themselves to a great cause – the fight for the poor and the oppressed.'

When the car finally outran the supporters and disappeared from view on its journey to Holloway, the crowd fell silent. The women councillors' arrests had been the peak of the week-long street theatre, which had boosted their campaign and embarrassed the government. But now they must continue their stand from inside prison.

Locked Up

The warder opened the gate of Holloway prison and Poplar's arriving prisoners asked him, 'Where's your union card?'[339] The prison then issued them with badges, which they refused to wear, so the prison's governor waived the requirement for them to do so. Holloway's governor had got an early indication that these were not typical prisoners, but neither were they the first political rebels hosted by his prison, where Sylvia Pankhurst had served a sentence earlier that year for sedition (for encouraging soldiers to refuse orders) and where hundreds of suffragettes had been locked up before the war. Julia Scurr suggested to Councillor Chris Kelly when he visited her the next day that campaigners make replica prison badges for supporters to wear in solidarity and to raise some funds. The five women councillors also demanded to be allowed to go to Brixton to meet with their male colleagues, reasoning that as they were imprisoned as members of the Council, they needed to meet as a Council to discuss their legal strategy.[340] That request was refused, at least for now. Putting their spirit of demand and defiance to dramatic and entertaining use, Minnie Lansbury even brightened up their prison stay 'by sliding down the bannisters to the horror of the wardresses.'[341]

However, if the spirit was strong, the body was less so, and within a day of her arrival at Holloway, Minnie was transferred to the sick ward.

---

[339] Tapper, 1960, p.62.

[340] *Daily Herald*, 7th September 1921.

[341] Tapper, 1960, p.62.

Put under 'special treatment', Minnie was exempted from the usual six o'clock rise and allowed to remain in bed.[342] While in the hospital wing, Minnie tried to contact Nellie Cressall, who was nearly eight months pregnant with her sixth child and had been placed in the wing as soon as she was admitted to prison only to then be ignored by the authorities. Exhausted and without exercise or edible food, Nellie was eventually rescued by Minnie kicking up a noise, calling Nellie's name and complaining to the authorities.[343] A week later, Minnie and Nellie were still in the hospital wing, but, so the authorities told the press, their condition was 'not such as to cause any alarm.'[344]

There had for some time been serious concerns about Holloway's standard of care for its inmates. Opened as a mixed prison in 1852, Holloway had become women-only in 1902, around the time that the penal system was supposed to be changing its ethos from punishment and deterrence to reform and welfare. But by 1919, concerns were so strong that the Duchess of Bedford was appointed to investigate conditions there amid allegations of neglect of prisoners' health and hygiene. Even after this spotlight, problems continued. After her most recent imprisonment, Sylvia Pankhurst had issued a statement revealing that women who had just given birth were lying on plank beds in cold, damp cells, and that diet was poor:

> The close confinement is bad for health, and the absolute discipline and lack of contact with the outer world and crushing of all initiative makes the struggle for existence on release far, far harder. It is no wonder that prisoners return time after time. [345]

Despite her situation, Minnie told her sister[346] when she visited on Tuesday 6th September that 'in the actual conditions of their imprisonment they had little cause for complaint – though the sense of deep injustice that they were imprisoned at all naturally prevented any feeling of gratitude for that.' Minnie insisted on hearing news of Edgar's wellbeing before she spoke of her own, and was 'greatly relieved to hear that he had been ordered a milk ration.'

---

[342] *The Scotsman*, 7th September 1921.

[343] Branson, 1979, p.75.

[344] *The Northern Whig*, 14th September 1921.

[345] *Workers' Dreadnought*, 28th May 1921.

[346] *The Scotsman*, 7th September 1921 – the report does not specify which of her sisters.

The other councillors also received visitors on their first full day in Holloway, and talking through wire netting, Julia Scurr told Chris Kelly that they had 'become more determined than ever since our arrest to see this fight through.' Minnie and Julia both told of courteous treatment by prison staff, and Minnie added that the governor was using his discretionary powers to allow them more visitors.[347] When Marion Phillips of the Women's Labour League visited on 9th September, she confirmed that the women councillors were 'all well and cheerful' and with no complaints, although Minnie and Nellie were still in the sick ward. The five women were allowed to wear their own clothes and to talk with each other during morning and evening exercise, and Jennie Mackay was even allowed out to visit her sick father. A Press Association reporter seemed to think they were enjoying a holiday, telling newspapers that 'The imprisoned ladies appeared to accept prison life with more equanimity than their male confrères, and at times they were almost enthusiastic over the attention they had received.'[348]

However, as time progressed, their visitors became increasingly concerned. Minnie's sister found her 'in excellent spirits' but observed that the authorities at Holloway were 'more officious' than those at Brixton.[349] A week into their imprisonment, the free councillors resolved to go to the Home Office to complain, having visited and found that Holloway's conditions were 'not so good' as at Brixton, with 'less freedom permitted', and that the prisoners 'had acknowledged that the food was atrocious.'[350]

Brixton's Poplar prisoners had successfully insisted on improved conditions, with Edgar Lansbury reporting that, 'We are now allowed to have paper and pencils, and also to have our own books sent in. But we are going on asking for newspapers, letters, and the other rights of political prisoners.'[351] Years later, Edgar would write that, 'After three days all pretence of discipline had gone, prison regulations were scrapped, and we became the virtual masters of Brixton prison ... The place became a pandemonium and our imprisonment degenerated into a farce.'[352] Councillor George Cressall described his 'vivid recollection

[347] *Daily Herald*, 7th September 1921.

[348] *The Scotsman*, 7th September 1921.

[349] *Daily Herald*, 10th September 1921.

[350] *Hartlepool Northern Daily Mail*, 13th September 1921.

[351] *Daily Herald*, 10th September 1921.

of our prison experience and how [Edgar's] spirit kept us alive, and I remember that when we were in the exercise yard we used to get in a ring and he used to sing a song about "Wrap me up in an old tarpaulin jacket".[353]

But Minnie, Edgar and the others still did not know how long they would be inside. And Minnie now had another legal issue to deal with.

'A Damnable Lie'

Lena Sybil Hunziker, a 'smart-looking woman' of twenty-five, had worked for the War Pensions Committee in Poplar, had been caught defrauding it of money, and now, facing trial at the Old Bailey, tried to deflect the blame onto Minnie Lansbury.

Hunziker had worked for the Air Ministry during the war, and had then transferred to the Pensions Ministry, which sent her to work in Poplar as a clerk to the War Pensions Committee. She stole sums of forty and seventy pounds, using various fraudulent methods, including entering fictitious names and addresses of pensioners, entering false figures in the accounts, forging receipts, and adding ten pounds to figures by placing the figure 1 in front of the true amount. The court, sitting on Wednesday 21st September, heard evidence from pensioners who were not paid what Hunziker's accounts showed that they were paid.[354]

After evidence from former servicemen whose pension payments she had defrauded, it became clear that Hunziker could not deny the charges, so she changed her plea from 'not guilty' to 'guilty' and her barrister, Sir Ernest Wild, launched an extraordinary defence. Wild was the Conservative MP for Upton (West Ham) and a former Municipal Reform member of the London County Council, and put his political bias against Minnie and Labour to full use, arguing that Hunziker was 'a most respectable woman' who had found the Poplar War Pensions Committee's accounts to be:

> hopelessly muddled, and with interference from Mrs. Minnie Lansbury and other people of that kind she got hopelessly muddled. She got wrong in her accounts and then took the

[352] E.Lansbury, 1934, pp.74-5.

[353] *East End News*, 31st May 1935.

[354] *Daily Telegraph*, 22nd September 1921.

> wrong method of trying to get them right. If the governors of
> Poplar had realised that it was their duty to manage the affairs
> with proper supervision instead of defying the law, this woman
> would not have been in her present unhappy position.[355]

Wild did not specify what he meant by 'people of [Minnie's] kind'. Most probably, he meant rebellious Labour councillors, but he may not have minded if some people also inferred 'Jews' and were reminded of the Russian jewels affair of just a year before.

Wild's defence did not fit the timeline of the crime. Hunziker had stolen the money from the Committee while it still operated under the auspices of the LCC's London War Pensions Committee and thus had no connection to Poplar Borough Council. Reverend Kitcat attended the trial and 'felt the keenest of indignation as I listened in court to [the defence barrister's] speech, with its disgraceful charges and innuendos … the suggestion that the affairs of the Committee are in chaos and that Mrs. Minnie Lansbury was responsible for any muddle is – consciously or unconsciously – a damnable lie.' These were strong words from a man of the cloth and a political opponent of Minnie's, but Kitcat had reason to be confident in Minnie's integrity: 'As Chairman of the Committee I have the right and the knowledge to speak: and I say that the whole Committee and its officers owe Mrs. Lansbury a great debt of gratitude for her untiring, orderly, and self-sacrificing assistance.' Even the *East London Observer* took a dim view of the defence case, editorialising that 'It is all very well to drag in the Lansburys. Any stick is good enough for some people to beat the rebellious Borough Council.'[356]

Minnie wrote to the *Daily Herald*,[357] expressing her personal indifference at Wild's accusations against her but making the point that 'to use a position of privilege to make manifestly untrue statements is not very courageous, but to do so when the person slandered is in prison is particularly cowardly, and, I should have thought, a departure from the traditions of the Bar.' She explained in the letter that the government had only recently dissolved the London War Pensions Committee and transferred the duties and the staff of its sub-committees to local authorities. It was then that Poplar had become suspicious of Hunziker and had initiated an investigation which resulted in her prosecution.

---

[355] *Daily Herald*, 22nd September 1921.

[356] 3rd October 1921.

[357] 23rd September 1921.

'The misappropriation of money ... took place before her transference to Poplar': rather than causing or facilitating the fraud, Poplar Council had discovered and stopped it. Minnie concluded:

> I think, therefore, that no one but an advocate hard-pressed for a defence could argue that the governors of Poplar did not exercise proper supervision. Whether there was proper supervision originally is another matter. My experience in Poplar in connection with this case leads me to believe that there is much that is seriously wrong with the system of financial checks prescribed by the Ministry. My conviction is strengthened by the reports of similar frauds and similar prosecutions which have from time to time appeared in the press. This is a matter which should be investigated by the Treasury. A demand for such an inquiry will be made as soon as Parliament meets.

Despite the evidence and extent of her fraud, the court decided merely to bind Hunziker over, in other words to tell her to behave herself. The *Daily Herald*[358] could not help but draw attention to the double standards at work, suggesting that 'had [the Poplar councillors] been gentlemen and embezzlers they would perhaps have been bound over. But being by universal acknowledgement devoted public servants, whose only crime was to feed the hungry and visit the sick and refuse to rob the poor by unjust taxes, they are thrown into gaol. British justice must stink in the nostrils of every honest man.' Even the *East London Observer* expressed its concern that this outcome appeared to substantiate socialist agitation that there was one law for the rich, another for the poor.

For while a person guilty of defrauding the poor and the public remained at liberty, borough councillors remained imprisoned for defending those who elected them. Solidarity and action would be crucial to determining what would happen next.

Showing Solidarity

From the start of their champions' incarceration, Poplar's people loudly demonstrated their support. On Wednesday 7th September, five thousand people marched the seven miles from Poplar to Minnie's new place of residence in Holloway, where they were joined by a further three

---

[358] 24th September 1921.

thousand who had marched from Islington and St. Pancras. It was, according to the *Daily Herald*,[359] 'the most remarkable demonstration of loyalty to the cause of the suffering poor ever seen in the East End':

> Starting from central points in the different boroughs, the marchers carried banners demanding the instant release of the Poplar Councillors, and, to the tune of 'For he's a jolly good fellow', they sang, 'We all are going to Holloway … and you can come as well.' …

> Some of the women carried little children, and when Councillor Sumner invited them to place the little ones on the *Daily Herald* car, many accepted with gratitude.

Marching back to Poplar, the councillors' supporters shouted 'Will we pay the extra rates?' 'No!'

Poplar set up a Tenants' Defence League on the day after Minnie's arrest, organising local residents to protect their rights from exploitative landlords and extortionate rates. People joined in their hundreds, queueing at its headquarters at 141 Bow Road which it shared with the maintenance fund for the councillors' wives and children. Tenants' Defence League rallies attracted huge crowds of supporters to Poplar Town Hall and Bromley Public Hall.

Poplar's supporters gave money, distributed leaflets and sent letters of support to the councillors and of protest to the Home Secretary. And they marched – to the prisons, to Trafalgar Square, to local landmarks such as Bow Obelisk and Poplar Dock Gates. Labour and trade union bodies local to Brixton and Holloway took responsibility for ensuring a regular presence outside the prisons. Islington Labour Party and the local branch of the National Union of Railwaymen led numerous gatherings at Holloway, designed to keep the prisoners' spirits up, keep pressure on the authorities, and keep supporters mobilised.

In many other London boroughs, supporters flocked to public meetings and to town hall public galleries to demand that their councils take the same action as Poplar had. Despite their popular support, Minnie and her colleagues were still taking action in isolation. Sylvia Pankhurst asked rhetorically, 'Will it continue: will the Labour movement, will powerful organised Labour, permit this sentence to be served by 30 Labour councillors?' and insisted that 'Poplar should not be struggling alone.'[360] Pointing out that half the London boroughs had

---

[359] 8th September 1921.

Labour-majority councils, Sylvia particularly highlighted Bethnal Green and its Mayor Joe Vaughan, a Communist Party member who had represented the party at the recent Third International Congress in Moscow. When, she asked, would they take their stand alongside Poplar?

A mass meeting in Shoreditch urged its borough council to refuse to levy the precepts to the central authorities, but its Labour group rejected this call by one vote.[361] Battersea Borough Council defeated a proposal to do the same as Poplar also by just one vote.[362] Hackney Council, led by Mayor Herbert Morrison, voted to not even co-operate with Poplar in holding a protest for rates equalisation, lest it associate them with Poplar's defiance of the law. Hackney's Liberals wanted to back Poplar's protest, but their own Labour colleagues did not!

Herbert Morrison thoroughly disapproved of Minnie and her colleagues' law-breaking. He had spent much of the summer ensuring that the London Labour Party, of which he was Secretary, did as much as possible to dissuade other Labour councils in London from following the same course of action as Poplar. But now that Poplar's confrontational course was winning so much support, he was desperate to draw attention away from it and towards an alternative, law-abiding approach to tackling the government over unemployment. So Morrison led a group of his fellow London Labour Mayors to see the Prime Minister. But Lloyd George was not in London but convalescing in Gairloch, in the Scottish Highlands. The Mayors trekked to Scotland, tracked down the PM, and got nothing from him.

Back in London, two of Poplar's neighbouring boroughs had finally started out on the Poplar road to defiance. Three weeks after the Poplar arrests had begun – and seven months after Poplar's decision to defy the law – Bethnal Green's Labour councillors decided, after 'much heated discussion', to propose to the Council that it refuse to collect the precepts. The Council agreed.[363] By that time, Stepney Borough Council had also voted to threaten to stop paying the precepts, at a meeting on

[360] *Workers' Dreadnought*, 10th September 1921.

[361] *Hackney and Kingsland Gazette*, 16th September; *Daily Herald*, 8th September 1921.

[362] *Daily Herald*, 1st October 1921.

[363] Bethnal Green Borough Council Labour Group minutes, TH/8214, 31st August 1921 and 21st September 1921.

12th September at which only 'the most fiery half' of the councillors was present.[364] It turned that threat into a decision on 5th October, agreeing with twenty-nine votes in favour and twenty-one against to set the rates minus the precepts.

By this time, Minnie Lansbury had made very clear which strategy she preferred.

Action and Analysis

In an interview published in *The Communist* newspaper on Saturday 1st October, Minnie contrasted two tactics on offer and was definite about which she saw as the way to win:

> We in gaol want to say right out that we don't care twopence for Morrison's trips to Scotland to talk to the Premier. There is only one way in which the official Labour movement can help us, and that is the way Bethnal Green has chosen. It is – going to gaol in the same manner. Even Morrison knows that, at the bottom of his little heart.

Minnie also expressed her frustration at the lack of concrete action from the labour movement establishment, although she understood that it was in its nature to hold back rather than drive forward:

> We don't, in any case, rely particularly on the official Labour movement. We rely on the workers of Poplar, the unemployed, and even the small ratepayers. If the Poplar Publicity Committee has done nothing then they must just go ahead without it. Anyway – action.

Minnie's definition of the labour movement rank and file included 'small ratepayers' alongside wage workers and the jobless – a definition that placed her family in the labour movement economically as well as politically.

The Communist later asserted that Minnie 'was the only woman councillor with enough courage and clearheadedness to urge the workers to really strong action on the occasion of the arrests.'[365] Its interview with her revealed Minnie as thoughtful, knowledgeable, militant and sharp.

She spoke of her disappointment that the unemployed had not marched to the seat of government at Whitehall nor to the house of

[364] *East London Observer*, 7th September 1921.

[365] 7th January 1922.

190

Home Secretary Edward Shortt, believing that this would apply more pressure than marching to prisons and landmarks. She also showed that she had studied her movement's history in order to learn from it, telling her interviewer of an incident that took place three years before she was even born:

> In 1886 a crisis similar to this one, if less in intensity, was answered by a march from the East End up to Pall Mall, where the unemployed replied to jeers from the clubmen [members of gentlemen's clubs] by smashing the windows. They marched on up St. James' Street through Oxford Street, wrecking as they went. Then the Lord Mayor's Fund for the Unemployed, which had been vegetating at a wretchedly low figure, shot up twenty to thirty thousand pounds in one day, as a result of this exhibition of the unemployed's temper.

> I'm not saying that this should be done again to-day. I don't expect to dictate from prison. But I do say that something should be done and done at once.

Minnie's comments drew scorn from a regional newspaper, the *Yorkshire Post and Leeds Intelligencer*,[366] which presented her words as a sign of 'disillusion' among the Poplar councillors, suggesting that their strategy of going to prison as 'a pose of heroic martyrdom' was proving ineffective. Incorrectly referring to Minnie as George Lansbury's daughter, the paper declared that her proposal for militant action was a 'method of touting' that would only see more people imprisoned 'and assist nobody'. The *Post* praised Herbert Morrison's approach as 'far the better way'. Events would soon suggest otherwise.

The Impossible Becomes Possible

The more steadfast the councillors and the more negligent the government, the more public opinion swung behind the former and against the latter. On 10th September, the *East London Observer* observed that, 'It has dawned upon the London public that there is nothing clever or statesmanlike' in the councillors' imprisonment and added that 'anything more idiotic than the gaoling of Mrs. Cressall is inconceivable.'

Nellie Cressall was a month away from giving birth, and prison officials told her that they had been 'so overwhelmed with protests

---

[366] 4th October 1921.

against her incarceration and demands for her release that they could no longer keep her in prison.'[367] But Nellie did not want to break ranks. Suspecting an ulterior motive on the part of the authorities, she insisted on staying in Holloway with Minnie, Julia, Susan and Jennie. As the governor told her he had no choice, she asked him, 'You mean it is like an eviction?' and he replied, 'Yes.' Nellie carefully scrutinised her release papers and checked that there were no conditions attached before she signed them and, accompanied by a nurse, went home on Wednesday 21st September.

Free from prison, Nellie visited her husband George in Brixton Prison. She then spoke out about the cruelty of the prison system and the importance of securing her comrades' release. Nellie explained that Holloway's conditions for Poplar's woman prisoners were worse than Brixton's for its men: they had not been allowed to meet together in a large room as the men had; prison discipline was more rigorous; cell doors were shut for the night soon after six o'clock; and they exercised for only two hours each day. The authorities even kept the Poplar women away from the other women prisoners, lest they tell them of the injustice of imprisonment and encourage them to assert themselves. When they were in the hospital wing, Nellie, Minnie and Jennie had heard screaming from the women in the padded cells, so loud it had even drowned out the sound of a thunderstorm.

> 'Think of it, you mothers!', Nellie appealed to a women's meeting at Poplar Town Hall. 'Young girls, taken from a life of freedom and locked up in cells with doors as thick as the doors of a pawnbroker's safe! Can you wonder at them screaming themselves into madness?'[368]

The order for Nellie's release had come from the Official Solicitor, a little-known functionary whose duties included reporting on the condition of prisoners committed for contempt of court. A judge, and then the Home Office, endorsed the Official Solicitor's recommendation for her release, which the Home Office had probably asked for in the first place! Until then, the Home Office had insisted that it had no power to release the Poplar rebels. An 'impossible' action had become possible under the pressure of working-class militancy and steadfastness. Several more impossible developments were about to similarly become possible as Minnie and her fellow councillors pressed towards victory.

---

[367] History Group, Communist Party, 1953, p.9.

[368] *Daily Herald*, 22nd and 30th September 1921.

While Home Secretary Edward Shortt was responsible for the judicial process, the issue of rates inequality fell under the remit of his fellow Liberal, Health Secretary Alfred Mond. Described by George Lansbury as 'well fed, and with a bank balance supplied from the sweat and toil of thousands of workers',[369] Mond was known for his 'moroseness and gruff manner'[370] and had a family home called The Poplars which was a world away from the borough which shared its name. He had only recently become Health Minister after a five-year spell as Minister of Works, and his new post included responsibility for local government.

Looking for a way out of the difficulty that the troublesome councillors had caused him, Mond agreed to hold a conference to discuss changing the rating system, but thought that Minnie and the other councillors might attend it and then return to Holloway and Brixton prisons! He also reckoned that it was impossible to free the councillors unless they collected the rates and impossible to quickly introduce a law to make the rates more equal, because 'it is a big and complicated problem, which has been raised hundreds of times.'[371] This, of course, was precisely why Minnie and her comrades had taken direct action over the rates: because repeatedly raising the issue had got them nowhere. Mond suggested a Royal Commission to discuss rates reform, but having seen issue after issue kicked into the long grass of Royal Commissions, the *Daily Herald* dismissed this as 'a bad and time-worn joke'.

So the women stuck to their guns. When TUC General Council member (and future first Labour woman Cabinet member) Margaret Bondfield visited them in prison, they told her of their 'determination to fight to the end at no matter what cost.' They told Charles Key that 'they decline to take part in any conference or negotiations unless they can do so as free women. They prefer the alternative of continued imprisonment.'[372]

To decide its response to the government's proposals, Poplar Borough Council would have to meet with all its members present. This was another arrangement that the authorities had deemed impossible but which suddenly became possible – in this case, within

[369] *Daily Herald*, 11th February 1922.

[370] Bolitho, 1933, p.46.

[371] *Daily Herald*, 24th September 1921.

[372] *Daily Herald*, 26th September 1921.

just one day. The male councillors had been holding meetings practically every day since 11th September, first in George Lansbury's cell, then – after they objected that this was an unsuitable venue for a council meeting – in the prison's board room. From 23rd September the free councillors, including Nellie Cressall, joined them at these meetings, but still the imprisoned women councillors could not attend as the authorities deemed it impossible. Edgar Lansbury reported to the meeting on Monday 26th September that the authorities had also refused him permission to visit Minnie in Holloway to discuss the legal implications of the comments made about her in the Hunziker fraud trial: again, the Home Secretary had 'no power to grant the application.'

But the very next day, the impossible became possible as Minnie and the other women prisoners were driven to Brixton prison for a council meeting with their colleagues. This had been arranged with the help of LCC Labour group leader Harry Gosling, who later wrote that, 'They were counted out of Holloway in proper form, and ... I suppose for the first time women prisoners were counted into Brixton prison.'[373] Eleven London Labour Mayors also went to Brixton to take part in the meeting, and at the gate, met Minnie and the others, 'who had been brought from their cells in motor-cars, attended by wardresses'. George Lansbury wrote that, 'we were all glad to see the Mayors on Tuesday, and were more glad than any of us could express to see our women comrades. It was a very enthusiastic, cheery gathering of husbands, wives, comrades and friends.' Gosling recalled that, 'We sat long after ten o'clock that night considering the position, with the warders grimly stationed on the other side of the door.' They agreed to insist on the councillors' unconditional release before any conference.[374]

Poplar Council met again at Brixton Prison on Friday 30th September, after which a 'huge crowd gathered at the entrance to the prison to cheer the women Councillors as they left to return to Holloway.'[375] Over the next few days, the London County Council and Metropolitan Asylums Board agreed carefully-worded resolutions that they would not object to the councillors' release. Thousands of people

[373] Gosling, 1927, p.99 – his observation was not quite right, as Brixton had previously been a women's prison.

[374] *Daily Herald*, 28th September 1921.

[375] *Daily Herald*, 1st October 1921.

demonstrated their support for Poplar's rebels at and outside these meetings, targeting the seats of power as Minnie had recommended. At the LCC meeting, a woman heckler referred to the continuing imprisonment as 'torturing women'.[376]

As a warm September moved into a hot October, the temperature kept rising in the fight for work or full maintenance. Mond offered emergency legislation for the temporary equalisation of London rates – a measure that he had insisted just a few days previously could not be hurried. On Unemployment Sunday – 9th October – hundreds of thousands of people joined demonstrations around the country, and over that weekend, 'Enthusiasm for the Release of the Prisoners Movement reached fever point.'[377] Over five thousand people squeezed into Bow Baths Hall for a meeting which hundreds more could not fit into, necessitating overflow meetings in several adjoining streets. A public swimming pool temporarily converted to use as a hall was a large and loud venue: hundreds of seats lined in rows faced a stage with heavy curtains from where speakers projected their voices into a chamber more used to the sound of waves and splashes. Poplar Town Hall hosted a similar meeting, and many street corners in Poplar, Bromley and Bow saw impromptu gatherings.

Even Poplar's schoolchildren had joined in the movement, writing letters of support to their imprisoned councillors. On 12th October, the councillors wrote back together, each appending their name. Their letter explained the action they had taken against 'bad, wicked laws' and that they 'shall not do what the Judges told us we must do until Poplar gets money from the rich to help the poor.' Then it urged the children not to rush into the armed forces or domestic service, to join a trade union when they went to work, to attend branch meetings and to learn about the labour movement. It concluded that, 'Labour is the source of all wealth whether it is labour by hand or brain; it is the workers who should enjoy leisure, pleasure, holidays and all the good things of life ... We hope all you boys and girls will live to see the day when there will be no rich or poor, no paupers or millionaires.'

Minnie and her colleagues were themselves about to taste some of the good things of life: freedom and victory.

---

[376] *Daily Herald*, 5th October 1921.

[377] *Daily Herald*, 10th October 1921.

Three Cheers[378]

When a government finds itself in a tight spot, it will conjure a procedure to help it to get out. So it was that, under the irresistible pressure of working-class mobilisation in support of obstinate councillors, the government found a way to release Minnie and the other Poplar rebels from prison. For the details of the manoeuvring, see my book about the Poplar rebellion, *Guilty and Proud of it*.[379] Suffice to say, the prisoners submitted a carefully-worded statement, the lawyers presented an awkward case, and the court issued the release orders on 12th October on grounds that one newspaper described as 'not exactly plausible … [but] attractive,'[380] to allow the councillors to attend a conference on rates equalisation as free men and women.

With the release order in his hand, Harry Thompson set off to Holloway, accompanied by Councillor and Mrs. Key, Fulham Mayor Robert Gentry, Labour LCC member Harry Gosling, and a *Daily Herald* representative. Arriving at the prison, Thompson handed over the order, and Gentry and Gosling – both being magistrates – were allowed into the courtyard. The *Herald* representative reported that, 'A few minutes later … we thought we could hear the voice of Minnie Lansbury, but it was more than half an hour before the Councillors emerged from the grim building.'

Just after five o'clock, Susan Lawrence came out of prison, and Mrs. Key rushed forward and presented her with a bouquet of flowers. While they were exchanging greetings, Minnie Lansbury walked out, calling out 'Hooray!' as she moved towards the group that had come to collect her. 'Hooray!' she called again, this time to a group of workers who were carrying out repairs to the prison. Minnie was also given flowers, as was Julia Scurr, who came out soon after. Jennie Mackay was already out on parole following the death of her father, and would now not have to return to prison that evening as previously ordered. Minnie explained that the half-hour delay had been because they had been 'waiting for their money'. The four cross-London authorities were, of course, still waiting for theirs.

The three women councillors had a lot of luggage to be brought from their cells, so the prison authorities allowed the Mayor's motor-car into

---

[378] References in this section are from the *Daily Herald*, 13th October 1921, unless otherwise specified.

[379] Booth, 2009.

[380] *Dundee Courier*, 13th October 1921.

The councillors and their supporters outside Brixton prison immediately following their release (Minnie: front standing row, holding flowers)

the courtyard, where suitcases and books were loaded onto its roof and the women jumped in. Then came Minnie's third 'Hooray!' as she asked whether they would go straight to Brixton and was answered that they would. A photograph[381] shows Minnie and Julia leaning out of the car's windows, both holding their bouquets and smiling. Although the newsprint image is not very sharp, it looks to me that Minnie had lost weight in prison, and appeared pale and tired.

On their arrival at Brixton, Thompson again handed over the release order, and Minnie and her companions heard the sound of cheering and the singing of The Red Flag from inside the prison building. At around ten past six, the twenty-five men councillors stepped through the gates of Brixton prison to freedom. Minnie and Julia greeted their husbands and their comrades, and joined in the singing and cheering. A great 'team photograph' captured the councillors, their lawyer and other helpers posed outside the prison wall. Harry Thompson and Edgar Lansbury appear to be the only two men without moustaches!

Cars drove the councillors back to Poplar, and when they reached the borough boundary at around seven o'clock, a procession of thousands welcomed them home.[382] A brass band headed a throng of Poplar people carrying red flags and Sinn Fein banners, indicating both the support of the local Irish community and the drawing of links between the

[381] *Leeds Mercury*, 14th October 1921.

[382] Tapper, 1960, pp.64-5.

respective struggles. The cars took them to the Marches' house, from where the Irish band led each of them home in turn. Pipes, drums, music, cheering and celebration filled the poverty-stricken borough of Poplar, knowing that it had won a significant victory in its fight against distress.

Minnie Lansbury was back home at Wellington Cottage with her husband Edgar.

A 'Welcome Home' meeting the next day was followed by a mass meeting the day after, with Poplar Town Hall packed from floor to gallery, its two smaller halls also full, a huge gathering outside and even people standing on the outside ledges. Minnie received another bouquet of flowers, but was not among the speakers. The climax of the celebrations was a half-mile long procession to Victoria Park on Sunday 16th October, with five bands and fifty banners. As Mayor Sam March observed, 'After a six weeks' rest at the "Hotel de Brixton", most people would get slighted or scorned. Few coming out of prison would have so wonderful a welcome.'[383]

The promised conference began on 17th October – the Monday after the councillors' release – and agreed a radical reorganisation of the rating system. Daily meetings followed at the Ministry of Health, with Poplar, Stepney and Bethnal Green councils still refusing to levy the precepts until the t's were crossed and the i's dotted. The eventual outcome saw the grant for workhouse inmates increased from five pence to one shilling and sixpence per day, and the cost of outdoor relief pooled across London, with the common fund meeting payments to the destitute up to scales set by the Minister of Health. Poplar would benefit by around a quarter of a million pounds per year, and other poor boroughs would benefit too, although Herbert Morrison and a few others were not happy with the outcome, wanting a different formula for a victory which they claimed to have won but which everyone else knew was Poplar's. Richer boroughs would have to dig deeper into their well-filled pockets to help their poorer neighbours. Those who lived off the labours of working-class Londoners would finally have to contribute to their upkeep when they fell on hard times.

Even the politically-hostile *East London Observer* had to admit that, 'The only people who came out of this with flying colours and the bands playing [literally, in this case] are the Poplar Councillors, who have

[383] *Daily Herald*, 15th and 17th October 1921.

fought clean and straight throughout. They had the courage of their convictions and they have won, after great personal hardship.'[384]

Their victory sealed, but anticipating more battles ahead, Minnie Lansbury and her husband could take a break. It was not a typical East End working-class holiday, but a trip to the Swiss Alps.

Through an Oven to the Mountains[385]

It was probably in the latter half of October when Edgar and Minnie Lansbury set off on their trek. The first leg took them from London to Paris, with Minnie suffering acutely on the boat crossing the English Channel but unable to relieve her sickness by actually vomiting. 'Imagine the consequences,' Edgar wrote to his mother, 'I won't harrow your feelings further!' Perhaps this was evidence of prison having physically weakened Minnie; if so, it would have a much more serious impact when winter came.

For now, it was an exceptionally hot October in both Britain and continental Europe. When the travelling couple arrived in Paris, they became separated from their companions, and journeyed across the city in large buses, an experience that Edgar likened to 'driving through an oven with a big fire in the grate.' Paris was then at its peak size, with a population of nearly three million and enjoying the start of an economic boom following wartime hardship and post-war slump. Their buses passed through the Place de la Concorde and the Champs Elysees, but it was too dark to properly see what Edgar rather dismissively referred to as 'the things which students and fanatics get excited about.' When they arrived at their departure station, they found it 'worse than an Oven.' What happened next suggests an approach to personal difficulties similar to their uncompromising, irreverent and effective approach to municipal problems:

> We drifted about trying to find our train, & after various suggestions about staying in Paris the night, & sleeping on the platforms, Minnie & I made a dive for a first class compartment & swore we wouldn't move for anybody at all. We were rewarded for our determination, for after being shunted up & down for about an hour, we found ourselves moving out of Paris.

---

[384] *Daily Herald*, 15th October 1921.

[385] Letter, Edgar Lansbury to Bessie Lansbury, late 1921, undated.

They 'settled down to a jolly good sleep' as the Paris, Lyon and Mediterranean Railway carried them to Pontarlier, a town of around ten thousand inhabitants near the border with Switzerland. From there, the Swiss Railway took them on a journey of over eight-and-a-half hours through 'some of the grandest scenery [Edgar had] ever imagined let alone seen.'

> We simply wended our way slowly up towards the source of the Rhône, through narrow gorges, fast sparkling cascades, fast roaring torrents, & through beautiful valleys, over the sides of which the Swiss peasantry have planted row after row of vines.

Their journey took them past Lake Geneva – which Edgar described as 'a splendid stretch of water, blue as a summer sky, and clear as crystal' – to Stalden, a town of six hundred people nestled at the foot of the Dom mountain, part of the Mischabelhörner, the highest massif lying entirely in Switzerland. This was as far as the train could take them, so they disembarked and ate a good dinner. But their final destination was still fifteen miles away – 'out of civilisation's reach', wrote Edgar – along a route impassable by any wheeled vehicle. So they walked.

Although their four-hour hike was all uphill, Edgar and Minnie found it 'magnificent', Edgar explaining that 'The air is so fine that you don't feel the strain at all.' They were surrounded by snow-capped mountains, the snow having retreated to a much higher level than usual due to the hot weather. Their path wound alongside the river Rhône, never straying more than thirty yards from its banks. The river 'simply hurls along destroying everything in its path & even the rocks that got thrown down from the mountain don't hold out against its fury for more than, say a dozen centuries.'

Finally, they reached their destination: a hotel in the village of Saas-Grund at the source of the Rhône. What they did on their holiday we don't know, as only Edgar's letter home shortly after their arrival survives. Minnie's husband wrote detailed, descriptive, chatty letters, ending with love to his family from his wife and himself. If Minnie wrote to her own parents or siblings, then those letters are no longer to be found.

Soon enough, the adventurers were back in Poplar, and back in the business of battling on behalf of the working-class people who elected them.

Back to Business

With its members no longer residing at His Majesty's pleasure, Poplar Borough Council returned to its municipal business.

After voting itself a week's break, the Council returned to its own council chamber. Its first meeting back saw the councillors thank the people of Poplar, reflect on their time in prison, and record their objections to the government's proposed scheme of grants to provide work for the workless. The women councillors were presented with yet more bouquets of flowers, this time by a deputation of women from Poplar, Bow and Bromley.

The Council formally entered the records of its meetings in Brixton prison into the minutes, and re-elected to its committees those aldermen and councillors who had taken leave to go to prison. Minnie Lansbury returned to the Public Health Committee and the Maternity and Child Welfare Committee, but not to the Tuberculosis Care Committee, from which she had resigned on the day of her arrest. The Maternity and Child Welfare Committee reported spending £1,319 on free milk for babies and nursing mothers during the eight weeks up to 3rd September, a period when the committee's members were in courts and campaign meetings but still looking after the people who relied on them. Alfred Mond, wishing to avoid another fight with belligerent socialist councillors, dropped his plan to slash the government subsidy for the free milk to just seven-and-a-half per cent and pledged to keep it at fifty per cent for the rest of the financial year.[386]

Sam March presented his review of the Council's work during his year as Mayor. He would soon be replaced by Charlie Sumner, as Poplar continued its practice of electing a new Mayor each year. This policy, designed to enhance democracy and prevent entrenchment of power, was unusual even among Labour councils. Poplar's neighbours Bethnal Green and Shoreditch both re-elected their Labour Mayors, Joe Vaughan and William Girling respectively. It is perhaps not surprising that his year as Poplar Mayor had left sixty-one-year-old March in need of a rest, and on doctor's orders, he checked into a convalescent home for a month's recuperation.[387] The London Labour Party's Executive included in its conference report its wish 'that those among [the Poplar councillors] whose health has been impaired by incarceration may

---

[386] *East London Observer*, 22nd October and 5th November 1921; *Daily Herald*, 22nd October 1921.

[387] *East London Observer*, 5th November 1921.

speedily be restored, so that they may continue their work of devotion and service for the poor of London.' Prison had taken its toll on many of Poplar's 'Fighting Thirty'.

Other Council positions also changed hands. The Municipal Alliance's Clifford Knightbridge resigned as alderman, perhaps not having the stomach for years of opposition that Sumner, George Lansbury and others had shown before him. The Council appointed Helen Mackay to replace him, increasing the representation of both Labour and women by one. Labour candidate James Hunter won a by-election to replace Labour's John Clifford as councillor for Bow West, after Clifford had tendered his resignation (along with a postal order for one shilling) at the height of the summer's legal drama.

By now, winter was arriving, bringing with it a return of the influenza pandemic which had caused such a heavy death toll at the end of the war, having killed nearly a quarter of a million UK residents.

Chapter 7 – Loss, Legacy and Lessons

A Killer Returns

The 'Spanish flu' virus that broke out in 1918 had killed some fifty million people, three to four times as many as the war had killed (although, unlike the 'world' war, the 'flu pandemic actually affected the whole world). Unusually for 'flu, it caused a significant number of deaths among young adults. The pandemic came in three waves and then subsided, only to return in the following winters. In each of these returns, the death rate among young adults was lower than previously until, by the third recurrence in the winter of 1921/22, it was back to its usual very low level.

So it was telling that having gone through every post-war winter unscathed, Minnie Lansbury caught, and was so severely affected by, influenza at an age when in full health she could be expected to shrug it off. But she was not in full health: she was suffering the effects of six weeks in a prison described by one of her fellow councillors as a 'hell-hole'.[388]

Minnie fell ill in the middle of December 1921. Having attended the Poplar Borough Council meeting on Thursday 15th December, she and Edgar both missed the following week's meeting, which agreed to send to her 'an expression of the regret and sympathy of the Council at her absence, by reason of illness, with their best wishes for her speedy recovery.'

Minnie was cared for at home by Lucy Cole, who had visited her and Edgar every week during their time in prison. But her health worsened, and influenza developed into pneumonia. 'Christmas was a sad time at Wellington Cottage,' the *Daily Herald* later explained.[389] The council meeting on Thursday 29th December noted that Minnie was now 'far from well'.

On New Year's Eve, Minnie seemed to be getting better, and her family and friends hoped that she might recover. However, the next day – the first of the new year – her condition deteriorated again. Lying in bed, she asked in a whisper whether the children had had their New Year party, and smiled when she heard their happy voices though her window as they made their way home.[390]

---

[388] Councillor Jack Wooster, reported in the *Daily Herald*, 10th October 1921.

[389] 7th January 1922.

At around quarter to six in the evening of Sunday 1st January 1922, Minnie Lansbury died, aged just thirty-two.

Broken Hearts and Red Rosettes

On that New Year's Day in the evening, a thousand Poplar residents were seeing in 1922 as they meant to go on. They were at Bow Baths Hall, meeting and campaigning with Poplar's Labour councillors, celebrating their recent achievements and preparing themselves for further battles against poverty, unemployment and government neglect. But their discussions were interrupted when Mayor Charlie Sumner announced that Minnie Lansbury had died. 'The audience for a moment was stricken silent ... then out of the silence came a woman's cry of grief, followed by the weeping of many women.'[391] For a few minutes, the large crowd stood in soundless tribute. Then the meeting adjourned and the crowd dispersed in sadness.

Three days later, tens of thousands of people filled the streets of Bow

Mourners carry Minnie's coffin past St Mary's Church on Bow Road

[390] Letter, Edgar Lansbury to memorial meeting.

[391] *Daily Herald*, 2nd January 1922.

Poster advertising Minnie's
memorial meeting

for Minnie's funeral, a huge and impressive event reported by national newspapers from the left-wing *Daily Herald* to the right-wing *Daily Telegraph*. The people and organisations who brought themselves, their banners and their floral tributes to Minnie's funeral told of the social and political movements in which she had lived and died. A large crowd wearing red flowers and badges gathered outside Minnie's house in Wellington Road before the funeral cortège set off, headed by five hundred unemployed East Enders. The Boys' Band of the Shenfield School – run by the Poplar guardians of the poor – marched and played ahead of her coffin, which was draped in purple and carried in relays by Poplar councillors and ex-servicemen. A carful of memorial flowers included bouquets from council staff, the Women's Guild, the East London Labour Orchestra, Poplar Trades Council, local trade union branches, Labour Party branches and the Communist Party.

The Reverend Solomon Lipson of the Hammersmith United Synagogue conducted a short service outside her house, possibly chosen because the west London synagogues tended to be more tolerant and inclusive of Jews who did not follow all the Jewish religious rules and customs than those in East London, possibly because he was a chaplain to the armed forces and therefore aware of Minnie's work and reputation among former soldiers. Four Poplar councillors carried Minnie's coffin our of the house, from where it was carried in relays through Bow. Poplar's Town Clerk and the Mayors of Poplar, Bethnal Green and Stepney walked behind the coffin. Thousands of women, ex-servicemen, trade unionists and unemployed people marched in tribute, and when they reached the borough boundary at Bow Bridge and a motor hearse took the coffin to the City of London Cemetery, they 'fell out' of the

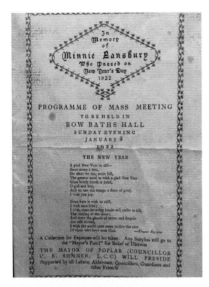

Programme for Minnie's memorial meeting

procession and lined the roadway.

None of Minnie's family or Labour colleagues felt able to speak at her funeral, so Reverend Kitcat had what he called the 'great privilege' of speaking about Minnie's life. He described the three qualities that most impressed him about Minnie: 'her brilliant intellectual power … her extraordinary liberal mind and generosity of disposition … [and] her love of justice, and the depth of her sympathy, for suffering and sorrow.'

The Christian Minister then handed back to the United Synagogue rabbi to inter the ashes of the non-religious Jew in the Jewish cemetery in East Ham. Her father-in-law observed that, 'Minnie was of the Jewish faith, but the glory of Minnie was that she belonged to them all. Sects and creeds and parties, in death could not divide them.'[392] In death, she united those of various religions and none in their grief, to the extent that her family's religion broke its own rules to allow her cremated remains to be buried in its holy ground.

A week after Minnie Lansbury's death, a memorial meeting packed into Bow Baths Hall. Councillor Sam March said that 'no one could say Minnie's stature was large, but all could say her heart was large'. Her Poplar Labour colleagues paid tribute; one read a letter from her husband Edgar, who was still too debilitated by grief to attend; a collection was held for the Mayor's Fund to relieve economic distress; and the crowd sang socialist anthems.

Cruelty to the Survivor

Francis Meynell and his wife Hilda were staying with their close friends Minnie and Edgar Lansbury over New Year 1922, while they looked for

[392] Memorial meeting, 8th January 1922.

a house of their own in London. Nearly fifty years later, Francis recalled that Minnie's death was the only one that he had personally witnessed during his life, and wrote that, 'Its cruelty to the survivor rather than to the dying bit into me.'[393]

London's East End was gripped by the shock and tragedy of losing their comrade at such a young age. George Lansbury wrote that, 'Minnie, in her 32 years, crammed double that number of years' work compared with what many of us are able to accomplish.' Tribute after tribute lauded her public service, not as a philanthropist but as a suffrage campaigner, working-class champion and rebel. *The Communist* eulogised that she 'had for a long time worked in Poplar on behalf of the left wing of the labour movement,' was 'much loved' and would be 'sorely missed.'[394] George Lansbury said that, 'Although big men carried her out, no big men could intimidate her.'[395] The *Daily Herald* wrote that Minnie had 'won a great reputation throughout London for her work in connection with the War Pensions Committee,' which had won her the epithet of 'the Soldiers' and Sailors' friend'. She was a fighter against the political and economic system who also looked after its victims.

Alongside a brief, factual obituary, the *Jewish Chronicle*[396] carried a notice recording that Minnie was 'Deeply mourned and sadly missed by her broken-hearted husband, parents, brothers, and sisters, brothers-in-law, nephews, and nieces, relatives and friends.' A further notice memorialised 'our darling auntie Minnie, [who] was called to heaven but will never be forgotten by Ruth and Harold Lazarus.' Young Ruth and Harold, just nine and five years old at the time, were true to their word. They preserved material about Minnie's life, and told her story to the next generation – Harold's daughter Selina. And in 2008 at the grand old age of ninety-two, Harold spoke at the rededication of the newly-restored Minnie Lansbury Memorial Clock on Bow Road. At the time of their aunt's death, Ruth and Harold lived with their parents, Minnie's older sister Selina and her husband Abraham Lazarus, in a block of flats in St. Martin's Lane in London's West End. Her sister Leah was now Mrs. Longman and lived in Amhurst Road in Hackney. Minnie's other

---

[393] 1971, p.134.

[394] 7th January 1922.

[395] Memorial meeting, 8th January, reported in *East London Advertiser*, 14th January 1922.

[396] 6th January 1922.

sisters, Kate and Ray, never married, and often talked to their great-niece Selina about their 'feisty' sister. The youngest of Minnie's siblings, Hyman, enjoyed life as something of a 'man about town'.[397]

Minnie's family sat *shiva* for her at her parents' house at 28 Golders Manor Drive in Golders Green, north-west London, Here, Minnie's father Isaac died just months later. Her brother Louis succumbed to the 'white plague', tuberculosis, a couple of years after.

Edgar Lansbury's loss was nearly unbearable, and he was deeply unhappy for some considerable time. Eventually, nearly three years later, he found happiness again, marrying Moyna McGill, an American actor and socialist with whom he went on to have three children: Angela, Edgar and Bruce, all of whom achieved success in theatre and film.

Movement and Martyrdom

Poplar had to continue its work and its battles with the government without Minnie Lansbury.

There would be fights over the level of relief given by the Guardians to the poor and over the wages paid by the Council to its workers. Edgar Lansbury would play a leading role especially in the former, as he became Chair of the Poplar Board of Guardians. In 1925, he would serve as Mayor of Poplar, but thereafter become less involved in politics. He died of stomach cancer in 1935.

Poplar Borough Council appointed Muriel Lester to replace Minnie as Alderman. Lester was a shipbuilding heiress, a Baptist pacifist and socialist who had moved from the prosperous suburb of Loughton to run Kingsley Hall in Bow with her sister Doris. The council also appointed Muriel to the Maternity and Child Welfare Committee, which elected her as its chair. Some sources[398] claim that it was under Lester's leadership that Poplar began providing services such as free milk to babies and nursing mothers, but we have seen that this work was already well under way when Minnie Lansbury was on the committee and Charles Key was its chair.

As the *Daily Herald* noted, 'For years ... [Minnie] had devoted herself voluntarily to the betterment of the conditions under which the poor ... live. By her death the Labour Movement and the Communist Party sustain a great loss.'[399] The movement which Minnie served and

[397] Interview, Selina Gellert with author.

[398] eg. McSwain, 2008.

championed extended beyond the borough boundary of Poplar. Her reputation across London was emphasised by the message of condolence from the London Labour Party and the attendance at her funeral of London Trades Council Secretary Duncan Carmichael. Her still wider recognition saw reports of her death in national newspapers and letters of condolence from far and wide. Many stressed her role in both her local working-class community and in the labour movement.

New Poplar Mayor Charlie Sumner, presiding over her memorial meeting, said that 'those whose pleasure it had been to work with Minnie Lansbury, those who had cause to make application to her, would realise that they had lost one of their best friends. She had gone like many more in the labour movement, she had sacrificed her life for the people she loved.'[400] He was alluding to what many of Minnie's friends and comrades believed: that 'flu and pneumonia had been able to kill her only because prison had weakened her. Minnie's sister-in-law Jessie Lansbury frequently and angrily said that 'they' had murdered her.[401] Councillor Thomas Blacketer wrote that Minnie had 'died for the cause' and blamed her imprisonment.[402] Muriel Lester's biographer Seth Kove wrote that Minnie's death 'accentuated awareness of state violence against those seeking justice for workers and the poor at home and abroad.'[403] And George Lansbury attributed the early deaths of Councillors Julia Scurr, James Rugless, Charlie Sumner and Joe O'Callaghan, as well as Minnie, to their time in prison.[404] When *The Times* had derided the Poplar councillors for their 'martyrdom' and Minnie had refuted the allegation, probably neither had imagined that it would become so literally true.

Moreover, it may have been a martyrdom which the movement itself might have avoided. Speaking to the Universities Socialist Federation shortly after the councillors' release, Harry Thompson argued that if other councils had followed Poplar's lead when it first withheld the precepts, then 'no councillor would have gone to gaol.'[405] The London

---

[399] 2nd January 1922.

[400] *East London Advertiser*, 14th January 1922.

[401] Interview with author, Jessie's son Terry Lansbury.

[402] *Daily Herald*, 2nd January 1922.

[403] 2015, p.191.

[404] 1928, p.157.

[405] *Daily Herald*, 15th October 1922.

Trades Council had made a similar point before the councillors were imprisoned. Poplar had wanted to fight alongside other councils but had been willing to 'go it alone' when it had to. When solidarity from other councils eventually came, it tipped the scales towards victory. But when solidarity hesitates and falters, victory can be harder to attain and the price more severe than it needs to be.

Tributes to Minnie came from people connected with the various events and movements around which her life had centred: from suffragettes including Emmeline Pethick Lawrence; her old college friend Edith 'Deano' Hellowy; the Secretary of the Poplar War Pensions Committee; from Coborn School for Girls, where she first studied to be a teacher; from the Jewish and British left; from the Communist Party and individual communists including Sylvia Pankhurst.

Minnie Lansbury's life was shaped by the large-scale political events of her time. Tsarist antisemitism drove her family out of Polish Russia and caused her to be born in London's East End. The expansion of education for working-class children enabled her to become a school teacher. The lack of political rights for women restricted the role she could play in society. Religious and communal conservatism made her marriage an act of rebellion. The outbreak of war brought fear into her life and pressure onto her family. Post-war economic slump brought mass unemployment and destitution into her community.

But Minnie Lansbury's life was also shaped by the movements of resistance that she encountered and in which she involved herself. Socialists and trade unionists in London's East End organised and educated working-class people such as Minnie about the causes and remedies of their oppression, and the more progressive ones reached across the communal divide to unite immigrant Jews and native English. The East End suffragettes mobilised not just wealthy, disenfranchised ladies but working-class women like Minnie who wanted the vote not just for its own sake but to improve their social conditions. Among them, Minnie found others like her committed to both ameliorating the impact of war on working-class women and men and challenging the basis for war itself. Workers' revolution in her parents' home country offered inspiration, and less radical steps forward in Britain at least saw a mass-membership, trade-union-based Labour Party gain strength and influence. And in Poplar, years of socialist activism, of building strong roots and clear political stances, enabled Minnie to become part of a borough council that truly fought for the people who elected it.

Mourners at Minnie's memorial event sang 'Hear a Word' by the late East London socialist William Morris, a secular hymn for the dead:

Some had name and fame and honour
Learned they were and wise and strong
Some were nameless, poor, unlettered,
Weak in all but grief and wrong
Named and nameless all live in us;
One and all they lead us yet,
Every pain to count for nothing.
Every sorrow to forget.

Minnie Lansbury was both 'named' and 'nameless'. She was not born with the name Lansbury, nor was she born into a propertied family like some better-remembered suffragettes. Born into an unknown and displaced family, she earned her name and reputation by her work, her kindness, her solidarity, her revolutionary commitment and her sacrifice. She gained national attention in her death and in the dramatic events of the last four months of her life. But this had grown from the deep roots she had planted in the community and the movement which had nurtured her.

None of us chooses the events that happen around us, whether close by or far away. But we do choose how we respond to those events, and whether and how we try to direct the future. Minnie Lansbury was the person she was because of the circumstances in which she lived, but also because the choices she made – fundamentally, the choice not to simply accept those circumstances but to fight to change them.

What If?

We can ask ourselves: what if? What if the Glassmans had not fled Zakroczym, or had fled to somewhere other than London's East End? What if Minnie had chosen – or drifted into – an occupation other than teaching? What if there had not been a local suffragette organisation that welcomed working-class women?

What if Minnie had come across only those labour movement figures who were hostile to Jewish immigration? Fortunately, other labour movement figures welcomed immigrants, and the movement gained many great activists from the ranks of immigrant families: indeed, two of Minnie's fellow imprisoned women councillors were also the daughters of immigrants, Julia Scurr of Irish parents and Jennie Mackay of an Italian father.

What if Minnie had not married Edgar Lansbury? The *Daily Herald*'s tribute to her described how her influence in Poplar had grown steadily 'since her marriage with Councillor Edgar Lansbury', and it may have been more difficult for a working-class woman to rise to prominence in the labour movement, or in politics more widely, were she not married to a prominent political man. Moreover, although her particular marriage challenged convention, the fact that she married was a choice to conform. There were others at the time who took more rebellious routes, for example living with (male or female) partners, or having a child without marrying as Sylvia Pankhurst did.

Probably the most significant 'What if?', though, is 'What if she had lived?'. Poplar Labour lost many of its key figures during the 1920s, and by the end of the decade, it had lost much of the popular respect and participation it had enjoyed at the start. Perhaps if Minnie had lived longer, she might have prevented that decline and her husband might have remained active in socialist politics for longer. Might Minnie Lansbury have gone on to become an MP, as several of her Poplar council colleagues – John Scurr, Susan Lawrence, Charles Key, Dave Adams and George Lansbury – did? It seems clear that she had the ability and the political commitment to do so. But Chris Sumner, grandson of Poplar councillors Charlie Sumner and Albert Easteal, believes that Minnie was too principled and uncompromising for mainstream politics.[406]

Minnie had been a member of both the Labour and Communist Parties, but in a series of votes during the 1920s, Labour eventually barred communists from Labour membership. Which would Minnie have chosen? Would her revolutionary zeal have kept her in the Communist Party despite its political deterioration, or would she have taken the same path as friends and comrades including Raymond Postgate, Francis Meynell and Harry Thompson, who were all members of the CP at the beginning but left after a few years?

We can speculate on these questions, but we cannot know for certain. We can, though, reflect on the personal and political qualities that Minnie Lansbury brought to her life's activities.

Qualities and Sides

Minnie Lansbury was an educator. She taught infant school children for four years, and also took part in a local socialist movement that valued

---

[406]   Letter to author.

and practised self-education about oppression and liberation. She studied what she needed to know to carry out her roles and to work out an effective line of march for the struggles she took part in. Her efforts at her own education made her a knowledgeable, articulate and effective campaigner.

She was a secularist. Brought up in a Jewish family, she was not herself a believer and worked politically alongside Jews, Catholics, Protestants and atheists. Her funeral reflected this, with elements of Judaism, Christianity and secularism. The *Jewish Guardian*[407] noted that she 'was greatly beloved by a very large circle of friends, both Jewish and Gentile.'

Minnie was a modern woman and in some senses a pioneer. Her age gave her the opportunity to ride the wave of the expansion of state education and become one of the first women to come from a poor, Jewish background to qualify at university and teach at a state school. As the daughter of immigrants, she integrated into the labour movement and the civic life of their chosen country. The few photographs of Minnie show her in a very contemporary and practical style, wearing her hair short and her dress comfortable.

She was brave. Minnie was prepared to do what was necessary to fight the causes to which she was committed, whether that was giving up her career or helping to dispose of donated Russian diamonds. Faced with prison, and with others wavering, she held them and herself firmly to their cause; and offered a way out of prison short of victory, she and her fellows refused it and went on to win.

Minnie was a hard-working community activist. She knew that socialists could not simply lecture working-class people about the need for social transformation to end their suffering if they did not also work to alleviate that suffering in the here and now. Reverend Kitcat spoke at her funeral of her 'life of toil and labour in the relief of distress, and the uplifting of her fellow men.' Edgar Lansbury wrote to his wife's memorial meeting that Minnie was 'supremely conscious of the happiness which her work brought to others … She loved her work.' And the *Daily Herald*[408] eulogised that 'by consistent hard work Mrs. Lansbury had earned the respect and esteem not only of her own political party, but also of many of her opponents … She spared neither time nor energy in carrying out the duties which she voluntarily assumed.'

[407] 6th January 1922.

[408] 7th January 1922.

Kitcat also spoke of Minnie's 'ability to recognise wholeheartedly the good points in those who might differ from her,' and Edgar of how 'Our poor and wretched streets were brightened up as she passed through … [and] brought into our rather dull politics and social work, so much sunshine and pleasure.' Her father-in-law George told her memorial meeting that Minnie was motivated not by personal ambition but by her love of justice, and argued that although she had many talents, 'one thought dominated her whole being night and day: How shall we help the poor, the weak, the fallen, weary, and heavy-laden, to help themselves?'[409]

Minnie Lansbury was happy, friendly, helpful and very popular. Crucially, she took sides. In her various roles, she sought not to administer in an even-handed, respectable way, as she knew that there was not a level playing field. She took sides with her people: the men and women; immigrants and natives; children and adults; workers, housewives and jobless; fighters and peaceniks of the East End and beyond.

Why does this matter? Minnie's life story remains relevant today, more so than we might wish. We still have poverty, inequality and residents of poor parts of London paying higher local taxes than those in richer parts. We still have both antisemitism and hostility to immigrants from Poland and elsewhere. Women are still under-represented and still struggling to be accepted as equal and separate individuals with or without husbands. We have attacks on pension rights and failure of government support for disabled people including, but not only, ex-soldiers. We still have deaths from the preventable and curable diseases influenza, pneumonia and tuberculosis.

Of course, there has been significant progress on some of the issues that Minnie confronted – such as housework, education and the welfare state – mainly due to the efforts and sacrifices of campaigners like her. But in today's Conservative Britain, we are now seeing a worsening of some of the issues that Minnie and her comrades were tackling a hundred years ago. Central government is stripping local council funding to the bone. And while the idea of barring recipients of welfare payments from voting may now sound as obsolete and laughable as barring women from voting, in 2018 the opinion poll company YouGov ran an online poll testing public opinion on this very proposal.

---

[409] *Daily Herald*, 2nd January 1922.

Remembering Minnie

Poplar remembered its champion for a long time.

Minnie's fellow councillor Dave Adams still had her photograph in a frame on his mantleshelf at home when he was a Labour MP in the 1930s.[410]

Ten years after her death, public subscription raised the funds for a memorial clock, attached to the wall of Electric House at 65 Bow Road. Electric House opened in 1925, its upper floors being flats and most of its ground floor showrooms for Poplar Borough Council's pioneering Electricity Undertaking. Its official opening on 29th May 1925 was addressed by John Wheatley MP, who had been one of the few ministers in the short-lived minority Labour government of 1924 who had supported Poplar and pursued radical policies.

The clock was added in 1932, the money raised through the public sale of small, floral tickets. It is a distinctive timepiece, with three clockfaces, framed in wrought iron and attached to the building with ornate brackets, 130 centimetres high and eighty centimetres wide and deep.

It suffered extensive damage during the Second World War, and again the Poplar public put their hands in their pockets, making up the shortfall between the cost of the repairs and the amount that the government's War Damage Commission was willing to pay.[411] In 1975, Tower Hamlets Council updated the clock's power supply from battery to mains electric, but thirty years later, it was falling into disrepair again. The Heritage of London Trust and the Jewish East End Celebration Society launched an appeal to raise the twelve thousand pounds needed to renovate it. With the help of donations including two thousand pounds from Edgar's daughter, the Hollywood star Angela Lansbury, it was repaired. The clock now has two plaques beneath it. The original one reads:

> The clock above was erected by public subscription in memory of Alderman Minnie Lansbury who after a life devoted to the service of the poor of this borough, died on New Year's Day 1922, aged 32 years.

Above it, a much newer plaque reads:

---

[410] Letter, Dave Adams MP to Ray Glassman, 24th February 1933.

[411] Poplar Borough Council minutes, 2nd December 1946 and 5th January 1948.

215

> On 16 October 2008 the restored Minnie Lansbury Clock was celebrated by those who helped to pay for its restoration, in honour of this East End suffragette and champion of local people.

Her closest family, friends and comrades agreed that the best tribute to Minnie Lansbury was to continue the battles to which she devoted her life. George urged the huge audience at her memorial meeting that 'If they wanted to erect a monument to her they should erect it in their own lives'; Charles Key that 'Helped by her example and strengthened by her memory, let them labour for the cause as she lived and fighting, die.' The last word goes to her husband Edgar: 'If we honour her memory let us do what we can to hasten the day of the emancipation of the workers.'

Bibliography

1. Printed Primary Sources

A. Contemporary Newspapers

Aberdeen Daily Journal
Auckland Star
Birmingham Mail
The Call
The Communist
Daily Herald (*The Herald* during wartime)
Daily Telegraph
Dundee Courier
East End News
East London Advertiser
East London Observer
Eastern Post and City Chronicle
Edinburgh Evening News
Gloucester Citizen
The Goldsmithian
Hackney and Kingsland Gazette
Hartlepool Northern Daily Mail
Illustrated Police News
Jewish Chronicle
Journal of Education
Labour Gazette
Leeds Mercury
Lloyd's Weekly Newspaper
London Gazette
The Morning Post
News and Chronicle
The Northern Whig
Nottingham Evening Post
Nottingham Journal
School Government Chronicle
The Schoolmaster
The Scotsman
Sheffield Independent

The Star

Straits Times

Studies in Mental Inefficiency, issued by the Central Association for the Care of the Mentally Defective

The Times

The Vote

Woman's Dreadnought

Workers' Dreadnought

B. Contemporary Books and Pamphlets

Board of Education, *Report of the Consultative Committee on The Education of the Adolescent*, HMSO, 1927

Charles Booth, *Life and Labour of the People vol.1*, Macmillan, 1889

Charles Booth, *Life and Labour of the People in London, vol. 3*, Macmillan, 1902-3

Independent Tailors, Machinists and Pressers' Union et al, *A Voice from the Aliens*, 1895 (reproduced by No One Is Illegal, 2006)

Charles Key, *Red Poplar: Six Years of Socialist Rule*, Labour Publishing, 1925

Jack London, *The People of the Abyss*, Createspace, 2016 (first published 1903)

Harry Pollitt, *A War Was Stopped*, Communist Party of Great Britain, 1925

Poplar Borough Municipal Alliance, *The Breakdown of Local Government: The Story of Poplar*, PBMA, 1925

Israel Zangwill, *Children of the Ghetto*, McAllister Editions, 2015 (second edition, 1893, first published 1892)

C. Archived Material

Held at Coopers' Company and Coborn School:
  Coborn School for Girls archive

Held at Goldsmiths' College archive:
  Information books
  Old Students' Association records
  Students' handbook

Held at the Institute of Education:
  National Union of Women Teachers

Held at the International Institute of Social History, Amsterdam:
  Sylvia Pankhurst papers: ELFS minutes and reports; WSF minutes and
    reports; articles; book drafts; publicity materials; War Emergency
    Workers' National Committee

Held at London Metropolitan Archive: records of:
  Boards of Guardians
  Jews' Free School
  London County Council
  London Labour Party
  Metropolitan Water Board
  Registers of teachers
  Rolls of sessions
  Schools admissions registers
  Schools inspections

Held at London School of Economics Library:
  Charles Booth's notebooks
  George Lansbury collection
  Raymond Postgate papers

Held at the National Archives, Kew:
  Isaac Glassman's naturalisation papers
  School Board for London

Held at Tower Hamlets Archive and Local History Library: records of:
  Bethnal Green Borough Council Labour Group
  East London Teachers' Association
  London Street Directory
  Medical Officer of Health reports
  Poplar Borough Council
  Poplar Borough Municipal Alliance
  Post Office London Directory

D. Photographs

Album of photographs presented to W. H. Thompson, Solicitor for the Defence of the Poplar Borough Council during the period of the Rate Strake 1921 – held by Thompson's Solicitors
Family photographs, Glassman and Lansbury families

E. Personal Materials

Letters and other materials held by Selina Gellert

2. Secondary Sources

A. Biography, Autobiography and Memoir

Steve Allen and Laurie Flynn, *The Search for Harry Thompson*, Thompson's Solicitors, 2007

Annie Barnes, *Tough Annie: From Suffragette to Stepney Councillor*, Stepney Books, 1980

Hector Bolitho, *Alfred Mond: First Lord Melchett*, Martin Secker, 1933

Harry Gosling, *Up and Down Stream*, Methuen, 1927

Martin Gottfried, *Balancing Act: The Authorized Biography of Angela Lansbury*, Little Brown, 1999

Jewish Women in London group, *Generations of Memories: Voices of Jewish Women*, The Women's Press, 1989

Seth Koven, *The Match Girl and the Heiress*, Princeton University Press, 2015

Edgar Lansbury, *George Lansbury: My Father*, Sampson Law, 1934

George Lansbury, *My Life*, Constable & co., 1928 (reissued 1931)

George Lansbury, *Looking Backwards — and Forwards*, Blackie, 1935

Muriel Lester, *It Occurred To Me*, Harper, 1937

William Lax, *Lax of Poplar: By Himself*, The Epworth Press, 1927

Francis Meynell, *My Lives*, Bodley Head, 1971

Lord Morrison of Lambeth, *Herbert Morrison: An Autobiography*, Odhams, 1960

E. Sylvia Pankhurst, *The Suffragette Movement: An Intimate Account of Persons and Ideals*, Virago, 1977 (first published 1931)

E. Sylvia Pankhurst, *The Home Front: A Mirror to Life in England During the First World War*, Ebury Press, 1987 (first published 1932)

Raymond Postgate, *The Life of George Lansbury*, Green & co., 1951

Rudolf Rocker, *The London Years*, Five Leaves, 2004

John Shepherd, *George Lansbury: At the Heart of Old Labour*, Oxford University Press, 2004

Barbara Winslow, *Sylvia Pankhurst: Sexual Politics and Political Activism*, Routledge, 1996

B. Modern Articles and Pamphlets

Julia Bard, Review of Jewish Women in London Group, 1989, in *Feminist Review* no.37, Spring 1991

David Englander, 'Policing the Ghetto: Jewish East London, 1880-1920' in *Crime, History and Societies*, vol.14, no.1, 2010, pp.29-50

M.E. Francella, 'Prisca Coborn and Her School', 1973

Michael Lavalette, *George Lansbury and the rebel councillors of Poplar*, Bookmarks, 2006

Hannah Renier, 'Streets of London', 2012, London Historians

Oscar Tapper, 'Poplar on Trial' in *East London Papers*, volume 3.2.57, 1960

Keith M. Wilson, 'The Protocols of Zion and the Morning Post, 1919-1920' in *Patterns of Prejudice*, 19:3, 5-14, 1985

Bronwen Walter, 'Irish/Jewish diasporic intersections in the East End of London: paradoxes and shared locations', in M. Prum (ed) *La place de l'autre Paris*, L'Harmattan Press pp.53-67, 2010

C. Local and General History Books

John Blake, *Memories of Old Poplar*, Stepney Books, 1995 (first published 1977)

Janine Booth, *Guilty and Proud of it: Poplar's Rebel Councillors and Guardians 1919-25*, Merlin Press, 2009

Noreen Branson, *Poplarism 1919-25: George Lansbury and the councillors' revolt*, Lawrence & Wishart, 1979

Julia Bush, *Behind the Lines: East London Labour 1914-1919*, Merlin Press, 1984

Martin Cloake, *Pride, Passion, Professionalism: The NUT and the struggle for education 1870-2017*, NUT/NEU, 2018

Katherine Connelly, *Sylvia Pankhurst: Suffragette, Socialist and Scourge of Empire*, Pluto Press, 2013

William Fishman, *East End Jewish Radicals*, Five Leaves, 2004 (first published 1975)

Lloyd Gartner, *The Jewish Immigrant in England 1870-1914*, Allen & Unwin, 1960

Derek Gillard, *Education in England: a history*, www.educationengland.org.uk/history, 2018

W.S. Hilton, *Foes to Tyranny: A History of the Amalgamated Union of Building Trade Workers*, AUBTW, 1963

Historians' Group of the Communist Party, *The Poplar Story*, 1921, 1953

Sarah Jackson and Rosemary Taylor, *Voices from History: East London Suffragettes*, The History Press, 2014

George Lansbury, *The Miracle of Fleet Street*, Victoria House, 1925

Larry L. McSwain, *Twentieth-century Shapers of Baptist Ethics*, Mercer, 2008

Ralph Miliband, *Parliamentary Socialism: a study in the politics of Labour*, Merlin Press, 2009 (first published 1961)

Kevin Morgan, *Bolshevism and the British Left: Labour Legends and Russian Gold Part 1*, Lawrence & Wishart, 2006

Winston G Ramsey, *The East End Then and Now*, After the Battle, 1997

Louise Raw, *Striking a Light: The Bryant and May Matchwomen and their Place in History*, Continuum, 2009

Huw Richards, *The Bloody Circus: The Daily Herald and the Left*, Pluto Press, 1997

Rosemary Taylor, *Walks Through History: Exploring the East End*, Breedon Books, 2001

Giles Udy, *Labour and the Gulag: Russia and the Seduction of the British Left*, Biteback, 2017

Laura Ugolini, *Civvies: Middle-class men and the English home front, 1914-18*, Manchester University Press, 2013.

Simon Webb, *1919: Britain's year of revolution*, Pen and Sword History, 2016

D. Websites

www.discovery.nationalarchives.gov.uk
www.historicengland.org.uk
www.islandhistory.wordpress.com

www.jewisheastend.com
www.jewishgen.org
www.karbatznick.com
www.leicesternut.org.uk
www.morningtongrove.com
www.sites.gold.ac.uk/goldsmithshistory
www.soundsurvey.org.uk
www.ssafa.org.uk
www.stetl.org.pl
www.surveyoflondon.org
www.victorianlondon.org
www.yeosociety.com
www.zythophile.co.uk

E. MODERN JOURNALS

BBC History

3. REFERENCE WORKS

House of Commons Hansard
Oxford Dictionary of National Biography
Poplar 1914, Old Ordnance Survey Maps, Alan Godfrey, 1990
Office for National Statistics

4. INTERVIEWS/CORRESPONDENCE WITH AUTHOR

Selina Gellert
Terry Lansbury
Chris Sumner
Steven Warren